RETURN OF THE COFFIN SHIPS
AND THE DERBYSHIRE ENIGMA

Bernard Edwards

Other books by Bernard Edwards:

Masters Next to God
They Sank the Red Dragon
The Fighting Tramps
The Grey Widow Maker
Salvo!
SOS, Men Against the Sea
Attack & Sink
Blood & Bushido
Dönitz and the Wolf Packs

RETURN OF THE COFFIN SHIPS

AND THE DERBYSHIRE ENIGMA

Bernard Edwards

Brick Tower Press
New York

in conjunction with
Bernard Edwards

Brick Tower Press, 1998

© Bernard Edwards, 1998

Edwards, Bernard
Return of the Coffin Ships
and the Derbyshire Enigma
Includes Index

ISBN 1-883283-19-1

Library of Congress
Catalog Card Number: 98-73939

Bernard Edwards

AUTHOR'S NOTE

The voyages of the ships described in this book are all reconstructions based on reports of official inquiries held into the casualties and, in some cases, eye witness stories. I have used my own knowledge of the sea and ships to add substance to the accounts, at the same time taking care not to stray beyond the bounds of credibility. Opinions expressed on the conduct of ships, organisations and individuals are mine alone. In order to compare like with like I have used deadweight tonnages throughout.

Dedication

For Douglas Brodie Foy, FNI MRIN, who for so long campaigned against the "rust bucket" bulkers. Doug has gone over the horizon on his last voyage. The "rust buckets" sail on.

Acknowledgements

The author gratefully acknowledges the help given him in the research for this book by the following people and organisations: Douglas Foy; Norman Hooke, Lloyd's Maritime Information Services; Captain D. C. Ramwell; Captain P. M. Cheek; Lee Curtis; Captain R. I. Newbury; Donald J. Sheetz and Dr. J. Cowley of Vanuatu Maritime Services Ltd.; Bergesen D. Y. Group; The Salvage Association; Nautical Institute; Department of Transport; International Transport Workers Federation; Bibby Line Ltd.; National Maritime Museum, Greenwich; University of Dundee; Times Newspapers Ltd.; National Oceanographic Data Center, Silver Spring USA; The Cork Examiner; International Registries (UK) Ltd.; Chemikalien Seetransport GMBH, Hamburg; International Maritime Organisation; Numast; Ministry of Mercantile Marine, Hellenic Republic; Marine Dept., Hong Kong; Wasser und Schiffahrtsdirektion Nordwest, Emden; Deutsches Seeschiedsgericht, Hamburg.

Contents

Widows of *Arctic Career* mourn their dead, page 122.
Photo: Nautical Institute

Heavy weather, North Atlantic. View from
bridge of tanker *British Wye*.
Photo: Nautical Institute

INTRODUCTION

In September 1980, the British ship *Derbyshire* sailed into the eye of Typhoon Orchid and on into oblivion, taking all on board with her. She is now no more than a pale ghost, appearing from time to time like a passing ship glimpsed through the morning fog.

It is known that she lies quiet in her grave more than 2,000 fathoms down in the Pacific Ocean, yet she still comes back to haunt us. To haunt those who mourn her dead, those who bear the burden of guilt for things undone, and those who over the years have shown so little enthusiasm to seek out the truth. For the misguided zealots who today preach with such passion the doctrine of "big is beautiful," her loss is a lesson yet to be learned. And the *Derbyshire* **was** big. At 169,044 tons deadweight, 970 feet long and 145 feet in the beam, she could well have accommodated the *Titanic*, that "unsinkable" marvel of early 20th century science and technology, on her foredeck. Both ships are now gone, mouldering on the bottom of separate oceans, but the *Titanic*, even with the passage of almost a century, still fascinates the historians and media men. Hardly an anniversary passes without her sunken ghost being resurrected to grip the imagination of the public anew. Many are the tales told of her going, of heroic deeds done and rescues that might have been; tales that grow in credence with every telling. The *Titanic* went down in the full glare of the publicity of her day–such as that was. News of her sinking was flashed around the world by Marconi's new wireless telegraphy, newspaper headlines screamed in horror, and much of Europe and America went into mourning. The *Derbyshire*, on the other hand, slipped beneath the waves almost unnoticed. But then, for all her great size, she was only a common carrier of oils and ores, her only passengers two officers' wives–no high-ranking diplomats, no bankers, no Hollywood stars. The national dailies gave her a column or two, radio and television made mention of her disappearance, but before the year was out she was largely forgotten, except by those who mourned for her crew. The question they continue to ask is, why?

The destructive power of a typhoon is awesome, but the *Derbyshire* was no small and ageing tramp, running red rust and manned by a bunch of "pierhead jumpers." She was a huge ship, only four years old, well-found, and crewed by British professional seamen of the highest standard. How, then, could she have disappeared so quickly and completely with no cry for help, and leaving only a thin film of oil on the sea to mark her passing?

Many theories have been advanced; of structural failure, shifting cargo, hatches stove in, of catastrophic explosions, yet none proven. The only good thing to come out of the appalling calamity that overwhelmed the *Derbyshire* was that it turned the spotlight on a hitherto unrecognised problem. Through her it became apparent that we had entered an era of shipping casualties unprecedented outside the two world wars of this century.

The carnage had begun in December 1975, when the 227,556-ton, Liberian-flag oil/bulk/ore carrier *Berge Istra* blew up in the Molucca Sea and entered the *Guinness Book of Records* as the largest vessel ever to become a total loss. Again, few outside the shipping industry were aware of her sinking, and no one could offer a plausible explanation for her loss.

One hundred years before the *Berge Istra*, when Samuel Plimsoll forced through the Merchant Shipping Act of 1875, the majority of merchant ships were poorly equipped and maintained. They were frequently overloaded, and more often than not manned by the sweepings of dock-side taverns and brothels. In the face of foul weather, fire and collision, a great many ships disappeared on passage with all hands. Others, using unreliable compasses and charts, came to grief on hostile shores like so much flotsam coming in on the tide. Across the oceans, as many as 2,000 ships and an equal number of seamen were lost every year. The tenacity of Plimsoll, manning by competent crews, and the advent of more reliable navigational aids changed all that. As the 19th century drew to a close, seafaring was fast becoming an occupation in which its inherent dangers ceased to promise only a hard life and a short one.

The golden age of shipping dawned soon after the Second World War, when all the technological spin-off from that long conflict became available to even the most impoverished tramp. Gyro compass, radar and the new radio navigational systems took much of the risk out of voyaging.

With highly-trained, dedicated men manning most merchant ships, a quarter of a century of steadily increasing security and stability was enjoyed on the high seas.

And there were even better times to come. Radar improved in definition and accuracy until it was possible to safely manoeuvre a ship in crowded waters in nil visibility. The arrival of satellite navigation in the merchant ships in the early 1970s offered accurate position fixing day and night, in all weathers, and at the touch of a button. At the same time, ships were becoming bigger and ever more powerful. Whereas in the 1880s the average foreign-going merchantman tipped the scales at around 800 tons and relied on a fair wind to roll back the miles, the great 100,000-tonners powered by 25,000 horse power engines had arrived on the scene. "Big is beautiful" became the rule of the day, for it is cheaper by far to lift 100,000 tons in one supership than in a fleet of smaller ones. And so came the 200,000-tonners, then the 300,000-tonners. There was no limit to the size of ships at sea–or so it was thought. Unhappily, when faced by the breathtaking might of the ocean in a rage, sheer size and ability to thrust through the water at speed can become dangerous handicaps.

Hand in hand with the seaborne juggernauts came the proliferation of flags of convenience and the subsequent dumping of the rule books as ship owners engaged in a frenzy of cost-cutting. Farcical collisions became the order of the day, the oceans were littered with sinking derelicts, and tankers regularly spewed their noxious cargoes onto unsuspecting shores. It was as though shipping had stepped back into the past. The primary causes of this return to the chaos of pre-Plimsoll days were not hard to discern. Poorly maintained ships manned by cheap, barely competent crews can only be a recipe for disaster. And it was in the ranks of the new breed of bulk carriers that this lethal combination of inadequacies became most prevalent.

In the twenty years following the sinking of the *Berge Istra* while on passage to Japan, no fewer than 340 bulk carriers, many of them bigger than the *QE II*, went down, taking with them over 1,300 men. This grim harvest of the sea is disturbingly consistent. Even today, in this magical age of proliferating technology, at least one of these ships is lost every month. The circumstances surrounding the loss of no two ships are exactly the same, but there are links common to all these appalling maritime disasters not difficult to perceive. This is all the more worrying in the light of the fact that, except for on rare occasions, these great ships go down with so little publicity, sometimes without even a mention outside Lloyd's. The *Derbyshire*, perhaps because she was a British ship, British built and British manned, is an exception to the rule. Her story continues to run–if only in the pages of the maritime journals. It may be that the others have scattered enough clues to lay her ghost once and for all–but first her story.

1

Enigma

"The loss of the MV *Derbyshire* in September 1980 is one of the great unsolved mysteries of the sea."
—Lord Donaldson of Lymington 1995

In late summer and early autumn there is menace abroad in Japanese waters. It is in these otherwise tranquil months that the destructive typhoons—taking their name from the Chinese "Tai-fung," or "Big Wind"—are spawned in the steamy tropics of the North Pacific, where the sea is at its warmest, and the air above dangerously unstable. It requires only an updraft from one of the scattered islands of Micronesia to act as a trigger, sending a pocket of warm, moist air soaring skywards to form a lazy spiral of low pressure. This embryo storm then moves west-northwestwards with the rotation of the earth, sucking up enormous energy from the sea as it goes. Malevolence breeds rapidly in the dark, swirling clouds. When a typhoon is fully formed, gale force winds are felt at 200 miles, while in the centre, or "eye" of the storm, all hell is let loose, with winds gusting to 200 knots, and visibility reduced to nil by driving, torrential rains. The typhoon is nature's nuclear holocaust, releasing energy equivalent to a one-megaton hydrogen bomb exploding every minute.

On 11 September 1980, Typhoon Orchid struck the southernmost Japanese island of Kyushu, killing six people and laying waste to thousands of acres of paddy fields and pine forests. After running clear of the land, Orchid roared on into the Sea of Japan and sank an entire fishing fleet in the Korea Strait with the loss of 112 men. The storm then cut a swathe of destruction through the Korean mainland and took three more lives, before blowing itself out in the empty canyons of the mountains of Mongolia.

The passing of Typhoon Orchid on 11 September was felt 300 miles away in busy Tokyo Bay. On the west shore, the port of Kawasaki, built on land reclaimed from the sea and squeezed in between the advancing sprawls of the cities of Tokyo and Yokohama, was swept by heavy rains. The port came to a brief standstill; passive while the rain washed away some of the grime deposited by the massed chimneys of the oil refineries, chemical plants and steelworks that come down to the sea at this point. As soon as the rain passed and the hot sun returned to set the steam rising from the wet concrete wharves, hordes of white-helmeted stevedores broke cover to resume work on the numerous ships alongside the quays. Only the main iron ore berth remained idle, its giant grabs swaying gently in the dying wind. The British ship *Derbyshire*, inward bound from Canada with 150,000 tons of iron ore, was expected on the berth, but she had yet to arrive. Two days earlier, a radio message had been received from the *Derbyshire's* master indicating that the ship had encountered Typhoon Orchid and her arrival would be delayed. In a hotel in downtown Yokohama, thirty officers and ratings waiting to relieve those of the ore carrier's crew due for leave, whiled away another day watching execrable Japanese television. The four wives who had flown out to join their husbands in the ship prevailed upon the Agent's representative to arrange yet another shopping trip to the Ginza, Tokyo's "Oxford Street." This was just another ship running late on her ETA, as ships always have, and always will. No concern was yet felt for the *Derbyshire's* safety.

Two months before, on the other side of the world, the *Derbyshire* had arrived in the Canadian port of Seven Islands, on the St. Lawrence river. She was under charter to load a cargo of iron ore concentrates for Kawasaki, Japan. The *Derbyshire*, an oil/bulk/ore carrier of 169,044 tons deadweight, was owned by Bibby Tankers Ltd. of Liverpool, flew the British flag and was entirely British manned.

Bibby Tankers, it must be said, was in 1980 far removed from the prestigious shipping company it had once been. Founded by John Bibby in 1807, Bibby Line, at first in sail, then in steam, had built up a first-class mail and passenger/cargo service between British ports and the Far East. Such was the company's record for efficiency and reliability, that it had been entrusted with most of the carriage of troops for the British Army in the days of the Empire. The ships, with their four tall masts and distinctive pink funnels with black tops, became well known throughout the world. They served their country well in two world wars and various colonial skirmishes. Sadly, like all British shipping companies, Bibby went into slow decline in the 1970s. One by one, the loss-making general cargo ships were dispensed with, and the company moved into the more lucrative bulk trades.

The *Derbyshire* was built at Swan Hunter's yard on the River Tees in 1976 as the *Liverpool Bridge*, one of a series of six oil/bulk/ore carriers in the "Bridge" series. She was part of a brave experiment to solve the dilemma of the tanker and bulk carrier owners who in those days of increasingly cutthroat competition were unhappy that their highly specialised and expensive vessels spent 50 percent of their time sailing empty. The oil/bulk/ore carrier, or OBO as it became known, was constructed with large, hopper-style holds with oil-tight hatch covers, these holds being flanked by side ballast tanks. The optimum aimed at was for the ship to carry oil in her holds on one leg of the voyage, and ore in the same spaces on the return passage. In this way, she earned freight for every hour spent at sea—the ship owner's dream of the ultimate in profitability. The *Derbyshire*, ex-*Liverpool Bridge*, was the last of a series of six similar OBOs built for Bibby Line by Swan Hunter, her sisters being named *Furness Bridge*, *Tyne Bridge*, *English Bridge*, *Sir John Hunter*, and *Sir Alexander Glen*.

Reality is often far removed from expectation, and to date the *Derbyshire's* earning capability had not been impressive. A dearth of cargoes resulted in her being laid up in a Norwegian fjord from March 1978 to April 1979, and when she again appeared on the high seas the demand for her services had not been great. She carried a cargo of crude oil from the Persian Gulf to Trinidad, and then made three more "one-way" voyages with cargoes of iron ore and coal. She dry docked in Japan in April 1980 for a routine survey and maintenance work, then sailed to Australia, where she picked up another cargo of coal for Fos-sur-Mer, on the Mediterranean coast of France.

On the seven-week passage north, the *Derbyshire* ran into heavy weather in the South Indian Ocean and sustained minor damage on deck, which led to the forecastle space being flooded. The damage was made good at sea, and the ship reached Fos on 20 June, where Captain Geoffrey Underhill assumed command. Following the discharge of her cargo of coal, she crossed the Atlantic to New York in ballast. Here she took on bunkers, and then sailed for Seven Islands, where she arrived on 10 July, 1980. The *Derbyshire* was covering a great deal of ocean for precious little return in freight.

The port of Seven Islands—or Sept Iles as it is called in this fiercely French corner of Canada—lies on the north shore of the St. Lawrence River, and is sheltered to seaward by seven small islands, from which it takes its name. The port is the termination of a 350-mile-long railway from Knob Lake, on the border between Labrador and Quebec, reputed to be one of the world's richest iron ore fields.

On arrival at Seven Islands, the *Derbyshire* was berthed at the loading terminal of the Iron Ore Company of Canada, and soon two travelling boom conveyors were spewing ore into the carrier's empty holds at the rate of 8,000 tons an hour. At the same time, water ballast was pumped out to avoid the ship grounding at low water. Throughout the loading operation, the weather was dismally overcast, with rain, which did not make the task of Captain Underhill and his officers any easier. As it was, with the cargo pouring into the ship at such a prodigious rate, they worked round the clock, performing the delicate balancing act of keeping the *Derbyshire* on an even keel, upright and off the bottom. At the same time, they were required to keep a constant check on the enormous levels of bending stresses the carrier's 970ft-long hull was being subjected to. And then there was the almost impossible task of distributing the ore cargo in the holds to minimise heavy rolling and pitching on the voyage ahead, not only for the good of the ship, but for the comfort of those sailing in her. By the time the *Derbyshire* completed loading her cargo of 157,447 tons of iron ore concentrates on the 11th, Underhill and his team were exhausted.

When she sailed from Seven Islands that same day, bound for Kawasaki, the *Derbyshire* had on board a total complement of forty-two British officers and ratings and two officers' wives. Ahead of them lay a voyage of 15,320 miles, with no intermediate ports of call. They would be out of sight of land for the best part of two months, with only a brief rendezvous with a helicopter off Cape Town to pick up stores and mail.

Uppermost in Captain Underhill's mind, as he navigated his ship down the Gulf of St. Lawrence towards the open sea, was not the immense challenge of this long voyage, but the danger of boredom setting in amongst his crew. For the old sailing ships, which had regularly engaged in similar long, lonely voyages, the possibility of the devil finding work for idle hands rarely existed. Tending sail and fighting the elements left little time for much beyond snatched meals and the blessed oblivion of sleep. In the modern ship, sophisticated equipment makes for light work and long periods of leisure time. The *Derbyshire* had a good-

Derbyshire–This photograph shows her while sailing
under her original name–*Liverpool Bridge.*

sized swimming pool, an ample supply of books, sufficient
films for two shows a week, and shortwave radio in every
cabin. Even so, Underhill knew he had to be constantly on
the lookout for the tell-tale signs of discontent. On prolonged voyages, minor grievances not quickly dealt with can
so easily fester and blow up into open warfare between fac-
tions in the ship. At the completion of this particular voyage, however, there was a carrot on offer. The majority of the
bulk carrier's crew were to be relieved on arrival in Japan and
would fly home for leave. Of those remaining, Underhill

and three of his officers looked forward to being joined by their wives at Kawasaki.

The *Derbyshire* passed through the Cabot Strait on the night of 12 July and entered the open Atlantic, swinging her blunt bows southeastwards for the Cape of Good Hope, 7,000 miles away. The weather was fair, with only the ever-present North Atlantic swell flexing its powerful muscles as it took the measure of this latest intruder into its domain. The deep-laden ship rolled lazily, her 34,000 horse power Burmeister & Wain diesel increasing its beat as it worked up to full speed. The acceleration was slow, for the ship and cargo displaced well over 200,000 tons, and like most merchantmen, the *Derbyshire* was very much underpowered for her size. In the open sea, she would manoeuvre well enough, but when up to full speed, her momentum became enormous, requiring nearly 2 miles stopping distance when going from full ahead to full astern. The *Derbyshire* was, in effect, an awkward giant requiring very careful handling. Fortunately, she was well endowed with all the modern navigational aids, having two high-performance radars, Decca Navigator, Satellite Navigator, two echo sounders, gyro compasses, weather facsimile receiver, and the latest in radio and telex equipment. And, in the unlikely event of all this failing, the officers on her bridge were well versed—as had been their sailing ship antecedents—in navigating with sextant, magnetic compass and chart. In her engine-room, led by Chief Engineer Norman Marsh, were men who knew their machinery well, and were capable of coping with every conceivable emergency. In all aspects, the *Derbyshire* was an eminently seaworthy ship.

The North-East Trades were light, and making good a speed of 12 knots, the heavily laden ship passed 350 miles to the west of the Cape Verde Islands on the 22nd. She crossed the Equator in fine, warm weather four days later and almost immediately ran into the South-East Trades, these blowing fresh at this time of the year. Head-on to wind and sea, the *Derbyshire* lost some of her speed, and spray began to climb over her bows, creating beautiful rainbow arcs in the bright sun. This was the "flying fish weather" all seamen cherish. Cotton-wool clouds chased each other across a flawless blue sky, and not another ship was to be seen on a sharp horizon that stretched to infinity and beyond. Isolated in an idyllic world of their own, far removed from the pressures and excesses of life ashore, the forty-two men and two women of the *Derbyshire* worked and played, slept and sunbathed untroubled.

And then, into this tranquil world intruded a problem that began to concern Geoffrey Underhill and his senior officers. For some days there had been a noticeable build-up of water in the ship's bilges calling for the frequent use of the pumps, sometimes as often as six times in a day. The *Derbyshire* had not sprung a leak, but it was clear that much more water was draining off her cargo than would normally be expected.

The ore loaded by the *Derbyshire* had been mined some 350 miles inland from Seven Islands, then washed and screened at the Iron Ore Company of Canada's plant at Labrador City until it was a fine metallic, sand-like substance containing 65 percent pure iron. This is known as "Carol Concentrates." Transported by rail in open trucks, the concentrates were already damp when they reached

Seven Islands, where they were stored in open stockpiles until required. June and July being rainy months in Quebec province, it is not surprising the concentrates loaded aboard the *Derbyshire* had a high moisture content, calculated to be around 3.6 percent. This seems a comparatively insignificant figure, but in relation to a cargo of 157,447 tons it represents 5,668 tons of water. Little wonder the carrier's hold bilges were filling up. Her powerful pumps would deal with this, but it was the more sinister problem of liquefaction that troubled Underhill. If sufficient water gathered at the bottom of the holds, his cargo would be afloat on its own moisture content and free to shift with the roll of the ship. This might well have a serious effect on the *Derbyshire's* stability, even rendering her liable to capsize.

On the 29th, the 2,800ft-high volcanic peak of the island of Ascension was visible to starboard. The sighting was brief, and the *Derbyshire*, with several giant albatrosses wheeling and dipping in her wake, ploughed on southwards, pitching easily in a rising swell generated by the unflagging trade wind. By the morning of the 30th, she was shipping green water over the bows with sufficient force to break adrift the inflatable life raft on the forecastle head. Prompt action saved the raft from going overside. The night that followed was an uncomfortable one as the deep-loaded ship fought to push her way through a heavy swell and rough sea. It was with some relief that next morning Underhill received a message from the charterers, instructing him to "reduce to a minimum speed consistent with safety, prudent seamanship and engine operations." This did not mean that any concern was felt ashore for the comfort of those on board; rather the ship was running ahead of schedule, which for those who controlled the paperwork constituted a threat to their finely judged market calculations. Underhill ordered the engine-room to reduce to 69 revolutions, and once more the *Derbyshire* rode easily. On the first day of August, she passed within sight of St. Helena. The remote island was the last land they would see before the Cape of Good Hope.

The final southeasterly leg of the passage to the Cape was covered at 10 knots, at which speed the great ship hardly seemed to be moving. It was the morning of the 8th before a dark blue smudge on the horizon announced that the southern tip of Africa had been reached. After four weeks sailing down an empty ocean, the call of the land was strong, and envious glances were cast ashore. But only one man, a sick seaman, would set foot on African soil, and then only very briefly.

Underhill had been in radio contact with the shore for some hours, and a helicopter carrying stores, mail and a change of films was quickly overhead. It was not necessary for the ship to stop, or even slow down, for the helicopter was back with the balance of the stores and the one man privileged to go ashore before Slangkop Point, 20 miles south of Table Bay, was abeam. This traditional off-limits call could well have been dispensed with on most voyages, but the air of excitement it created on board, with the resultant lifting of morale, was in the opinion of Bibby Line's management, money well spent.

The *Derbyshire* rounded the Cape of Good Hope in the early afternoon and entered the warmer waters of the Indian Ocean, but the weather that greeted her was far from welcoming. It was winter at the Cape, and by the time the light on Cape Point was disappearing astern in the gathering gloom, it was blowing a near-gale from the northwest. Soon, the ship was rolling ponderously in the grip of the long Cape Rollers. These giant swells, born in the Roaring Forties of the Great Southern Ocean, presented a real danger, not so much for their power—and this is awesome—but for the inshore set they create. Many an unwary ship's captain has dropped his guard once rounding the Cape from the west, only to be driven ashore on the rocky South African coast by the relentless thrust of the Cape Rollers.

It was nearing midnight when the *Derbyshire* rounded the notorious Cape Agulhas, southernmost point of Africa, and set course to the east. The weather had deteriorated, and the 12 million candle power light on the cape was visible only occasionally through the driving rain. In such weather Underhill was appreciative of his radar and Decca Navigator, with which the ship's progress was plotted with unerring accuracy. Her progress was slow, however, for she was now steaming in the teeth of the Agulhas Current, flowing westerly at around 3 knots. Underhill might have been tempted to edge closer to the coast to pick up the east-flowing counter current, the accepted practice for regular traders on this run, but his ship was too big for "rock-dodging." He held his course, taking take the *Derbyshire* outside the 100 fathom line, where the effect of the west-going current was less.

But even in deeper waters there was danger, a danger that first became apparent in July 1909, when the 9,000-ton British liner *Waratah* disappeared in the area with 221 passengers and crew. No trace was ever found of her, no wreckage, no bodies. Expert opinion was that she was the victim of a freak wave, a phenomenon now recognised as occurring off this coast when the conditions are right. A south-westerly gale, frequently met with in winter, clashing head-on with the powerful sweep of the Agulhas Current, sometimes gives birth to a monster wave of frightening proportions. The wave advances with the trough before the crest, creating, in effect, a deep valley backed by an incompressible wall of water up to 50 feet high. Any ship which has the misfortune to stumble into such a valley is unable to lift her bows to meet the oncoming wave, and is in danger of being overwhelmed. Since the unexplained loss of the *Waratah*, at least twelve ocean-going ships are known to have fallen victim to freak waves off the South African coast. In the winter of 1973, a ship bigger than the *Derbyshire*, the 286,981-ton Swedish OBO *Svealand*, had her foredeck set down by two feet and two of her heavy steel hatches were smashed open. She survived only by virtue of her great size.

Underhill proceeded with caution, and on the morning of the 10th the *Derbyshire* was to the south of Port Elizabeth, outside the 100 fathom line and clear of all local dangers. Her course lay along the arc of a great circle across the South Indian Ocean to the East Indies, over 5,000 miles away. On instructions from her charterers, the bulk carrier was from this point onwards to be weather-routed by Ocean Routes Inc of California. This entailed following courses laid down by planners ashore, which, in theory, should take her clear of any bad weather. In the opinion of many shipmasters, weather routing is a doubtful blessing, and Captain Underhill was no exception to the rule. Being an experienced navigator, and having on board a weather facsimile machine which gave him up-to-date weather charts on demand, he would have been happier choosing his own courses.

The *Derbyshire* was also participating in the AMVER (Automated Mutual-Assistance Vessel Rescue) programme operated by the United States Coast Guard. This involves filing a route plan before sailing–much like an aircraft's flight plan–and updating it from time to time by radio. The information, along with that from all ships participating world-wide, is fed into a computer in New York, which then produces an overall picture of the whereabouts of ships at sea. In the event of a participating ship going missing, then her approximate position is on the plot. Likewise, when any ship is in distress, the AMVER plot will show what other ships are in her vicinity and able to go to her aid. The system is simple, and for all the imponderables involved, works remarkably well.

Once well clear of the South African coast, with engine revolutions adjusted for 10 knots, the *Derbyshire* followed her long, curving course across the empty ocean, passing midway between Mauritius and Amsterdam Island on the 18th. Soon afterwards, she picked up the South-East Trades, which at this time of the year were blowing fresh, sometimes touching gale force. Belts of showery rain swept across from time to time, but for the most part the weather was no more than boisterous. The sun shone, the air was warm, and the passage would have been idyllic, had it not been for the persistent heavy swell on the beam. The *Derbyshire's* very low centre of gravity gave her a jerky roll that turned mealtimes into a farce and made sleep hard to come by. The ordeal lasted for eight days and nights, until on the 26th the ship at last came under the shelter of

Australia. The swell flattened, the wind fell away, and the sun shone hot out of a blue sky. The miseries of the days past were soon forgotten.

On the morning of the 29th, there was land again at last, the tip of the 12,379ft peak of Lombok Island showing up ahead at 80 miles. Then, on the port bow, the mountains of Bali rose out of the sea. That afternoon, with the sun dropping towards the horizon astern, the *Derbyshire* passed through the Lombok Strait and entered the Java Sea. Now, all around her was the lush paradise of Indonesia, the fabulous Spice Islands of the old Dutch East India Company, scattered like precious jewels across a sea of unsullied blue.

The channels between the islands are wide and deep, but contain hidden coral heads, and careful navigation was required. Having crossed the Java Sea, the *Derbyshire* entered the 400-mile long Macassar Strait, which separates the islands of Borneo and Celebes, recrossed the Equator on the night of the 31st, and on the morning of 1 September broke out into the Celebes Sea.

The Celebes Sea, 2,000 fathoms deep and sheltered on all sides by islands, was like a vast shimmering lake, through which the ore carrier sliced a path towards the northeast, her wide, frothing wake stretching behind her to the far horizon like a ploughed furrow in a field. It was hot and humid, with no breath of wind to stir the air, other than that made by the movement of the ship, but after the incessant rolling of the Indian Ocean the calm was a welcome relief. And with summer at its height in the northern hemisphere, such weather might prevail into the Pacific and to Japan, now just ten days steaming away. There was a danger, however, not yet apparent, but clearly recognised by Captain

Underhill. Once clear of the islands, the *Derbyshire* would move into the domain of the rampaging typhoons, which at this time of the year were at their most frequent. For some days Underhill had been watching the weather scene closely, receiving regular weather facsimile charts from Japan, while the *Derbyshire's* radio officer, Royal Waller, monitored the shore radio stations for warnings.

Underhill's healthy respect for the vagaries of the North Pacific weather was not misplaced. On the evening of 3 September, soon after the *Derbyshire* emerged from the Celebes Sea into the open ocean, he received a Japanese weather facsimile indicating a tropical depression was forming over the Caroline Islands, some 1,200 miles to the eastward. This may have seemed a very distant danger, but Underhill knew from experience the pattern this embryo typhoon was likely to follow. Moving initially to the northwest, and sucking up energy as it crossed the open sea, it might be expected to slow down when reaching latitude 20° North. Then it would either recurve and run northeastwards up the coast of Japan, swinging to the west and sweeping across into the South China Sea, or continue on a northwesterly course and end up on the Chinese mainland. There were unpredictable variations on these possibilities, but whichever track the gathering storm followed, there were strong indications that it would cross the *Derbyshire's* path.

Assuming the disturbance would develop into a full blown typhoon–and to err on the side of caution this he must do–there were only two options immediately open to Underhill. He could either reduce speed–hang back and wait for the typhoon to pass ahead–or increase speed and attempt to outrun it. He chose the latter, increasing to 12 knots and informing Ocean Routes of his action.

On the morning of the 4th, the *Derbyshire* was 80 miles off the coast of Mindanao and on a north-north easterly course, making 11 knots. Weather forecasts from Hong Kong and Japan, confirmed by facsimile charts, showed the depression then to be some 1,000 miles due east of the ship, north of the Carolines and moving west-northwest at 4 knots. At noon that day, Ocean Routes sent the following warning to Underhill:

FORECAST TROPICAL DEPRESSION 9.5N 145E AT 04/0000Z MOVING WESTNORTHWEST AT 10 KNOTS WITH MAXIMUM WINDS OF 30 KNOTS AND IS FORECAST TO INTENSIFY. RECOMMEND CONDITIONS PERMITTING BEST NORTHERLY HEADING AND SPEED CLEARING TROPICAL BY AT LEAST 200NM THEN DIRECT TO DESTINATION. PLEASE ADVISE POSITION DAILY UNTIL CLEAR.

Ocean Routes, aware of the danger threatening this huge, unwieldy ship they were charged with guiding, were clearly worried. But they could do no more. If their advice was correct, the *Derbyshire*, steering a course at right angles to the track of the depression, and making a speed of, say, 12 knots, should pass ahead of it in about 24 hours, with a clearance of around 900 miles. That was, of course, assuming the depression held its own course and speed. It did not. During that night, the whirling mass of warm, moist air veered to the northwest and speeded up. Ship and storm were then on a collision course.

By noon on the 5th, the *Derbyshire* was 250 miles east of the San Bernardino Strait, with the centre of the gathering storm 830 miles to the east-southeast. The information Underhill was receiving from various weather stations, based on satellite tracking, indicated the depression had turned north and was heading directly for the island of Guam, in the Marianas. There was a strong possibility that it might now be recurving to the northeast, as such tropical depressions often do. Playing for time, Underhill altered course to due north and ran parallel with the danger, watching it closely. That night, Ocean Routes were again in contact:

TROPICAL DEPRESSION NO.16 IS LOCATED NEAR 12.9N 141E AT 0511800Z MOVING NORTHNORTH-WEST AT 11 KNOTS. THERE ARE MULTIPLE CENTRES IN THE TROUGH AREA AND SHOULD BE ORGANISED IN NEXT 24 HOURS AND BECOME STORM INTENSITY BY 061200Z. FORECAST NEAR 15.3N 137.2E 061800Z MAX WINDS 45 KNOTS AND NEAR 17.4N 132.2E BY 071800Z MAX WINDS 50 KNOTS WITH 30 KNOTS RADIUS OF 125 NM. PRESENT ROUTE STILL VALID MAINTAINING 200NM FROM CENTRE.

At noon on the 6th, the *Derbyshire* was in the Philippine Sea, some 400 miles east of Luzon, and steering a northerly course at 11 knots. The depression was nearly 900 miles to the east-southeast, and apparently stalled over the Marianas, possibly on the point of recurving. Underhill now felt safe to assume the danger was moving away, and resumed a north-northeasterly course directly for Tokyo Bay. He did not increase speed, hanging back, still suspicious of the storm's intentions. His caution was justified, for during that night the depression, possibly thrown off balance by updrafts from the islands it was crossing, suddenly swung back to the northwest and speeded up to 13 knots. The *Derbyshire* was once again on a collision course with the storm.

At 0113 GMT on the 7th, Ocean Routes once more made radio contact. The message was urgent and unambiguous:

FORECAST TROPICAL STORM ORCHID BECOME TYPHOON, LOCATED NEAR 22.7N 132.7E AT 0900Z MOVING AT 10 KNOTS FOR 48 HOURS, THEN RECURVING NORTHEASTWARD AND ACCELERATING WITH RADIUS OF FORCE 7 CONDITIONS 25 NAUTICAL MILES.

It is probable that the *Derbyshire* was by then already feeling the effects of Orchid. The ship was 180 miles due south of the Daito Islands, steering a north-northeasterly course and making 10 knots. The typhoon was only 580 miles to the east, and was heading due west, not recurving to the northeast as Ocean Routes had advised. Orchid had executed a 90-degree turn and was charging directly at the *Derbyshire*. More serious still, the ship seemed likely to be caught in the dangerous semi-circle of the typhoon.

The dangerous semi-circle of a typhoon lies on the side of the path towards the usual direction of recurvature, in this case on the northern side. It earns its name from the

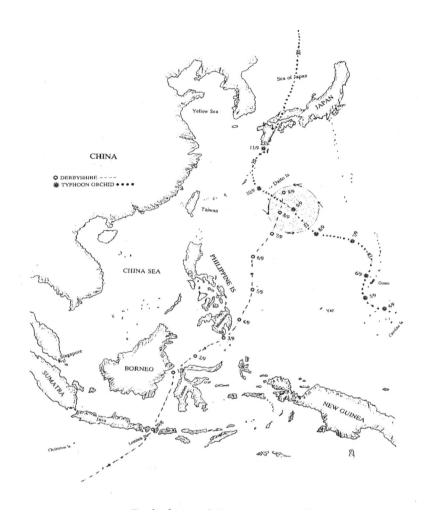

Derbyshire and Typhoon Orchid.

very real danger a ship caught in this semi-circle faces of being blown into the eye of the storm by the direction of the wind. For any ship thus trapped, the *Mariner's Handbook* advises: "The ship should proceed with all available speed with the wind 10 to 45 degrees, depending on speed, on the starboard bow. As the wind veers the ship should turn to

starboard, thereby tracing a course relative to the storm...."
This formula dates back to when men first began to understand the behavioural pattern of the weather at sea, and
holds good today as it did then. In the case of the *Derbyshire*,
the advice was to go south, where she would at least avoid
being sucked into the eye of the storm.

No communication reached the shore from the
Derbyshire on the 7th, but she appears to have held her course
for Tokyo Bay. It may be that Underhill, realising Orchid
was coming straight for him, had again decided to attempt
to cross ahead. His message to Ocean Routes on the 8th was
very brief and gave no clue to his intentions:

080300Z 23.34N 132.57E 8 KNTS.

The position given put the *Derbyshire* about 90 miles
southeast of Okino Daito Island. Typhoon Orchid was 375
miles further to the southeast in latitude 20 North longitude 139 East, and moving between north and northwest at
10 knots, apparently intent on a rendezvous with the bulk
carrier. By this time the effects of the approaching storm
must have been evident, as indicated by the *Derbyshire's* stated speed of only 8 knots. The wind will then have been no
more than a strong breeze, but it will have been from ahead,
and accompanied by rough seas. Underhill should now have
been aware that he was running into the dangerous semi-circle of Orchid, and it can be assumed he was taking the best
avoiding action possible. It is probable that during the following night he attempted to head due south with the wind
on the starboard bow, as was the recommended procedure in
such a situation.

And it must surely have been a dreadful night. The *Derbyshire* was no clipper-bowed destroyer, built to slice her way through the waves. She was 145 feet in the beam, with bows as blunt as a canal barge, the length of three football pitches, and drawing nearly 60 feet of water. Having only a single screw driven by an engine barely adequate for the size of the ship, in bad weather she had the maneuverability of a windjammer in irons. Underhill faced a stiff fight to prevent his ship being drawn deeper and deeper into the malevolent beast stalking her.

At 1023 local time on the morning of 9 September, Ocean Routes, acting on information gathered from various weather stations and satellites, sent the following message to Underhill via Choshi Radio:

09-SEP-80 0123 GMT REF/CABLE 20 KPH/SITOR ORCHID FORECAST TYPHOON STRENGTH BY 090600Z NEAR 24.5N 133.5E MAXIMUM WINDS 80 KNOTS FORECAST NEAR 25.5N 132.5E 091800Z MOVING NORTHWEST AT 13 KNOTS MAXIMUM WINDS OF 85 KNOTS WITH 50 KNOT WIND RADIUS 65 NAUTICAL MILES AND 30 KNOT RADIUS OF 400 NAUTICAL MILES NORTHEAST SEMI CIRCLE AND 120 NAUTICAL MILES ELSE-WHERE. ORCHID IS FORECAST 28.8N 132.9E BY 101800Z AND 32.1N 137.4E BY 111800Z MAXIMUM WINDS OF 80 KNOTS.

The warning had come too late for the *Derbyshire*. At noon on the 9th, Radio Officer Waller sent the following:

DERBYSHIRE/GULK/CHOSHI RADIO 9 0600090300Z 25.19N 133.11E VESSEL HOVE TO VIOLENT STORM FORCE 11 WIND NExE SEAS APPROX 30 FEET OVERCAST CONTINUOUS RAIN PRESSURE 995 MB.

From this message it was evident that the *Derbyshire* was caught in the dangerous semi-circle of Typhoon Orchid and was close to the eye of the storm. Under the circumstances, Underhill could only try to hold his ship up into the wind and wait for the centre to pass over her. Some idea of conditions aboard the ore carrier at this juncture may be gained from this report from the Master of the 11,000-ton American container ship *Mobile*, who two years later found himself in the path of Typhoon Faye in the South China Sea.

"At 1730 the wind was from the east at more than 60 knots and the barometer was dropping precipitously. The ship would not hold a westerly course in the wind and high sea and swell. Her head fell off to the southwest, and at 1805 maximum speed was needed to hold the southwesterly course.... Blinding rain reduced visibility to zero and made the radars ineffective. By 1830 the wind speed had increased to a steady 80-90 knots with gusts estimated at 100 knots.... Both radar antennas refused to turn in the high wind. At about 1945 *Mobile* entered the eye of the typhoon. One radar began functioning and the eye could be clearly seen encircling the ship, but the heavy rain of the storm attenuated the radar so that the targets beyond the eye wall could not be detected. At about 2030 *Mobile* entered the southern wall of the eye. The wind jumped to an average steady wind of 80-90 knots with gusts well over 100 knots.

Spray and torrential rain reduced visibility to near zero. Seas were mountainous. The radar ceased functioning again as the wind increased. Many of the ship's parts and fittings could be seen blowing away or bending in the wind with water coming across the ship. The masthead and range lights were lost around 2045."

The *Mobile* lost some of her deck cargo and suffered substantial damage on deck before escaping from the clutches of Typhoon Faye. Undoubtedly, the worst part of her ordeal must have been when her radars ceased to function, for she was then close to land. Fortunately, the wind was blowing her away from the shore at the time.

The report sent to Ocean Routes by Captain

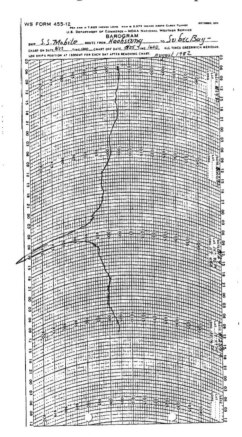

Typhoon Faye's barograph trace recorded aboard s.s. *Mobile* when passing through eye of Typhoon Faye, August 24, 1982.

Underhill at 0300 GMT on the 9th, although it spoke of a "violent storm," gave the wave height at only 30 feet, which seems too low for the conditions prevailing. This probably should have been 30 metres. The motor vessel *Alrai* was in the vicinity and in contact with the *Derbyshire*. Chief Officer Last, of the *Alrai*, later reported: "The *Derbyshire* was 80 miles distant from *Alrai*. It was calculated that the *Derbyshire* would be approximately 60 miles from *Alrai* at 2300/9th. Storm was deepest on *Alrai* at that time, barometer 962, waves hts 60-100 ft. Wind force 12 vis nil."

Weather experts consulted voiced the opinion that the *Derbyshire* was "caught in the most severe and dangerous quadrant of Typhoon Orchid and would have been seriously hampered by the weather and exceptionally high seas. The weather actually experienced locally may well have been very much more severe than scientific hindcasting can support. It is possible that during the night she could have experienced confused seas with an occasional mountainous wave as high as 20 metres (66 feet) or more. Swell waves of more than 6 metres (20 feet) would probably be coming from a different direction from the wind waves. In those confused conditions, accompanied by darkness and continuous rain, visibility nil, the *Derbyshire* would have found it very difficult to maintain a hove-to heading in any particular direction and could, quite readily, have fallen off the wind and ended up more or less beam-on to it."

The last message of any kind received from the *Derbyshire*, timed at 0930 GMT on 9 September, was addressed to her owners, Bibby Tankers, and read:

NOW HOVE TO DUE SEVERE TROPICAL STORM, ESTIMATED TIME OF ARRIVAL KAWASAKI 14TH HOPEFULLY.

There was nothing in this message to cause serious concern, and Underhill's choice of "hopefully" in respect of arrival Kawasaki may have served to allay any fears there might have been for the vessel's safety. She was, after all, a very big ship, well-found and well-manned. In the event, no attempt was made by the shore to contact the *Derbyshire* after the receipt of her message of the 9th.

It was not until Saturday the 13th, when the consignee of the *Derbyshire's* cargo began to make anxious inquiries about the whereabouts of his iron ore, that it became apparent something might be wrong. Radio contact could not be established with the ship, prompting Bibby Tankers in Liverpool to instruct their Tokyo agent, John Swire & Sons, to request the Japanese Maritime Safety Agency to mount a search for the vessel. The MSA, Japan's Coast Guard, politely refused, pointing out that a full scale search could not be set in motion until the ship's arrival was at least 24 hours overdue. Ships in the area were asked to keep a lookout for the *Derbyshire*, but no other steps were taken. This was at odds with the usual Japanese reaction to a crisis, which led Sir Derek Bibby, Chairman of Bibby Tankers, to comment at a later date: "I was advised that contact had been lost with our oil/bulk/ore carrier *Derbyshire*. While no one knew whether it was only a matter of the wireless having broken down, or whether the ship had been lost, the decision had to be made to alert the rescue authorities. The Japanese would do nothing until the ship was overdue, whereas if one alerted the American rescue operations the whole world would know within a few minutes. We decided to alert the Americans, but before doing so, we assembled all the personnel staff on that afternoon, and tried to get in contact with the next of kin. Police and clergy were involved where no contact could be made. Needless to say, one wife was on holiday and could not be contacted, but, sure enough, someone told her they had heard the news that her husband was reported missing. The Press seized on this and ranted about the heartless owner not informing the next of kin...."

Sunday, 14 September came and went with no sign of the *Derbyshire* in Tokyo Bay or any reply to the frequent calls put out by Japanese radio stations for her to report her position. By nightfall, the ship's agent, her owners and the consignee of her cargo were showing great concern, some of which must have filtered through to the relief crew and wives waiting in a hotel ashore. All by now feared that a major tragedy was about to unfold. The terrible anxiety suffered by the four wives does not bear contemplation.

At daylight on the 15th, with the weekend over, the Japanese Maritime Safety Agency at last came to life. Two of its patrol vessels, *Osumi* and *Motobu* and two reconnaissance aircraft were dispatched to search the area where the *Derbyshire* was last reported. At 1530 local time, one of the aircraft spotted a large oil slick on the water in approximate position 25° 50,–N 133° 30,–E. This was only 20 miles northeast of the position given in Underhill's last message to Ocean Routes on the 9th. The *Osumi* arrived in this area at 0545 on the 16th and discovered oil bubbling to the surface in approximate position 25° 48,–N 133° 37,–E, a further 20 miles to the northeast. The Japanese ship reported no signs of wreckage, lifeboats, life rafts, survivors or bodies. The enormity of what must have happened now began to be realised, although there were those who refused to believe that such a huge ship as the *Derbyshire* could have disappeared with no trace except a slick of oil.

The search was suspended on the 17th as Tropical Storm Sperry swept across the area, whipping up rough seas, but was resumed on the morning of the 18th. When the sun went down on the 20th, with no further sign of the

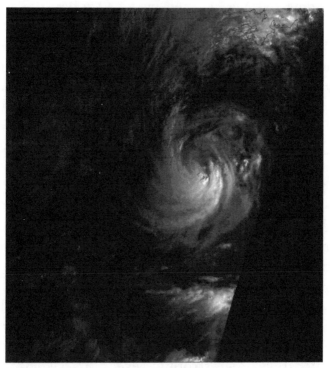

Satellite image of Typhoon Orchid centered over Daito Island, 9/9/1980. Photo: National Environmental Satelite, Data & Information Service, Washington D.C.

Derbyshire or her crew having been found, the Japanese called off the search. Samples were taken from the oil slicks, which when analysed were found to be similar, but not identical to the bunker oil the ore carrier had shipped in New York two months earlier. Given that the samples were diluted by sea water, it seemed safe to assume that the *Derbyshire* would never take up the ore berth waiting for her at Kawasaki. Her relief crew and four grieving wives were taken to Narita Airport and flown back to the UK. Their long vigil had been in vain.

Some five weeks later, on 24 October, the Japanese tanker *Daiei Maru* sighted an empty lifeboat drifting off the east coast of Taiwan. She was unable to recover the boat, but the name *Derbyshire* and port of registry Liverpool were positively identified on the bow and stern. The lifeboat was nearly 700 miles west-southwest of the last known position of the *Derbyshire*, and had therefore drifted at the rate of about half a knot over a period of 44 days. This is consistent with it having been carried on the west-going North Equatorial Current.

The *Daiei Maru* reported the derelict lifeboat to the Japanese Maritime Safety Agency, which in turn alerted the authorities in Hong Kong and the Philippines. A search was carried out, but the boat was seen no more. One day, it may be found cast up on the shore of some uninhabited atoll in the South China Sea, but whether its discovery will do anything to help solve the mystery of the loss of the *Derbyshire* and her crew of forty-four remains a matter for conjecture.

Whatever catastrophic event overwhelmed the *Derbyshire*—for it must have been so—it then seemed that the truth would never be known. As far as could be established, she lay 2,000 fathoms deep in the Pacific Ocean, and there was no one left to tell of her last hours. A preliminary inquiry held in Liverpool by the Department of Trade reached the weighty conclusion that, in the absence of wreckage and survivors, the cause of the loss of the bulk carrier could not be established. On the basis of this finding, the Public Inquiry called for by the bereaved relatives was refused. It was, however, recommended that research be carried out to establish the cause of the loss of the ship, but there was no real urgency to this recommendation. The *Derbyshire* seemed fated to enter the history books as yet another unsolved mystery of the sea, soon to be forgotten.

Onomichi Maru

On 30 December 1980, the 56,341-ton Japanese bulk carrier *Onomichi Maru* broke in two in the Pacific 400 miles north of the island of Minami Tori. The 15-year-old ship was on a voyage from Mobile to Sakaide with a cargo of 53,000 tons of coal, when huge cracks suddenly appeared in her decks and hull immediately abaft the forecastle head. Two hours later, the forecastle section dropped off and sank, leaving approximately 80 percent of the ship's length still afloat. The weather at the time was not particularly severe, the wind being force 8 and the waves around 20 feet high. The *Onomichi Maru's* crew of 29 were rescued by another Japanese bulk carrier, the *Dampier Maru*. The remainder of the abandoned ship floated for another 40 days, but sank after being taken in tow.

2

The Beginning

"The ritual single stroke on the Lutine Bell at Lloyd's yesterday confirmed that the insurers accept the loss of the supertanker *Berge Istra*. The thousands of underwriters, who had bought a share in its insurance, will now set about collecting the money and sending it to the owners of the ship, Sig. Bergesen D.Y. of Oslo. They say that it will be the most expensive maritime claim in the history of shipwrecks.

–The *Times* January 20 1976.

The *Derbyshire* was not the first of her kind to come to a sudden and unexplained end—nor would she, by any means, be the last. There had been been a few isolated instances of big bulk carriers foundering before, but the alarm bells did not begin to ring until five years before the *Derbyshire*.

The sun was low on the western horizon when, late on the afternoon of 30 December, 1975, the 227,556-ton oil/bulk/ore carrier *Berge Istra* emerged from the Celebes Sea on the final leg of her long voyage to Japan. The wind was light from the northeast, the sea mirror-like, but undulating gently with the first of the long Pacific swells coming in from the east. Overhead, the sky was flecked with high cirrus, while off to port the tall cumulo-nimbus building up over the distant island of Mindanao were dark with monsoonal rain.

It was nearing five o'clock, the end of the working day for those not on watch, and the party of five sailors working in isolation far forward in the bows of the ship laid down their chipping hammers with obvious relief. The men were all Canary Islanders, and no strangers to the hot sun, but the stifling humidity of the East Indies was new to them. After a long afternoon shifting rust they were physically drained and relishing the cold shower they would take before the evening meal now cooking in the galley far aft. But first the steel deck plates they had laid bare must be covered against the damp night air. While others swept up the rust flakes and paint chippings, Boatswain Avelino Hernandez began the long trek aft to the paint locker for pots of primer and brushes.

Able Seaman Imeldo Leon, who had been using a suction hose to pick up the debris, switched off his machine and stretched his aching back, idly watching the bosun as he made his way aft along the uncluttered foredeck. The distance from the forecastle to the bridge was nearly a fifth of a mile, and in the late afternoon haze the tall block of accommodation seemed to be part of another world. Forty-year-old Leon had never ceased to marvel at the sheer size of this great vessel that was his temporary home. Being so big, and having a crew of only thirty-two, she was a hard taskmaster, but the pay was good, and anything was better than hauling nets on a superannuated fishing boat running out of Tenerife. Leon's philosophy was simple but sound.

With the clatter of the chipping hammers stilled, the silence of the late afternoon was disturbed only by the swish of the *Berge Istra's* bow-wave, as her 31,000 horse power twin Burmeister & Wain diesels pushed her through the water at a speed approaching 14 knots, their measured beat barely audible so far forward in the ship. Soon, like any establishment ashore, the ship would be putting up the shutters for the night. The doors of the engine-room would close, leaving engines and auxiliaries in the hands of banks of monitors linked to alarms in the accommodation, and only two men, an officer and a lookout on the bridge, would stand watch through the night. The remainder of the *Berge Istra's* crew of 32 would be free to while away the time playing cards, listening to the radio–perhaps discussing the impending arrival in Japan, now only five days away. Then they would sleep soundly in their gently oscillating bunks. In contrast to the small general cargo carriers of yesteryear, life in a large OBO of the 1970s was a very ordered existence, dull even, most of the time being spent on the high seas. Although the *Berge Istra* carried over 200,000 tons of cargo, she was rarely more than 24 hours in port, loading or discharging. The strange and exotic lands Imeldo Leon had dreamed of as a boy in the remote Canaries remained unexplored in the hurly-burly of the turn-round.

Leon heard a faint rumble and turned his gaze to port, where the storm clouds gathered over Mindanao, suspecting thunder. Then the deck beneath his feet trembled and he felt a hot blast fan his cheek. He looked quickly aft and saw flames and smoke pouring from the port side of the accom-

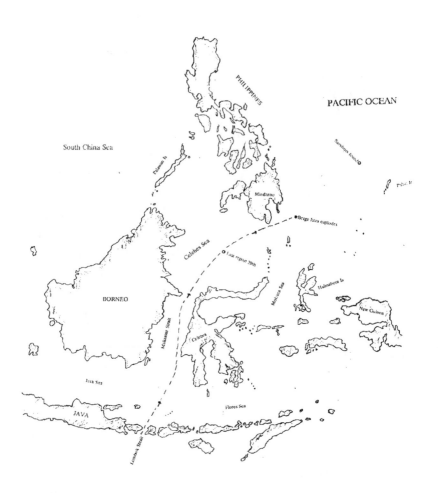

Berge Istra's path on her voyage to Japan.

modation block. As he watched open-mouthed, Leon felt another shock wave, and the *Berge Istra* leaned gently to port.

The others had stopped work and were huddling together in bewildered silence when, some 15 seconds later, another, more violent explosion shook the after part of the ship. Black smoke billowed out from behind the bridge, and flames shot high in the sky. The *Berge Istra* took a heavier list to port.

Gripped by panic, the first instinct of the four men was to run aft to the bridge, where the authority of the ship lay. The officers would know what to do. But aft lay only catastrophe, the bridge and accommodation being wrapped in smoke and flames. The only escape was forward. Silently, the men fought each other to be first up the ladder leading to the *Berge Istra's* raised forecastle deck. By the time they reached the forecastle, cooler heads reigned, and with the list to port increasing rapidly, they knew they must look to their own salvation. Three of them clawed their way up the sloping deck to the starboard side, then scrambled down the ladder to the main deck again. Their goal was a six-man glass fibre life raft stowed in the shelter of the forecastle bulkhead.

Imeldo Leon remained on the port side of the forecastle, staring aft, mesmerised by the the holocaust enveloping the stern of the ship. And so he was witness to the third, and most terrible explosion that ripped apart the *Berge Istra's* accommodation block, sending a mushroom of smoke and flames high into the air. The ship began to roll to port and sink by the stern.

Meanwhile, the others had released the straps securing the life raft and returned to the forecastle; leaderless and uncertain of what their next move should be. Leon, still stunned by the enormity of the catastrophe he had witnessed, gripped the ship's side rail with white knuckles, bracing himself against the increasing list. Then he saw the sea come rolling up the slanting main deck like an incoming tide, swallowing the *Berge Istra* whole, pulling her down into the depths.

Coming to his senses at last, Leon tore his eyes away from the approaching disaster and looked around for his companions. They were huddled in a frightened group on the starboard side of the deck, high above him. Hand over hand, he began to pull himself up the steeply sloping deck towards them. As he did so, the *Berge Istra* sank under him.

In the days prior to the First World War, the carriage of bulk cargoes by sea—iron ore, coal, bauxite, manganese, phosphates and grain being the most common—did not pose any particular problems for the ship owner. The size of the shipments required was not great, and the distance to carry not long. In fact, the main iron ore trade at that time was between Northern Spain and British ports, a three-day passage at the most. Any run-of-the-mill tramp was used, and so long as roughly one third of the cargo was stowed in the tween decks to avoid stiffness, and therefore heavy rolling, the ship was none the worse for the experience. A quick wash down of the holds and she was ready to return to carrying general cargo, produce, or whatever was on offer. The only real burden fell on the ship's crew, who were worked off their feet—but then seamen were cheap and easy to come by.

The first ocean-going steamer designed specifically for the carriage of cargoes in bulk was built in 1888 at Newcastle by C.S. Swan & Hunter for the Angier Line of London. She was the 3,300-ton *Gellivara*, a twin-screw ship with accommodation for twelve passengers employed on the Swedish iron ore trade. She had wide, uncluttered holds without tween decks, high wing tanks to counteract stiffness, and two 20-ton derricks for handling cargo.

Almost forty years were to pass before the forerunners of today's huge bulk carriers appeared. They were the Swedish-owned *Amerikaland* and *Svealand*, built in Germany in 1925 for the copper ore trade between Chile and the east coast of the USA. For their day, the *Amerikaland* and *Svealand* were ships on a gargantuan scale, each being of an unheard of 20,600 tons deadweight. They were also among the first ships to have engines and accommodation aft, which left a clear foredeck. Their hatchways were large to facilitate fast loading and discharge, and they were fitted with steel hatch covers, another new innovation. Generally, the idea did not catch on with other ship owners, but the *Amerikaland* was still carrying ore cargoes in 1942, when she was torpedoed and sunk by a German U-boat off Chesapeake Bay.

The same war that brought about the end of the *Amerikaland* became the catalyst for the birth of the large, dedicated bulk carrier. When the fighting was over, much of the world's industrial base outside America was in ruins, and in the late 1940s this led to a rebuilding boom and an unprecedented demand for metallic ores, particularly iron ore. In Europe, demand soon overtook supply, and it was necessary to look further afield for ore, to Australia, South America and South Africa. This involved steaming vast distances, and as it was already evident in the case of oil tankers, the bigger the ship the lower the freight per ton mile. Before long, 60,000-ton ore carriers were a common sight at sea.

When Ferdinand de Lesseps built the Suez Canal in 1869, he shortened the voyage to the Indies by nearly 4,000 miles. The result was a huge saving in time and fuel for the fleets of steamers that then joined Europe to the East. Under joint British and French control, the Suez Canal remained open for the use of ships of all nations for the next 87 years. Even during the two world wars, although access was restricted, the canal was never closed to shipping. Then, in 1956, Gamal Abdul Nasser seized power in Egypt, one of his first acts being to nationalise the Suez Canal. British and French troops went in to regain control but, fortunately, the conflict was short and the canal was soon reopened. Eleven years later, however, Egypt and Israel went to war and Nasser blocked the canal by sinking dredgers, tugs, barges and small ships along its entire 103-mile length. This time it stayed closed for eight years, all shipping between Europe and the East being obliged to take the long route around the Cape of Good Hope. This immediately raised the cost of transporting all cargo between East and West. Oil from the Persian Gulf was particularly hard hit, the long haul around the Cape adding another $5 per ton to the ship owners' costs. The only solution was to employ bigger ships, and by the early 1970s, 200,000-ton tankers were a common sight at sea. The bulk carriers followed suit, and soon matched the size of the tankers. It quickly became obvious, however, that there was an enormous waste involved in huge bulkers making one leg of their long voyage in ballast. This led to the introduction of dual-purpose vessels, carrying oil one way and bulk ore on the return passage.

The idea was not new. As early as 1950, Grängesberg-Oxelösund, of Gothenburg, built the *Porjus*, a combination oil tanker/ore carrier of 15,600 tons deadweight. She carried ore in her holds and oil in wing tanks and a deep double-bottom tank beneath the holds. The *Porjus* proved a commercial success, and others followed, but another twenty years would pass before the big oil/bulk/ore carriers of today came into service. One of the first of this new breed was the *Berge Istra*.

Built in 1972 at the Uljanik yard in Pula, Yugoslavia for the General Ore Navigation Company of Stavanger, when she took the water, the *Berge Istra* was one of the biggest ships of her day. She had a deadweight tonnage of 227,556, measured 1,030 feet long, 166 feet in the beam, and had a draught of 67 feet when fully loaded. She was managed for General Ore by Sigval Bergesen of Oslo, registered under the Liberian flag, and manned by Norwegian officers and Spanish ratings from the Canaries. She was thus a flag of convenience ship—although her owners would have denied this vehemently—and therefore open to all the corner-cutting abuses the flag legitimised.

In construction, the *Berge Istra* was not dissimilar to the *Porjus*. Her bridge, engine-room and accommodation were located right aft, and forward of this there were five centre holds capable of carrying either, oil, ore or water ballast. Each hold had two hatchways fitted with side-opening steel water and oil-tight covers. Outboard of the holds were twenty wing tanks, ten on each side, for the carriage of oil or water ballast. Bunker oil was carried in two deep tanks forward of No. 1 hold, in two side tanks extending two thirds the length of the engine-room, and in double bottom tanks beneath the engine-room.

The *Berge Istra* had three sister ships, *Berge Adria*, *Berge Brioni* and *Berge Vanga*, all managed by Sigval Bergesen and engaged on a regular trade carrying oil and ore in turn. The usual schedule for these ships was Persian Gulf to North

Europe with crude oil and from Europe in ballast to Brazil, where they would load a cargo of iron ore for Japan, sailing always via the Cape of Good Hope. The third leg was from Japan in ballast back to the Persian Gulf for another cargo of crude. The cycle was then repeated. This was a steady and lucrative trade, but the ships and their crews were hard run, with very little time in port for maintenance, and on the ballast passages the cleaning of holds and tanks ready for the next cargo involved a great deal of hard work.

The *Berge Istra* sailed in ballast from Tobata, on the west coast of Japan, on 17 September 1975, bound for Kharg Island, at the head of the Persian Gulf. In command was 45-year-old Captain Kristoffer Hemnes, who had under him a crew of 31, including three stewardesses, one Belgian, one Swedish and one Yugoslav. Hemnes' officers were, like himself, Norwegian, with the exception of the British radio officer Roland LeMarche, and First Electrician Egidij Sevrlica, also a Yugoslav. Of the fourteen deck and engine-room petty officers and ratings, twelve were Spanish, one a Brazilian and one Belgian. This was a cosmopolitan mix that must have given rise to communication difficulties. The ship herself, only three years old, was well found and well equipped for the voyage.

Arriving at Kharg Island on 6 October, the *Berge Istra* loaded a full cargo of Iranian crude, sailing again on the 7th for Rotterdam. The long haul around the Cape, a distance of 11,200 miles, took just over five weeks, and she arrived in the great Europort complex, at the Hook of Holland on 12 November with the northern winter fast closing in. She discharged her oil cargo, took on some 9,700 tons of heavy fuel oil, and sailed in ballast on the 14th, bound for Tubarao, Brazil.

Having on board a total of 64,104 tons of water ballast, bunkers, fresh water and stores, the *Berge Istra* was drawing 32 feet of water when she cleared the River Maas. Her passage across the shallows of the Southern North Sea and through the hazards of the narrow Straits of Dover was not an easy one for Captain Hemnes and his navigating offi-

Oil/Bulk/Ore Carrier *Berge Istra*–227,556 tons.
Note crew members on portside of forecastle head. It was from this spot that Imeldo Leon witnessed the explosions that sank the ship.
Photo: Bergesen D.Y. ASA.

cers. Keeping to the mandatory "traffic lanes" designed to separate incoming and outgoing ships, they carefully threaded their way towards the open sea, always on the alert for "rogue" ships going against the flow of traffic and fishermen, who consistently ignored all rules. Ten hours after sailing from the Maas, the bulk carrier was running the gauntlet of the unending stream of ferries criss-crossing the Dover Strait, a frightening experience when viewed from the bridge of a 1,000ft-long ship drawing over five fathoms of water and severely restricted in her room to manoeuvre. When, some two hours later, she finally ran clear of the Varne Shoal and into deeper waters, a cloud lifted from the *Berge Istra's* bridge.

Once clear of Ushant, on the 16th, and therefore outside the limits covered by the Oil of Navigable Waters Act, the work began to convert the *Berge Istra* back into an ore carrier. This was a formidable task, involving washing holds and tanks clean of the black oily residue left after the discharge of the crude oil in Rotterdam. It was a well practised routine, the bulker's deck and engine-room crew working continuously, day and night, under the supervision of Chief Officer Almar Ratama and Boatswain Avelino Hernandez.

The cleaning began forward with No. 1 wing tank, working aft. Each tank had up to ten manholes, through each of which was lowered a "Butterworth" machine with rotating nozzles blasting the inside of the tank with cold sea water under high pressure from the main cargo pump. The dirty water and oily residue, as much as 1,000 tons per hour, were continuously pumped out from the bottom of the tank being cleaned and transferred to No. 10 starboard wing tank, designated the "slop" tank. Here the oil and water were allowed to separate out, the water being then pumped over the side, and the oil residue remaining in the tank. All holds and tanks, including the slop tank, were maintained under inert gas during the washing process to avoid a build up of explosive gases. On completion of cleaning, which occupied seven days and nights of the Atlantic passage, all spaces were gas-freed using turbine-driven ventilating units. No. 10 tank, by then containing 584 tons of oil "slops," was kept under inert gas until the oil could be pumped ashore.

When the *Berge Istra* arrived at Tubarao Roadstead, 250 miles northeast of Rio de Janeiro, on the morning of 28 November, she was in all respects ready to load cargo. She was granted pratique and went alongside the iron ore berth in the early afternoon. Before the sun went down the conveyors were pouring ore into her centre holds at the rate of 8,000 tons an hour. By 1300 on the 29th, just 21 hours after berthing, she was ready to sail again. She left Tubarao at 1450, having on board 185,244 tons of iron ore consigned to Nippon Steel's plant at Kimitsu, in Tokyo Bay. Her mean draught on sailing was 60 feet 2 inches, which gave her a total displacement of 232,157 tons.

Very little is known about the *Berge Istra's* voyage from then on, except that it apparently passed without serious incident. She was instructed by her operators to maintain a speed of 13 knots, and as she had a service speed of 15 knots, it must be assumed that she had no difficulty in complying with this instruction. As a matter of routine, she radioed Oslo every Wednesday, giving an update on her ETA Kimitsu but, strange as it may seem, this weekly message did not contain the ship's position, nor her course and speed. It transpired that Bergesen's office used this weekly report to calculate the ship's position at any particular time, allowing for a speed of 13 knots. This was dead reckoning carried to a ridiculous degree—pure guesswork, in fact. It is difficult to understand why Sigval Bergesen, fifty years in the shipping business, should adopt such a slipshod method of keeping track of their ships.

The question also arises as to why on this particular voyage the *Berge Istra* was not particpating in the AMVER scheme. On previous voyages she had always taken part, Captain Hemnes being known as an enthusiastic participant with an impressive record of reporting. A simple coded message sent off twice weekly and fed into the AMVER computer would have given a reasonably accurate picture of the bulker's movements. As it was, this huge ship, although undoubtedly competently commanded and manned, appeared to be crossing the wide oceans virtually untracked by those ashore who should have been concerned for her safety.

From best estimates, it can be assumed that the *Berge Istra* rounded the Cape of Good Hope on the morning of 9 December, and then entered the South Indian Ocean. Her crew, very appropriately, celebrated Christmas Day off, and perhaps in sight of, Christmas Island, which lies 250 miles south of the western tip of Java. At sometime on the 26th she passed through the Lombok Strait and into Indonesian waters.

At 1924 Japanese time on Monday 29 December, Captain Hemnes broke with routine and passed a message to Oslo, through Nagasaki Radio, giving his position as 174 miles southwest of Mindanao, with an ETA Kimitsu of 0800 on 5 January 1976. This was the last word ever received by the outside world from the *Berge Istra*.

On Wednesday 31 December, when the *Berge Istra's* weekly ETA was due, her radio was silent. In Sigval Bergesen's office in Oslo this lack of communication from the ship appears not to have caused undue comment. Later, the reason advanced for the lack of concern was that, it had all happened before. Two years earlier, the bulker had broken down off Okinawa and drifted for four days without contacting the shore. This seems a very thin premise for deciding to do nothing. A more likely explanation is that the Wednesday in question being New Year's Eve, with the weekend following closely behind, the absence of a report from the *Berge Istra* was not noticed in Oslo. Whatever the reason, it was not until late on 5 January that suspicions were aroused–and then only because Bergesen's agent in Japan informed Oslo that the ship had failed to arrive in Kimitsu. On the same day, the Monday after the New Year holiday, Oslo radio reported having been unable to contact the *Berge Istra* to deliver messages since 31 December.

It now at last began to dawn on those ashore that all might not be well with the *Berge Istra*. Captain Ingolf Stangeland, Marine Operations Director for Sigval Bergesen, then radioed several of the company's other vessels known to be in the vicinity of the *Berge Istra's* last reported position, including the 86,179-ton OBO *Marshall Clark*. Stangeland directed these ships to search until further notice. He also contacted AMVER in New York, only to learn that the *Berge Istra* had not been participating, and that her possible whereabouts were not known.

On 7 January, Stangeland informed the Liberian Bureau of Maritime Affairs that the ship was overdue. He also alerted the US Air Force and the Japanese Maritime Safety Agency. Both these authorities then called for information from ports and ships along the route believed to have been taken by the *Berge Istra*. The inquiries bore no fruit.

An intensive air and sea search was then mounted, involving the United States and Philippines Air Forces, the Japanese Maritime Safety Agency and Australian search and rescue agencies. On the 11th, an American aircraft sighted debris in the water in the Western Pacific, but this could not be identified as being from the *Berge Istra*. The search continued in daylight hours. By the 13th, with the bulk carrier now eight days overdue in Japan, nothing conclusive had been found, and the Japanese MSA withdrew its ships and aircraft. American and Filipino planes continued to scour the ocean for another four days, but on the 17th, having covered many thousands of square miles without a sighting, they also gave up. The *Berge Istra*, one of the world's biggest ships, had apparently vanished into thin air. Then, on the 18th, the Japanese fishing vessel *Hachimo Maru* radioed that she was heading for Koror Island, in the Palau Group, with two survivors on board.

When Imeldo Leon fought his way back to the surface again after being dragged under by the sinking *Berge Istra*, he found he was within about 50 feet of the fibreglass life raft released by his companions. The raft had apparently floated clear when the ship went down, but was badly damaged. Leon, who had suffered no physical injury, struck out for the raft and hauled himself on board, discovering to his great relief that much of the equipment on board was intact.

Looking around him, he saw the sea was littered with floating wreckage, mostly broken pieces of wood, but with a few chairs clearly indentifiable as belonging to the seamens' mess of the *Berge Istra*. This pathetic flotsam brought home to Leon the terrifying events of the past minutes, and the enormity of the disaster he had lived through. His ship, a ship so enormous that she rode the waves like a colossus no natural enemy could overcome, had suddenly gone from under him–literally swallowed up by the sea, leaving only scattered debris behind.

It did not occur to Leon that he might be the only survivor of a crew of 32, and he began to search for others, standing upright on the damaged raft and balancing himself against the roll. In addition to this raft, the *Berge Istra* had carried two 51-person motor lifeboats, a smaller work boat, and two 20-person life rafts. It seemed inconceivable that no others had survived. But as far as the eye could see nothing moved.

Leon, filled with a terrible sense of loneliness, was about to sink back on the raft, when he saw a head bobbing on the water only a few yards away. He used his bare hands to paddle the raft towards the other man, whom he now recognised as Epifanio Lopez, one of the men working on the foredeck with him when the ship sank.

Lopez was unconcious and seemed near to death when Leon pulled him aboard the raft. He clearly had serious head and leg injuries, and did not appear to be breathing. Desperate that he should not be left alone on this empty ocean, Leon called on his sketchy knowledge of first aid and applied mouth-to-mouth resuscitation. His fumbling efforts were successful, and Lopez began to breathe again, shallowly at first, then normally as he regained consciousness.

For the next nineteen days the two survivors drifted on their small raft, with Leon caring for Lopez, who because of his injuries was unable to move. The constant rocking of the raft, the hot sun during the day and the chill wind at night compounded the nightmare. After twelve days, the food and water on the raft gave out, and the two men began to give up hope. Then Leon discovered a fishing line and hooks amongst the raft's equipment, enabling him to catch sufficient fish to appease their hunger. Rain water collected in a canvass canopy quenched their thirst.

Despite their proximity to the shipping lanes, only on two occasions did the survivors sight a ship. Each time Leon tried to set off distress flares, but the directions for the use of the flares were printed only in English and Norwegian, neither of which he could read, and his efforts came to naught. The ships sailed on without seeing the drifting raft. Throughout the long ordeal, the men saw no sign of the aircraft searching for them. This was not surprising, for their raft was being carried by a current running at the rate of 25 miles per day, and when the alarm was finally raised on 7 January, they were well to the east of the search area.

Rescue came soon after sunrise on 18 January, when Leon sighted a fishing vessel close by. Only one distress flare remained, and by this time he had solved the problem of igniting it. When the two men were picked up by the *Hachimo Maru*, they were both in a desperately weak condition.

Leon and Lopez had been found some 400 miles to the northeast of the *Berge Istra's* last reported position, and when news reached Japan of the rescue, a full sea and air search was reinstated, backtracking along the estimated drift of the life raft. On the 20th, aircraft from Okinawa sighted a 90-mile long oil slick about 550 miles southeast of Mindanao. Twenty-four hours later, the bulk carrier *Marshall Clark*, which had remained in the area, found a piece of a life raft and two fragments of a lifeboat, all of which were positively identified as having come from the *Berge Istra*. And that, it seemed, was all that remained of the 227,556-ton oil/bulk/ore carrier.

On 22 January, Sigval Bergesen announced that there was no longer any hope of finding any more survivors and the air and sea search, which by this time had covered more than 500,000 square miles, was called off. At Lloyd's, in the City of London, a single stroke on the historic Lutine Bell announced to the world that the insurers were prepared to accept the total loss of the *Berge Istra*. At this solemn signal, anxious underwriters who had a share in the £13.5 million cover for the ship and cargo began to mobilise their assets to meet the claims soon to come in. The *Berge Istra* was the largest vessel ever to become a total loss, and she would be the subject of the most expensive claim ever made in maritime history.

Although the *Berge Istra* was Norwegian-owned and Norwegian-officered, she sailed under the Liberian flag, and it was therefore the responsibility of the Republic of Liberia to hold an inquiry into her loss. After a preliminary inquiry in Monrovia, the Liberian Marine Board of Investigation held a formal hearing in London in June 1976. Having taken evidence, the Board summed up as follows: "It is now necessary to consider what could have been the cause or causes of the devastating explosions which led to the sinking of the *Berge Istra* in such a short space of time, and what may have been the reasons why only two members of the crew succeeded in escaping with their lives. The Board has found this task most perplexing. Any conclusion must be based on such facts as are known from the evidence of the survivors, and on other such inferences as may be legitimately drawn from other known facts...including the evidence as to the usual routine followed in the past when the vessel was making the same or a similar voyage. A number of possibilities have been considered, but it is fair to say that none of them appears to carry any great degree of probability, at any rate to the extent of producing such a catastrophic result. However, it is well known that the improbable does sometimes happen, and the Board is not blind to the possibility that this may be just such a case. It could be that the casuality is not to be attributed to any single cause, but rather to a combination of causes, none of which individually would have been sufficient to result in disaster. Though the Board is satisfied that the *Berge Istra* was manned by efficient and well qualified officers, it would be a mistake to rule out the possibility of human error. Similarly, though the *Berge Istra* was, as stated above, a well found ship, this is not to say that she was completley free of defects."

In reaching this not very enlightening conclusion, the Liberian Board of Inquiry was forced to rely on rather thin evidence. This consisted mainly of the opinions of experts who were not on board the ship during her last voyage, and the observations of the two surviving Spanish ratings whose knowledge of the day to day running of the ship was very sketchy indeed. It was found that "there must have been an extremely violent explosion involving the engine-room. This conclusion is also supported by the fact that none of those in the bridge structure, engine-room or accommodation were able to escape. It seems possible that one and all were instantaneously killed, or it may be that their failure to escape was due to the fact that the vessel was sinking so quickly."

The likelihood of the *Berge Istra* hitting a floating mine left over from the Second World War was examined and discounted. Although mines were laid in large numbers in these waters during the war, the majority of which had not been swept, it did not seem possible that a 30-year-old mine could blow the stern off a 220,000-ton ship. In the end, attention was centred on the *Berge Istra's* No. 10 port wing tank, which was believed to contain 584 tons of oil slops remaining from the tank cleaning following the discharge of the cargo of crude oil at Rotterdam. Although it was the practice to inert slop tanks, expert witnesses were of the opinion that there may have been a massive build-up of inflammable gas in this tank that had somehow gone unnoticed. In other words, it was suggested that No. 10 port wing tank had over the weeks at sea become a huge time bomb, ticking away below decks and waiting for a stray spark to set it off. Evidence suggested that repairs involving welding and burning were taking place in the vicinity of this tank on 30 December. The report of the Liberian Board of Inquiry speculated: "....a violent explosion in No. 10 port wing tank could have ruptured the engine-room bulkhead and led to an explosion in the port bunker tank, which could not only devastate the engine-room but would also open up the side of the ship to admit sea water in large quantities..." In view of the fact that Imeldo Leon first saw smoke and flames pouring out of the port side of the bridge and then ship then took a list to port, this theory seems at least feasible.

As it is most probable that the wreckage of the *Berge Istra* lies scattered on the sea bottom six miles deep in the Mindanao Trench, it is unlikely that the reason for her loss will ever be clearly established. What is certain, though, is that her going signalled the beginning of an era of ship disasters never before experienced.

Exotic

On 31 January 1977, the 152,179-ton oil/bulk/ore carrier *Exotic* was ripped apart by a series of violent explosions in her tanks that killed nine of her crew. The Liberian-flag *Exotic*, built in Japan in 1971, and owned by the Northwind Shipping Company, was on passage in ballast from Fos-sur-Mer to Brazil. The ship was off the west coast of Morocco when the explosions occurred, and thirty survivors, some of them injured, were picked up by the Spanish ferry *Juan March*. A helicopter transferred the injured to hospital in Las Palmas. The abandoned ship eventually beached herself on the coast near Agadir, but was refloated a few days later by tugs. She was towed to Lisbon, but found to be so badly damaged as to be declared a total loss. Insurance of $15 million was paid by the underwriters, and the *Exotic* ended her short career in a Taiwanese breaker's yard.

3

Encore

"A tragedy can be defined as a drama in which the protagonist is unaware of the fate in store for him and is the victim of forces outside of his control."
–Douglas Foy FNI, MRIN

The *Berge Istra* was an early example of a flag of convenience ship operated by an old established European shipping company. Sigval Bergesen were not seriously in the business of cutting corners, and although she carried mainly Spanish ratings, the *Berge Istra's* deck and engine-room officers were Norwegian, all highly trained men with recognised certificates of rank. It may have been that the Spanish ratings were not as competent as Norwegians–and they were certainly cheaper to employ–but in the end it was the officers who ran the ship, and standards were maintained. Bergesen were doing no more than following the example set by many first-rate European companies, who had for many years employed Indian, Chinese or African ratings with perfectly satisfactory results.

Four years after the loss of the *Berge Istra,* in line with the modern trend, Bergesen's manning policy changed. When, in July 1979, the *Berge Istra's* sister ship, *Berge Vanga,* entered dry dock in Sasebo, Japan for her special periodic survey and voyage repairs, she was beginning to look like a true flag of convenience mongrel. Commanded by Captain Hakon Johnsen, the 227,912-ton oil/bulk/ore carrier had only five other Norwegians on board, namely her chief officer, chief engineer, first engineer, second engineer and third engineer. The remainder of her 36-man crew were all Filipinos, then the world's cheapest seamen. Flying the Liberian flag, she was engaged on the same triangular run as the *Berge Istra,* carrying oil from the Persian Gulf to Rotterdam, and ore from Brazil to Japan.

Being built at the same yard and only two years after the *Berge Istra,* the *Berge Vanga* was almost indentical in construction, but she incorporated some improvements prompted by the loss of the other ship. The most significant was a gas detection device designed to trigger an alarm on the bridge had been fitted in the large double bottom space under her cargo holds. This space, 825 feet long, 66 feet wide and 12 feet deep, had been identified as a place where pockets of hydro-carbon gas might build up sufficiently to produce an explosion of the magnitude of that thought to have sunk the *Berge Istra.* Her life-saving equipment had also been updated in the light of her sister's untimely end. She now carried three lifeboats, each sufficient to accommodate all on board, and two 20-man inflatable life rafts designed to float off and inflate automatically in the event of the vessel sinking rapidly. She also had a 6-man rigid life raft housed below the forecastle head, similar to that which saved

Imeldo Leon and Epifanio Lopez. Emergency communications were provided by five position indicating radio beacons stowed in the wheelhouse. When thrown overboard, these beacons were designed to transmit continuous radio signals audible to ships and aircraft for a period of 150 hours. Also on board was another floating radio beacon capable of being used for voice communications. However, none of these beacons was so arranged to float off the ship and begin transmitting automatically if she went down quickly. They all required to be first activated and thrown overboard, which in the light of the catastrophic events that overwhelmed the *Berge Istra* seemed hardly adequate.

The *Berge Vanga* was also in the process of having new tank washing equipment installed, a requirement born out of a disastrous happening of twelve years earlier.

Early on the morning of 18 March, 1967, the 120,000-ton supertanker *Torrey Canyon* was approaching the Scilly Isles from the south, inward bound for Milford Haven with a cargo of 119,193 tons of Kuwaiti crude. The weather was fine and clear, and all the tanker's navigational equipment was operating well.

It had been the intention of Captain Pastrengo Rugiati, the *Torrey Canyon's* Italian master, to pass to the west of the Scillies in his approach to the Bristol Channel. But when, at 0645, the ship's radar picked up the southernmost of the islands right ahead, Rugiati changed his plan. During the night he had received a cable from his agent at Milford Haven warning him that if he was not able to catch the high tide at 2300 on the 18th, his deep draught would preclude him from entering the harbour for another five days. It was obvious to Rugiati that his charterers, Union

Oil of California, would not take kindly to the tanker lying idle at anchor off Milford Haven for five days. He therefore decided to take what looked like a short cut. Altering course to starboard, Rugiati opted for a more direct route which would save vital time. His new course would take the *Torrey Canyon* between the Scillies and the Seven Stones, a group of submerged rocks 8 miles northwest of the islands. The channel was deep and the Seven Stones were clearly marked by a light vessel. Rugiati anticipated no difficulty.

Unfortunately, Captain Rugiati and his officers were not familiar with these waters, and they failed to make sufficient allowance for the run of the tide. At 0850, despite the clearly visible light vessel, the *Torrey Canyon* ploughed into the Seven Stones at 16 knots, ripping open her bottom on Pollard Rock, the northernmost of the Stones. Millions of gallons of Kuwait crude oil spewed out into the clear waters of the South-Western Approaches. The golden beaches of Cornwall and Brittany turned black, one of Europe's richest fishing grounds was devastated, and in Cornwall alone 25,000 sea birds perished. The disaster was compounded by the misguided use of 2 million gallons of detergents on the polluted waters and beaches, and ten years were to elapse before the blight of the *Torrey Canyon* was lifted from the English Channel.

The *Torrey Canyon* stranding, the world's first great maritime pollution disaster, was attributed to a lethal mix of commercial pressures, incompetence and deplorable navigation. Outrage and horror was expressed on all sides, but those who knew the true facts would not have been too surprised. The *Torrey Canyon*, owned in the USA, managed in Bermuda and sailing under the convenience flag of Liberia, was operating on the fringe of legality. She was a warning of things to come. Meanwhile, the humiliating end of this big ship and the widespread damage her cargo of crude oil caused provided a major impetus for the "Green Revolution" of the Sixties. From then on, oil tankers became a primary target in the sights of the anti-pollution legislators.

When any tanker discharges her cargo, whatever the grade of oil, a considerable residue is inevitably left behind, clinging to the sides and bottoms of her tanks. If a different grade of oil is to be loaded at the next port, then these tanks must be first washed out. Up until well into the 1960s, it was permissible to begin washing tanks as soon as the ship was outside territorial waters, the resulting oily water being pumped straight over the side to disperse in the wide ocean. At the time it seemed a perfectly acceptable arrangement, but as the increasing demand for oil resulted in many more tankers at sea, beaches and estuaries began to suffer the blight of oil pollution. The cries of protest from the shore were long and loud.

The *Torrey Canyon* fiasco was the final straw, and in 1971 the Oil in Navigable Waters Act was introduced by the Government. The act prohibited any British ship from discharging oil or oil residues anywhere at sea. Other countries followed with similar legislation, and although some rogue ships continued to dump their tank washings under the cover of darkness, the sea became a cleaner place.

In the 1970s, the standard procedure for cleaning dirty oil tanks was by cold water washing using Butterworth type machines. The tank washings were transferred to a "settling" tank on board, where the mixture was allowed to separate out, the oil rising to the top of the tank. The clean sea water was then pumped overside, a monitoring device ensuring that the permitted parts per million of oil to water was

Oil/Bulk/Ore Carrier *Berge Vanga*
227,912 tons on passage with full load.

not exceeded. The oil residue recovered was then transferred to a slop tank for further treatment, more water being extracted by the use of a centrifugal separator. The uncontaminated oil remaining was then retained on board, either to be mixed with the next cargo, or pumped ashore for recovery. When properly carried out, this procedure avoided pollution of the sea and saved a considerable amount of oil that would otherwise have been lost. It did, however, involve a great deal of time and labour.

Crude Oil Washing (COW), introduced in the late 1970s, was a further step forward in tank washing, which in this age of the supertanker had become a major operation. The COW process made use of Butterworth machines, but instead of sea water, oil recycled from the cargo was used to wash down the tanks as they were being discharged. In comparison with water washing, this resulted in a 70 percent reduction in oil sediment remaining in the tanks after washing, leading to a great saving of time and money. It was still necessary to water wash tanks needed for clean ballast, but an oily water separator on deck took care of the small amount of oil remaining to be held on board.

When the *Berge Vanga* entered dry dock in Sasebo in the summer of 1979, the introduction of mandatory Crude Oil Washing in all tankers was imminent. With the ship gas-freed and immobilised in dry dock, this should have been the ideal opportunity to fit the COW equipment, which involved a considerable amount of burning and welding. Some preliminary work was carried out, but it was decided that the bulk of the work would be put into the hands of experts in the field, Tofte & Jorgesen of Copenhagen, when the ship next reached Europe.

Having completed her voyage repairs and special survey at Sasebo, the *Berge Vanga* received a certificate from the classification society, Norske Veritas, confirming her class as 1A1. This is the equivalent of 100A1 at Lloyd's, and indicates the highest standard of seaworthiness. The *Berge Vanga* sailed from Sasebo on 2 August, 1979, and proceeded in ballast to the Persian Gulf, arriving at the Iranian off-shore oil

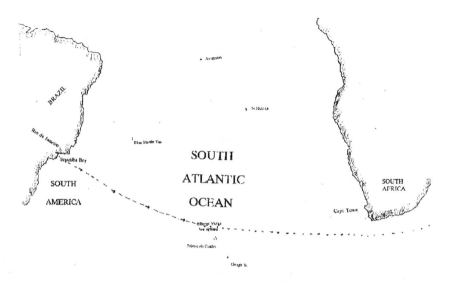

terminal of Kharg Island on the 21st. There she loaded a full cargo of Iranian crude, part heavy and part light, for North Europe. She left Kharg on 22 August.

The long haul around the Cape of Good Hope passed without undue incident, and when abeam of the Straits of Gibraltar, on 20 September, Captain Johnsen received orders to make for Lyme Bay, in the English Channel, to discharge part of his light crude. Thereafter, as expected, the *Berge Vanga* was to proceed to Rotterdam to off-load the remainder of her cargo.

Rounding Ushant on the night of the 22nd, the *Berge Vanga* anchored in Lyme Bay on the morning of the 23rd. There, within sight of the ancient port and watering place of Lyme Regis, which sits astride the border between Devon and Dorset, she discharged part of her cargo into a smaller British tanker which came alongside her. The weather was fair, and the discharging operation went without a hitch. That same evening, the *Berge Vanga* weighed anchor again, and with a North Sea pilot on board, began her passage up Channel.

The English Channel is the gateway to Northern Europe, and consequently one of the busiest through waterways in the world. Of it the Admiralty *Pilot* book has to say: "The mariner, on entering the Channel, should bear in mind that, owing to the traffic in these narrow waters one of the greatest dangers to its safe navigation lies in the risk of collision, especially in hazy or foggy weather. It is well to remember that, in addition to the vessels following the ordinary track, fleets of trawlers and yachts, there are fast cross-channel vessels and hovercraft plying between English and French ports, and crossing the track nearly at right angles." The *Pilot* also mentions numerous hidden shoals and rocks, fierce tides and unpredictable currents, fog and gales, the latter seeming to alternate as though vying with each other to increase the hazards of the passage. For the 1,030 foot-long *Berge Vanga*, drawing nearly 10 fathoms of water, the English Channel presented the ultimate test. She came through with no more than a few jangled nerves on the bridge.

The Maas pilot was reached early on the 25th, and the *Berge Vanga* berthed in Europort later that morning, commencing discharge of her cargo at once. Supervising the operation on board was Chief Officer A. Johansen, who had been with the ship since her last call at Rotterdam some four months earlier. When the last tank was empty, the receiver of the oil claimed to be about 3,000 tons short of the quantity on the bill of lading–the amount of oil signed for by Captain Johnsen before leaving Kharg Island.

When dealing with the vast tonnages of oil carried by a ship the size of the *Berge Vanga*, the absolute accuracy in the amount loaded or discharged is not possible, and a margin of error must be allowed for. In this case, however–a shortfall of 3,000 tons, or about 1 percent of the total cargo–the error was too substantial to put down to a mistake in the loading calculations. A leak was suspected, and it was at first thought that the missing oil might be in the *Berge Vanga's* double bottom tank, which ran most of the length of the ship beneath her cargo tanks. It would not be the first time that this had happened, as Chief Officer Johansen was well aware. It was for this reason that he had regularly inspected the double bottom for leaks during the voyage from the Gulf and during the discharge of the cargo. At no time did he find any significant amount of oil in the double bottom, but he had during the passage discovered a small leak in one of the cargo lines passing through the tank. A temporary repair cured the leak, and when Johansen left the ship to go on leave after completion of the discharge at Rotterdam, he informed his relief, Chief Officer Alf Lauritzen, of the need for a permanent repair to be made to the leaking pipe on passage to Brazil. This would not present a problem for Lauritzen, as it had been arranged for the installation of the new Crude Oil Washing equipment to begin as soon as the ship left Rotterdam. Torben Pedersen, one of Tofte & Jorgensen's engineers, had already joined the ship, and would go with her, using welders in the *Berge Vanga's* crew to begin the job on the Atlantic passage.

Lauritzen added the leaking double bottom pipe to his work list.

When the *Berge Vanga* sailed from Rotterdam, she had on board a total complement of thirty-nine. Her crew of six Norwegians and thirty Filipinos had been supplemented by Torben Pedersen, Munck Nielsen, one of Tofte & Jorgensen's works managers, and Nigel Page, a representative of Shell International Marine. The ship was usually under charter to Shell when she carried oil, and Page was aboard to observe the method of tank cleaning used.

Page had ample opportunity to become involved in the tank cleaning, which began as soon as the *Berge Vanga* was well clear of the land. He struck up a good relationship with Alf Lauritzen, but he was later critical of the method used to clean tanks in the *Berge Vanga*. As might be expected, the centre tanks, or holds, which were entirely free of obstructions, were easily cleaned to Page's satisfaction. Not so the wing tanks. One of these still contained some oil after washing and it was necessary to rewash. Several other wing tanks, Page noted, contained a substantial amount of residue in the form of a "sticky deposit," and to the best of his knowledge, no attempt was made to remove this by hand. He also noticed that some of the tanks contained dangerous pockets of gas after washing, and that the so-called "clean" tank washing water was far from oil-free. When this was being discharged overside, the ship's wake showed up as an oil slick stretching back right to the horizon. It was Page's stated opinion that the *Berge Vanga's* officers were more easily satisfied than he was accustomed to in the case of Shell officers, and that they generally showed some laxity in their procedure for testing and entering tanks.

Despite Nigel Page's reservations, the *Berge Vanga* was granted a gas-free certificate soon after she berthed alongside the ore terminal in Sepitiba Bay, near Rio de Janeiro on 22 October. The ore terminal surveyor noted that the ship's slop tank contained 2,361 tons of oil, the residue accumulated from the tank washing on voyage. This was far in excess of what would be expected from a normal tank washing operation, and perhaps goes a long way towards explaining the alleged shortage of 3,000 tons on completion of discharge at Rotterdam.

Loading commenced within a few hours of arrival at Sepetiba Bay, and was completed at 1420 on 24 October, a total of 208,396 tons of iron ore having been loaded into the *Berge Vanga's* five central holds. When she sailed for Japan shortly after completion, she was on her maximum summer draught of 67 feet fore and aft. Nigel Page and Munck Nielsen had by then left the ship, while three Norwegian welders, Hakon Slettum, Magne Bulaeg and Martin Haland, had joined. The three men, under the supervision of Torben Pedersen, would complete the installation of the Crude Oil Washing system on the long voyage to Japan. There was still a great deal of work to be done on this, and Pedersen anticipated being kept busy for much of the month-long passage, weather permtting.

Five days later, at noon on 29 October, the *Berge Vanga* was 200 miles northwest of the lonely island of Tristan da Cunha, and roughly midway between Sepitiba Bay and the Cape of Good Hope, when she was sighted by the 39,000-ton British bulk carrier *La Ensenada*. The two ships exchanged greetings by VHF radio, and at the request of the master of the *La Ensenada*, Captain Johnsen passed across his noon position, as determined by the *Berge Vanga's* satellite navigator. At the time, it was blowing force 6 from the north-northwest, with both ships rolling and pitching in a rough sea. The smaller British ship was shipping spray overall and generally making heavy weather of it. She was soon overtaken by the *Berge Vanga*, and 44 minutes later, at 1345, the Norwegian ship disappeared out of sight over the horizon. She was never seen again.

In accordance with Sigval Bergesen's standing orders, the *Berge Vanga* was due to radio in a routine positional message at 1600 that day. At the same time, she would have been expected to make an update on her progress to AMVER in New York. Neither message was received, and in the light of what had happened to the *Berge Istra* four years earlier, it might have been thought that suspicions would have been aroused in Oslo. Until then, the ship had been reporting regularly, and her silence should have been immediately noticed. But, once again, as with her ill-fated sister ship, the alarm bells did not ring in Sigval Bergesen's Oslo office.

It was not until 31 October, two days later, that any steps were taken to contact the *Berge Vanga*, but she made no reply to calls sent via Rogaland Radio, the Norwegian coast station. AMVER was contacted, and early on the morning of 1 November confirmed that no report had been received from the ship on 29 October. And still Bergesen's office did not come alive. It was not until late on 1 November that it was admitted the *Berge Vanga* might be missing. Even then, any sense of urgency was lacking, and another 24 hours passed before a definite move was made.

The alarm having been at last raised, the *La Ensenada* was contacted via Durban Radio, her Master replying with the following message:

FIRST SIGHTED BERGE VANGA 0300GMT APPROX 8 MILES ASTERN. 29/10/79 BERGE VANGA ABEAM 2 MILES SOUTH US AT 0830 GMT 29TH OCT. EXCHANGED NOON WITH BERGE VANGA AT 1310 GMT POSITION OF BERGE VANGA AT THAT TIME WAS 34.33S 15.27W. LOST SIGHT OF BERGE VANGA 1345 GMT DISTANCE APPROX 12 MILES AHEAD OF US. VISIBILITY AT THE TIME WAS ABOUT 12 MILES. CONVERSATION BETWEEN OUR 2/O AND 2/O OF BERGE VANGA AT ABOUT 0300 WAS ABOUT NATIONALITY OF CREW ON OUR SHIP AND THEIRS. ALSO WHERE BOUND AND LAST PORTS OF CALL. 2/O OF BERGE VANGA ALSO STATED HIS COURSE WAS 108 DEGREES TRUE. LAST CONVER-SATION WITH BERGE VANGA WAS AT 1310 ONLY THE POSITIONS WERE EXCHANGED AT THIS TIME. THERE WAS NOTHING UNUSUAL ABOUT THE SHIP OR THE CONVERSATIONS–MASTER

The *Berge Vanga* was by this time overdue passing the Cape of Good Hope, and fears for her safety were growing, prompting the South African authorities to take action. A chartered aircraft flew out to scour the seas off the west coast of Cape Province, while three Shackletons of the South African Air Force went deep into the South Atlantic to search for the missing ship. All other ships in the area were asked to keep a lookout for wreckage or survivors. No trace of either was found, but in the early hours of the morning of the 5th, the Swedish bulk carrier *Aleppo* reported sighting an 8-mile long oil slick some 45 miles east of the *Berge Vanga's* last reported position. For those assembled in Sigval Bergesen's Oslo office, the pattern was all too familiar.

The search, now coordinated by the Search and Rescue Centre at Stavanger, was concentrated in the area of the oil slick, which was about 1,600 miles due west of Cape Town. The first sign was the discovery by the research vessel *S.A. Agulhas* of small pieces of wreckage, including a short length of rope, a chair, splintered pieces of a lifeboat and large quantities of broken timber, none more than a few feet long. The implications of the state of the wreckage were ominous.

It was now learned that two ex-crew members of the *Berge Vanga*, a Norwegian female radio officer and a Filipino seaman, were aboard the tanker *Bahrainiah*, which was also engaged in the search. The *S.A. Aghulas* closed with the *Bahrainiah*, and at 0035 GMT on 9 November the Master of the tanker sent the following dramatic radio message to Stavanger:

NOVEMBER 9; DECLARATION AT SEA NOVEMBER 8. WE RADIO OFFICER INGUNN SOLLI AND ABLE SEAMAN JUAN M. HERNANDEZ GONZALES, PRESENTLY ON BOARD BAHRAINIAH, HAVE BOTH SERVED PREVIOUSLY ON BERGE VANGA AS RADIO OFFICER AND ABLE SEAMAN WE HAVE TODAY INSPECTED WRECKAGE FOUND BY THE MOTOR RESEARCH VESSEL S.A. AGULHAS ON NOVEMBER 7 IN LAT 34° 15,–S LONG 15° 20,–W

AND FOUND THAT IT DOES ACTUALLY ORIGI-
NATE FROM THE BERGE VANGA. IN PARTICULAR
WE WISH TO EMPHASISE THAT THE EASY CHAIR,
WHICH WAS PARTLY SMASHED BUT NOT BURNT,
CAME FROM THE CREW'S LIVING ROOM OF THE
BERGE VANGA AND THE ORANGE COLOURED
LIFEBOAT THWART HAS SMALL GREEN FLECKS OF
PAINT ON IT WHICH ARE BERGESEN GREEN
PAINT.

There now seemed to be little doubt that the *Berge
Vanga* had suffered a similar fate to that of her sister ship,
and at 0800 GMT on the 9th Stavanger declared her to be a
total loss. That same day, for the second time in four years,
the Lutine Bell at Lloyd's tolled for a Sigval Bergesen ship.

The search for survivors was about to be called off,
but within a few hours came the startling report that a ship
and an aircraft had heard faint SOS transmissions near
Tristan da Cunha, emanating, it was thought, from a
lifeboat or life raft radio. This led to the search being
extended for another three days, but nothing further being
heard and nothing having been found by the 12th, it was
then called off. It is possible that the signals heard on the
9th may have come from one of the *Berge Vanga's* emergency
radio beacons, which had been activated and thrown overboard. But if anyone in the ship had survived long enough
to carry out this last desperate act, then it had done him no
good. No survivors or bodies were ever seen.

The inquiry into the loss of the *Berge Vanga*, held by
the Liberian Marine Board of Investigation in November
1981, followed a similar pattern to the one held for the *Berge*

Istra. Masses of evidence were presented by people involved with the vessel on her last voyage, and by "experts" with an opinion to offer. But this time there were no eye-witnesses, for no one lived to tell the tale. Wild theories had already been advanced. The South African press, always mindful of the disappearance of the liner *Waratah* off East London in 1909, suggested that the *Berge Vanga* might have "dropped into a hole in the sea." While such a explanation might perhaps be accepted for the disappearance of a 10,000-tonner, it is most unlikely that it would have any credence in the case of a ship twenty times the size of the *Waratah*. Sources in Brazil hinted at the possibility of a bomb being planted in the ship while she was loading at Sepetiba Bay–but who on earth would wish to blow up a ship carrying a cargo of iron ore?

Captain Ingolf Stangeland, Sigval Bergesen's Marine Operations Director, appearing before the Board for the second time in three years, confessed that he was completely baffled by events. The only explanation he could offer for the loss of the ship was an explosion caused by some unknown reaction between the iron ore and a pocket of hydrocarbon gas. Stangeland stated that the *Berge Vanga's* tanks had been so thoroughly cleaned after she discharged her cargo of oil in Rotterdam that it was not considered necessary to fill them with inert gas on the ballast passage. This conflicts directly with the report of the Shell representative Nigel Page, who observed that dangerous amounts of oil residues remained in the wing tanks after washing. Page was on board the ship during the tank cleaning operation, Stangeland was not.

That the *Berge Vanga* was destroyed by catastrophic explosion of some sort seems to be beyond doubt. Yet, when this explosion is thought to have occurred—between 1345 and 1600 on the 29 October—she cannot have been much more than 20 miles ahead of the *La Ensenada*. Those on the British ship neither saw nor heard anything untoward.

Having examined all the evidence, the Liberian Board accepted an explosion or explosions as the cause of the loss of the *Berge Vanga*. The Board found that: "...the primary explosion probably took place in the double bottom space. It is probable that secondary and tertiary explosions of a massive nature would take place in the double bottom, pump room and the slop tank, blowing out the bottom and sides of the ship and also the bulkhead between the pump room and engine room, which could then also become involved. The resulting flooding of these and possibly other compartments would cause the ship to sink with extreme rapidity. An explosion in the engine room could well have killed many of the officers and crew in the accommodation above, and it is to be inferred that any who survived must have been trapped, since they were apparently unable to make use of any of the life-saving equipment provided. The recovery of a large chair, identified as being from the crew's day room, tends to confirm that at least some parts of the accommodation were blown open by the explosion, in which case any persons therein—possibly assembled for a tea break—could well have been instantly killed."

Assuming there had been pockets of gas in the ship, the most likely source of ignition leading to the explosions was found to be the burning and welding thought to have been taking place on board the *Berge Vanga* in connection with the installation of her Crude Oil Washing system. The Board concluded that the three Norwegian welders carrying out this work under the supervision of Torben Pedersen might not have been fully aware of the danger present when burning and welding in a ship that had recently carried a cargo of oil. They were not seamen, and they could well have thought that no precautions were needed. If this was so, then some responsibility must fall on the ship's officers for not keeping a careful watch on the operation.

Bearing in mind that on a previous voyage a substantial amount of oil had found its way into the *Berge Vanga's* double bottom, and that Chief Officer Johansen had found a leaking pipe in the space on passage from the Gulf to Japan, it is highly likely that the double bottom was the seat of the explosions. The slop tank was known to contain around 2,000 tons of oil left over from the tank washing, and it might be that some of this leaked into the double bottom while at sea. Test made later showed that only a small quantity of oil was required to produce an explosive mix of hydrocarbon gas and air. The double bottom was not inerted, and the fans used for ventilating the space were so placed that they might change the air in the centre sections, but leave pockets of gas in the wings. Only one air sampling unit was fitted, and that was at the extreme after end; a build-up of gas further forward could well go undetected. There is no evidence either way as to whether the welders were working in or near the double bottom, but it remains a distinct possibility. Only one spark in the right place would have been necessary to detonate the sleeping bomb.

All this is, of course, just speculation based on assumption. The secret of the *Berge Vanga's* end lies buried deep in the cold waters of the South Atlantic.

Hae Dang Wha

The 102,805-ton, South Korean-flag bulk carrier *Hae Dang Wha* sailed from Dampier, West Australia on 16 July 1980, bound for Pohang, South Korea with 98,802 tons of iron ore. On 23 July, she radioed her position as 120 miles east of Samar Island, in the Philippines. From then on, nothing further was heard from her. When she failed to arrive at Pohang on the 28th, as expected, the alarm was raised. Search aircraft sighted debris on the water off Catanduanes Island and to the east of Luzon, but no positive identification was possible. The *Hae Dang Wha*, a 12-year-old ship owned by the Korea Line Corporation, and her crew of 30 were subsequently posted missing. No trace of them was ever found. The ship was insured at Lloyd's for $7 million.

Deifovos

On 24 January 1981, the 70,341-ton Greek-flag oil/bulk/ore carrier *Deifovos* sailed from Narvik, bound for Dunkirk with a cargo of 66,108 tons of iron ore. Soon after sailing she encountered storm-force winds and developed a serious list. She sank on the 25th when 40 miles off the Norwegian coast, near Vega Island. Mountainous seas, and a blizzard which reduced visability to almost nil, hampered rescue operations, but twenty-nine crew were rescued from life rafts by heliocopters. The frozen bodies of five missing crewmen were found on a raft two days later. Four other men were believed drowned. Built in Japan in 1964, the *Deifovos* was owned by the Deifovos Shipping Corporation of Monrovia.

4

A Matter of Convenience

"The coffin ships of the last century have returned to haunt us."

–Peter Morris, Australian Federal Minister of Transport, 1992

In 1788, William Wilberforce–a rogue politician for his day if there ever was one–badgered the British Parliament into accepting the Act to Abolish Slavery. In doing so, he became an unsuspecting party to the creation of what is now known as the "flag of convenience."

The slave trade was a vast source of income for Britain, her ship owners and ports growing fat on the huge profits made, and such a lucrative business was not to be cast aside lightly. When Wilberforce's bill became law, certain indignant, but unquestionably enterprising, merchants immediately transferred their offices and ships across the Channel to France. Here they were free to take advantage of the still flourishing slave markets on the Continent and were, in effect, using a flag of convenience to circumvent the law of their own country. It is poetic justice indeed that

British ship owners unknowingly assisted at the birth of a system that, some two centuries later, would substantially assist in bringing about their own demise.

During the crippling depression of the late 1920s, some of the more hard-pressed ship owners of Europe again resorted to "flagging out," this time to avoid costly manning and safety regulations imposed by their governments. But this, again, was only a temporary expedient. Most of the ships drifted back into the fold when the profits began to flow again.

The flag of convenience, as it exists today, was first used in earnest in the early days of the Second World War by the United States of America. Being officially neutral, she was unable to openly use her own-flag ships to supply Britain with the war materials she so desperately needed to hold the line in Europe. The US Government therefore transferred the necessary ships to the flag of its near neighbour and protectorate, the tiny state of Panama. The U-boats, being largely flag-blind, sank these ships all the same whenever the opportunity occurred, but most got through and American neutrality was preserved.

The end of the war saw the Stars and Stripes flying over the largest merchant fleet in the world, with 43 percent of all US maritime trade being carried in American bottoms. Needless to say, American merchant seamen enjoyed the best working conditions and drew the highest pay of all the world's seafarers. An ordinary seaman in a US merchantman earned a wage equivalent to that of a British shipmaster. But this apparent Utopian state of affairs failed to satisfy the militant American seaman. Urged on by his powerful trade unions, he became a sea-going Oliver Twist, ever demanding more and offering less in return.

By the 1960s, American national crews had become too expensive even for the world's richest nation to employ, and for US ship owners the need to flag-out became imperative. This time they turned to the West African state of Liberia. The operating costs of a ship under the Liberian flag, which allowed her to carry a crew of any nationality, or mix of nationalities, were only about one quarter that of a ship under US jurisdiction. Consequently, the freight charged by a Liberian flag of convenience ship was less than a third that demanded by an American ship. In just a few years, the Liberian register increased from two ships to 10 percent of the world's merchant shipping.

Ironically, Liberia was founded on slavery, which, largely due to the insatiable demand for labour in the cotton plantations of the Southern States, died hard in America. Efforts to suppress this odious practice eventually led to the bloody civil war between North and South of 1861-65. But before that, as early as 1821, freed slaves were being returned to West Africa and settled on land purchased by the American Colonisation Society. In 1847, the Republic of Liberia was constituted, and by 1860 the coastal strip around the port of Monrovia held a large and thriving community of emancipated black Americans. However, the land they settled was no Shangrila. Situated five degrees north of the Equator, Liberia was a hot, steamy jungle teeming with ferocious animals, and plagued by every nasty disease know to man, and others unknown. Notwithstanding, the new Afro-American settlers took all this in their stride, and then promptly set about enslaving the indigenous tribes with all the enthusiasm of their late masters.

Today, Liberia is Africa's oldest independent state, and holds the distinction of being the only country of that great continent never to have been ruled by a foreign power. It is also the poorest country in Africa, heavily in debt and torn by internal strife; there is no visible government and anarchy rules. Three quarters of the population make a subsistence living out of the land, a great deal of iron ore is exported, but Liberia's main source of income is the hire of its national flag to ship owners seeking a liberally inclined tax haven. The capital and main port, Monrovia, is home to more than 2,000 separate shipping companies, almost one per fifty head of the population of this impoverished country. Monrovia is the hub of the flag of convenience world, and plays host to such internationally unknown shipping companies as Universe Rainbow Marine, Morning Glory Navigation and Poppy Bulk Transport, to name but three of the one-ship concerns that hang their brass plates from every convenient wall.

America set the example, and over the years following the end of the Second World War, ship owners of other established maritime trading nations, strangled by high crew costs, taxation and unrealistic regulations, followed suit, quietly transferring their ships to other flags. The power-hungry Gulf OPEC countries raised the price of marine fuel oil from $20 to $150 a ton, creating a further burden, and by the late 1970s, nearly 30 percent of the world's commercial shipping was sheltering under one flag of convenience or another. Liberia had the lion's share, with Panama trailing in second place, while an ever-increasing number of other countries climbed onto this lucrative bandwagon, offering their national flags for sale. The list is now long, and in addition to Liberia and Panama, comprises Antigua and Barbuda, Aruba, Bahamas, Belize, Burma, Bermuda, Cambodia, Cayman Islands, Canary Islands, Cook Islands, Cyprus, Gibraltar, Honduras, Lebanon, Malta, Marshall Islands, Mauritius, Netherlands Antilles, St Vincent, Sri Lanka, Tuvalu and Vanuatu. Most of these are inconsequential territories having only very tenuous links with the shipping industry, but they offer tax-free, no-questions-asked havens for the enterprising maritime entrepreneur.

It must be said that some ships flying a flag of convenience are owned by reputable companies, and are well-manned and operated. However, lack of governmental control does give scope for ship owners to cut corners, flout safety regulations and employ sub-standard crews. The casualty figures over the years bear witness to this, FoC ships being persistently top of the league table with over 50 percent of losses. As a result of this, and a number of high profile shipping disasters involving environmental pollution, flags of convenience earned themselves a very unenviable reputation. This in turn led to the setting up of "second registers."

The "second register" may be defined as a flag having close links with the origins of the ship, but offering the benefits of lower taxation and the freedom to employ a crew of any nationality. There is a commitment to comply with all international safety regulations, but enforcement is left largely in the hands of the ship's owner—a most convenient arrangement for the owner. The second register can be said to be a "respectable" flag of convenience, operating more openly, but still with considerable scope for cutting costs. The British second register is based on the Isle of Man, which although part of the United Kingdom, still clings to its Scandinavian origins. The island enjoys a measure of self-government, which includes the power to enact certain legislation and set taxes independent of the rest of Britain. Although its main port, Douglas, serves only fishing boats, yachts and the occasional ferry from Liverpool, the Isle of Man is geographically and historically ideally suited as a second register for British ships. This it became in the 1980s, offering ship owners dramatically lower taxation and a more relaxed regime. At the same time, the need to comply with international conventions was stressed, and it was necessary for a ship's owners or managers to be based on the island for accountability.

Shell Tankers, with a long and proud history of sailing under the Red Ensign, were one of the first to put their ships under the Manx flag. In 1986, Shell set up a management company in Douglas, and thirty-five of its UK fleet of forty ships were transferred to the Isle of Man register, hoisting an ensign practically unknown outside the British Isles. The crews of the ships involved were made redundant and then offered new employment on a self-employed basis—meaning cash-in-hand, from which they would be required to pay their own income tax, health insurance and pensions contributions. Tour lengths were increased from four to five months, and leave pay was cut. The change to the Isle of Man flag may have helped to balance Shell's books, but for the men who sailed the ships it was a step back in time. Unfortunately, they had no other option open but to accept the new terms, for the spectre of mass unemployment had laid its hand heavily on Europe. A job in a British-owned ship, even if it did mean a cut in pay and conditions, was well worth holding on to.

Far removed from the Isle of Man–on the other side of the world–Vanuatu, a chain of small islands in the South Pacific formerly known as the New Hebrides, once supported its 138,000 inhabitants by growing coconuts and rearing fine beef cattle. When this proved to be not enough, it also put its national flag up for rent, gathering in ships from all around the Pacific. Today, Vanuatu has over 400 ships on its register, many of them owned in Japan and Hong Kong.

In 1991, the Luxemburg register was launched, offering shelter mainly to Belgian-owned ships. How it can be that a small, completely landlocked European state can be judged to be a maritime nation is beyond comprehension–but so it is. The French, not to be outdone, have taken to registering their ships under the flag of Kerguelen, which is no more than a cluster of barren rocks deep in the Roaring Forties, and home only to a few meteorologists and flocks of itinerant penguins. Cambodia, said to be the poorest country in the world, is one of the latest to join the second register circus. This ex-French protectorate has been in a permanent state of chaos since 1975, yet claims to be able to operate and supervise a ship registry. Aruba, a Caribbean island state of only 75 square miles, opened its second register in 1996 with two US-owned VLCCs under its flag. More will follow, for the second register, although for the most part legitimate and professionally run, offers licence to cut crew costs in the same way as a flag of convenience. Numbers are reduced and cheaper foreign nationals employed.

The shipping industry of the late 20th century has become, like most industries ashore, highly competitive. Merely to exist in this cutthroat world, let alone make a profit, the ship owner must keep his operating costs down to a bare minimum. Fuel and port charges he has little control over; which leaves only maintenance and manning, and it is the latter that in most cases proves to be the incentive for a ship switching to another flag. In a nationally-manned First World ship, crew wages can account for as much as 25 percent of the total running costs; under a flag of convenience, it is possible to employ the cheapest crew on offer, saving up to $300,000, or more, annually per ship. Little wonder more than a third of the world's merchant ships now fly one flag of convenience or another.

The Philippines, an archipelago of 7,000 islands ravaged by typhoons and plagued by erupting volcanoes, is the Latin America of the Pacific. Since gaining independence from the USA in 1946 and being pillaged by Ferdinand Marcos, the country has been in the grip of high inflation, unsustainable debt, social unrest and rampant unemployment. Jobs are like gold dust in the Philippines, hence the major export is people. Filipinos migrate to the four corners of the globe in search of work, and a great many of the men end up crewing flag of convenience ships. They now man nearly a quarter of the world's merchant ships, and predominate in the bulk carriers. A nautical academy set up in Manila turns out more than 400 "certificated" officers a month. These men are cheap, they are enthusiastic, but as with all in life, "you get what you pay for." A British master of a Filipino-crewed bulk carrier recently commented: "Among deck officers there is very scanty knowledge and, in many cases, a total inability to interpret and apply the Collision Regulations.... One Filipino bosun who had failed his Third Mate's ticket told me that the examiner told him he could pass for US dollars 50, if he so wished...." The chief engineer of a Hong Kong registered ship carrying Filipinos reports: "As Chief Engineer, I now have to instruct/demonstrate operations which would be second nature to (other) second, third and fourth engineers.... The standard of English with agency-supplied Indian and Filipino officers and Filipino crews is so poor that orders "passed down" lose sense."

Multinational crews often pose even greater problems, as the British master of a 130,000-ton flag of convenience bulker discovered:

"The ship had a Korean crew, none of whom could speak any English, a Filipino third engineer with poor English, a Hong Kong Chinese 2nd engineer with very poor English and a Republic of China cadet whose technical training language had been in Chinese and thus could not understand any technical terms.

"On this ship communications with the crew by any officer was impossible, except in sign language. When the 2nd Engineer was on watch communication between the bridge and engineroom was not possible and communications on the bridge between helmsmen, lookouts and officers was on the most basic terms.

"The most worrying aspect was safety. Our fire and lifeboat drills were farcical, as we often had situations where not only could none of the crew understand the officers, but the officers could not understand the commands they were given—nor each other.

"No instruction could be given in safety procedures and none of the instructional material on board was in all the languages required."

It has now come to the point in many flag of convenience ships where a competent master and chief engineer are carried, usually European, and the remainder of the crew, officers and ratings, are just makeweight, cheap labour to stand lookout and scrub and clean. The inevitable result is that the two senior men literally "carry" the ship, the master being the only man with any knowledge of navigation and cargowork, the chief engineer the only one capable of keeping the wheels turning. Consequently, the two men work unacceptably long hours and suffer very high stress levels. Mistakes are made, ships are lost. The British chief engineer of the 169,000-ton *East Bridge*, sister ship to the *Derbyshire*, then under the Hong Kong flag and managed by Zodiac Maritime Agencies, wrote of his one and only voyage in the ship: "I was the third chief engineer she had had in two months, and she is a wreck! ... This company expects all personnel to work a minimum 12-hour day. This includes myself and the Captain, and we are both in boiler suits working flat out dawn to dusk... The biggest shock to the system was the living conditions. I knew they didn't have uniforms, but when I walked into the saloon and found them all sitting at the tables in filthy boiler suits I felt physically sick."

These are the words of a senior officer brought up in a reputable cargo liner company where high standards prevailed on and off duty. In a large part of the world's merchant fleet that has all gone by the board, being replaced by a system which turns every voyage into a cheapskate operation involving clapped out old ships manned by semi-literate ex-fishermen from the warm waters of the East. It is well

Sir Alexander Glen–Sistership of the *Derbyshire*. Built April 1975.
Known to be still trading September 1995.
Probably still in service under another name.

known among seamen that worthless certificates of competency are on sale in the backstreets of Kaohsiung and Manila. Often only a small manipulation of the truth and a handful of US dollars are required to exchange these for Panamanian or Liberian certificates, which are internationally accepted. This can result in a 150,000-tonner in the hands of men whose expertise lies mainly in the field of casting and heaving nets.

It would be a wrong to blame the Third World seamen who flock to man the flag of convenience ships for their own inadequacies They are, in the main, semi-literate and naive, and they are exploited unmercifully. The International Transport Workers' Federation has strong views on this:

"The FoC countries do not enforce minimum social standards or trade union rights for seafarers. If they did, ship owners would soon lose interest in them. The countries from which the crews are recruited can do little to protect them, even if they wanted to, because the rules which apply on board are those of the country of registration. The result is that most FoC seafarers are not members of a trade union and for those who are, the union is often powerless to influence what goes on on board the ship.

"Many seafarers working on FoC ships receive shockingly low wages, live in very poor on-board conditions, and work long periods of overtime without proper rest. They get little shore leave, inadequate medical attention, and often safety procedures and vessel maintenance are neglected (in many cases reported to the ITF, ships have been unseaworthy). In some of the worst cases, seafarers are virtual prisoners on the ship, unable to earn enough for repatriation home which the company demands they must pay."

Even making due allowance for the known bias of the ITF, there are too many well documented instances of exploitation for this to be just anti-ship owner propaganda.

The situation has worsened since the collapse of Communist rule in Soviet Russia and Eastern Europe, which resulted in the maritime labour market being flooded with out of work Russian, Polish and Yugoslav seamen. These men, again, are ripe for exploitation; so demoralised that they are willing to work for little more than their keep. It is now common practice for ships manned by "Third World Europeans" to sign two sets of articles, one with the crew signed on at ITF wages to be presented on demand to visiting officials, the other with the wages actually being paid, usually less than half the going rate.

The distinction between flag of convenience and second register has now become so blurred that it is often hard

Sir John Hunter–Sistership of the *Derbyshire*. Built January 1974. Still trading 1997 as *Nafsikam* of Kykkos Navigation Co., Ltd of Limassol. Also known as Goodfaith Shipping Co.

to distinguish one from another. And lately, "bareboat chartering" has joined the growing list flag options. Under a bareboat charter a ship becomes the property of the charterer for the term of the charter. This allows him to appoint his own crew, including the master, and has led to ships flying the Red Ensign and other reputable flags being crewed by low-paid, second-rate foreign crews. This practice is on the increase.

Flag of convenience, second register and bareboat chartering all offer the ship owner a cover under which to operate substandard ships, should he be so inclined. It is claimed that all international regulations are complied with, but who is to police these ships, many of which never come within a thousand miles of the country whose flag they fly? How can any administration, however efficient and diligent, hope to enforce its rules on a ship it never sees, a ship perhaps owned in the USA, managed from Hong Kong and manned by Indian officers and Filipino crew? It might be said that the *Kowloon Bridge* was a typical example of such a ship, owned in the Netherlands, flying the flag of Hong Kong, and crewed by Indian officers and Turkish ratings.

In 1948, in the euphoria of new-found peace, the United Nations set up the International Maritime Organisation to oversee the world's merchant shipping. As with so many best laid schemes, the IMO turned out to be a toothless tiger, powered only to recommend, but not enforce the sea of paper regulations it churns out. Today, its ranks swollen by members who do not pay their dues, it teeters on the edge of bankruptcy; an expensive talk-shop for the free lunch brigade of the pseudo maritime nations of the Third World.

COFFIN SHIPS

One result of the proliferation of flags of convenience and cheap crews has been the wasting away of the fleets of the established maritime trading nations. The British merchant fleet, which in 1975 dominated the world's trade routes with 1,614 ships of 50 million tons, is at the latest count down to a mere 236 ships of 2.5 million tons, and still shrinking. The shortage of nationally-flagged British merchantmen ships has become so acute that, of the 143 ships chartered in by the Ministry of Defence over the past five years to support the armed forces, only one flew the Red Ensign. Trawlers fishing out of Milford Haven are registered in Belize, cross-Channel ferries in the Bahamas, tugs in Bermuda, North Sea coasters in Panama. At sea, obedience to a flag and its code of conduct has become a thing of the past.

London August 9, 1990

—A Seattle court ruling has obliged Mitsui OSK Lines Ltd. subsidiary Inui SS Co. Ltd. to pay $32.6 million backpay and other compensation to 21 Filipino seamen. The award against Inui for alleged double bookkeeping standards on board the bulk carrier *Pine Forest*, followed an International Transport Workers Federation investigation. The ITF alleged that the crew members were being paid around $276 a month, well under half the ITF rate stipulated in the vessel's articles and documented in false wages accounts. —*Lloyd's List*

London August 1996

—Described by safety inspectors as one of the worst ships they had ever seen, the Cyprus-registered bulk carrier *Ambassador 1* finally left the port of Aberdeen last month after 101 days detention. The 12,603gt vessel was detained by the Marine Safety Agency in March after 56 major defects were discovered—including holes in the deck, collision bulkhead and port hatch coaming, an inoperative lifeboat engine, a missing anchor, unhygienic galley, showers and toilets, blocked drains, and unheated crew accommodation. The ship was sold to an undisclosed Greek buyer last month, renamed *Leader* and switched to the St Vincent register. Holes were filled and defective fire fighting equipment repaired, to allow the ship's new Indian crew to sail the vessel to Poland for further repairs. —Numast *Telegraph*

5

Who Commands?

"To secure a high degree of success as a shipmaster a man must possess a rare combination of qualities. He must be physically sound and strong with a personality capable of commanding the necessary degree of confidence and willingness to obey on the part of his subordinates. He must be morally strong seeing that failure in an emergency so often results in disastrous consequences. No amount of experience will compensate for lack of nerve and will power and self restraint."

–H. Holman *A Handy Book for*
Shipowners and Masters

There was a time–now receding into the distant past–when Britain's merchant fleet reigned supreme on the high seas. Forming the backbone of this busy armada were the tramps, who dominated the cross-trades, wandering from port to port at the behest of the charter market. They were mainly ships of a very basic design, strongly built, easy to maintain and economical to run. The men who manned them were dedicated professionals with generations of seafaring in their blood. Their financial rewards were not great, the conditions they lived under were often harsh, but they were loyal to the astute ship owning families that provided their employment. This unique combination of affordable ships, tight management and long-suffering seamen was unassailable money-spinner for a nation that lived by its trade.

Prominent in the ranks of Britain's tramps was J & C Harrison of London, ship owners since 1888. With a sizeable fleet of 6,000-tonners, J & C Harrison carved out a reputation by chartering out its ships, mainly on the South America trade; coal out from the South Wales ports and grain home from Argentina. The profits earned were not spectacular, but for many years "Harrisons of London" provided a good living for a considerable number of people, ashore and afloat. Then, in the late 1970s, came the slump in world trade, bringing in its wake a surplus of shipping and abysmally low freight rates. What followed is history, an unending succession of long established ship owners going to the wall. J & C Harrison were no exception. Initially, they sold off their loss-making fleet of general cargo carriers and invested in medium-sized bulk carriers running wood pulp from Canada's west coast to Japan. For a year or two the new trade paid dividends, then, as freights fell further and competition from flags of convenience increased, so Harrisons, like so many British ship owners, were forced to sell their remaining ships and invest elsewhere.

Among the assets disposed of by J & C Harrison was the motor ship *Harfleet*, a bulk carrier of 26,044 tons built on the Clyde in 1973. She went to the Astarte Shipping Company, one of the many hundreds of "brass plate" companies based in Monrovia. The *Harfleet* became the *Antacus*, her Red Ensign lowered and the rent-a-flag star and stripes of Liberia hoisted at her stern. Her managers were named as the Chi Yuen Navigation Company of Taipei, indicating the *Antacus* was almost certainly Taiwanese owned. Her British crew of thirty were replaced by a Taiwanese master, five Taiwanese officers, three Filipino officers and thirteen Filipino ratings, a total complement of nineteen. Under a flag of convenience and with a minimal wage bill–some $300,000 a year less than under the British flag–the new-born *Antacus* obtained an 8-year time charter to the Atlantic Lines and Navigation Company. Her profitability was thus ensured well into the future.

In the summer of 1984, the *Antacus* was booked to load a full cargo of fabricated steel in three North European ports, Hamburg, Bremerhaven and Antwerp, for US Gulf ports. Captain Chen Ming-Chen was then making his second voyage in command; the other Taiwanese officers on board were Chief Mate Jean Jyi-Shyong, Chief Engineer Lee Chang-Jou, Radio Officer Lin Hung-Cho and Third Assistant Engineer Szu-Wu Chang. All held Liberian certificates of competency, presumably issued on the strength of the Taiwanese qualifications they were reputed to hold. As for the ship, the *Antacus* was now eleven years old, and, as would be expected of a hard-run bulker, she was showing her age. She was, however, still classed 100A1 at Lloyd's.

To the layman, it might seem that the stowage of a cargo of fabricated steel in a bulk carrier, which has wide, uncluttered holds and no tween decks, must be a fairly straight forward, if not simple operation. This is far from the truth. Fabricated steel comes in all shapes and sizes, plates,

girders, coils, brackets, and is a heavy, awkward cargo to handle and stow. Inevitably, the bulk of the weight is low down in the holds, resulting in a "stiff" ship liable to roll jerkily, even in a moderate seaway. In which case, the stow should be tight, avoiding empty spaces which might allow movement in the cargo. Particular attention must be paid to securing with wires and wood chocks. There must be no opportunity for any single piece to break adrift, for this could lead to disaster.

Captain Chen, who had carried steel cargoes on at least two previous voyages, should have been familiar with the loading procedure, but Chief Mate Jean, who would be directly responsible for the stowage and securing, had never before been involved with a cargo of prefabricated steel. In the event, it transpired that Jean's inexperience might not be of vital importance, for the charterers, as is often the practice, had appointed a cargo superintendent to the ship. Captain M. Tijan was to go with the *Antacus* to "supervise the loading, stowing and securing of cargo by the lashing gangs in all three ports." In reality, Tijan would be on board in an advisory capacity only. Under international law, the master of any ship carries the ultimate responsibility for the loading and securing of his cargo. In the case of the *Antacus*, this was clearly stated in her charter party, which said: "Charterers are to load, stow and trim the cargo under the supervision and responsibility of the Captain," and "...the stevedores remain under the direction and control of the Master, who will be responsible for the proper stowage and seaworthiness of his vessel." Clearly, as in the case of any merchantman, although Captain Tijan was in operational control of the cargo, it was up to Captain Chen, and his deputy, Chief Mate Jean, to see that Tijan and the stevedores did their job properly. They both held internationally recognised certificates of rank, and should therefore have been capable of doing this.

At Hamburg, the *Antacus* was inspected by surveyors for the charterers, who found her holds to be clean and fit to receive cargo. Her bilge suctions were tested and found satisfactory, while the manholes giving access to the pipe tunnel running under the holds were certified secure and watertight. The ship then loaded steel sheets and wire rods in No. 1 hold; steel sheets, wire rods and nails in No. 3 hold and steel plates and sheets in No. 4. She sailed from Hamburg on the night of 30 June, making an overnight passage down the Elbe and up the Weser, arriving at Bremerhaven in time to start work next morning. In this port, she loaded bundles of steel pipes in Nos. 2 and 5 holds and steel girders, steel wires and steel coils in No. 4 hold. Some containers were also loaded on deck.

The *Antacus* left Bremerhaven on 7 July, reaching Antwerp on the 9th after a 29-hour coastal passage. At Antwerp, steel pipes were loaded in No. 2 hold, steel girders and steel "I" beams in No. 4 hold and bundles of wire rods, steel sheets, steel plates and other steel products in No. 5. On completion, the ship had on board a total of 24,600 tons of cargo, and was drawing a maximum of 34 feet of water.

Throughout the loading operations in the three ports, Captain Tijan, who had drawn up the cargo plan, was in attendance from time to time, giving instructions to the stevedores regarding the stowage and securing of the cargo. The stowage was in accordance with the practice of the trade, the steel pipes and wire rods being stowed fore and aft, with the "I" beams athwartships in the centre part of the holds and fore and aft in the wings. The containers on deck were stowed on both sides of the vessel and on top of the hatch covers of Nos. 1 and 2 holds.

On completion of loading at each port, Chief Mate Jean checked the holds with the foreman stevedore and passed the stowage and securing of the cargo as satisfactory. This implied that all bundles of cargo, including the steel plates, were securely lashed with wires and turnbuckles, while any void spaces between the cargo and the ship's side or bulkheads were chocked off with timber. There is some evidence to suggest that Jean was unable to check all the lashings and chocks, but on completion at each port he reported to Captain Chen that all was secure. On sailing, both Chen and Jean had no hesitation in signing papers acknowledging that the cargo had been stowed and secured to their entire satisfaction.

When the *Antacus* sailed from Antwerp early on the morning of 11 July, the weather forecast was favourable. It was summer, and pressure over the North Atlantic was high, although a slow-moving shallow depression was reported to the west of Ireland. In the Southern North Sea and English Channel, light or moderate southwesterly winds were expected, with a possibility of some thundery showers. Chen had good reason to look forward to a fair passage to his first discharge port, New Orleans, which, allowing for an average speed of 12 knots, he anticipated reaching on the 28th.

With her cranes stowed and hatches battened down, the *Antacus* cleared the River Schelde in late morning, and dropped her pilot off the Wandelaar around noon. The barometer was high and a moderate northwester was whipping up a choppy sea, but visibility was excellent, which in these heavily populated waters was of paramount importance. Keeping to the mandatory traffic lanes, Chen eased past the West Hinder light vessel, crossed the northeast bound lane, and joined the procession of ships heading southwest into the Dover Strait. With the British ports in the grip of yet another dockers' strike, the traffic was fairly light, and by midnight the *Antacus* had cleared the Varne Shoal and was running into more open waters.

As it so often does around these unpredictable shores, the benign weather forecast received on sailing proved over optimistic. By noon on the 12th, when the *Antacus* was off the Channel Islands, she was heading into the teeth of a rising southwesterly gale. A long, heavy swell was running ahead of the wind, and in these comparatively shallow waters this soon built up into an ugly sea. The deep-laden bulker developed a most uncomfortable corkscrew-like movement, rolling and pitching, and shipping seas over her foredeck. The *Antacus* had a long sea passage ahead of her, and at this point Captain Chen had nothing to lose by slowing down to ease the strain on the ship. He did not do so, however, continuing at full revolutions, driving the ship into the seas at 12 knots. The barometer was now rising steadily, and it may be than Chen anticipated an early improvement in the weather. Perhaps he was not aware—although as a master mariner of some experience he should have been—that a rising glass does not always mean fair weather. In this case, a ridge of high pressure moving up from the Azores was pressing against the Atlantic depression, which had now come to a halt off the northwest of Ireland. The result was a tightening of the isobars in the Western Approaches, and an ever strengthening wind.

Land's End was abeam to starboard at midnight on the 12th, and the *Antacus* moved out into the open Atlantic in worsening weather. By noon on the 13th, she was 180 miles west of Ushant, steering a course of 236° and making 11 knots. The wind had veered to the west, and was blowing force 7 with a high sea and heavy swell running. The *Antacus* was labouring badly, rolling and pitching and burying her bows deep in the oncoming seas. Her decks were constantly awash, her engines racing each time her stern lifted, and yet Chen made no move to reduce speed. The ship was being driven into the storm regardless of the consequences.

The constant pounding the *Antacus* was subjected to inevitably took its toll. That night slamming noises were heard coming from below decks, seemingly forward of the crews' quarters. The thumps were accompanied by vibrations running through the hull that coincided with the roll of the ship. Something was adrift in the holds. This was the conclusion reached by Chief Mate Jean, and confirmed by Third Mate Santiago Realigue and Boastwain Nelson Morgal, all of whom agreed that the noises came from No. 4 or No. 5 hold. Yet none of these men, senior members of the crew, thought fit to report the matter to the Master. Chen was in his cabin below the bridge, and although he heard the noises and felt the shock-like blows, he made no effort to investigate.

The picture conjured up is a shameful one. Even to the most uninitiated, it should have been obvious that some heavy object had broken adrift and was careering from side to side, from forward to aft, and smashing against the bulkheads and ship's side like a gigantic battering ram. It was later revealed that everyone on board the *Antacus* was aware of what was happening, yet although they whispered together in groups, frightened by the threat below decks, no one made any attempt to take action. The prudent thing to do would have been to slow down, put the wind and sea fine on the port bow to ease the ship's movement, and then enter the hold to resecure whatever was causing the damage. But no action was taken, not even by the man supposedly in command, Captain Chen, who later described the sounds heard as "very heavy and dull," and similar to the noise made when cargo was lowered into the holds during loading. No log entries regarding this were made.

All through that long night, the *Antacus* ploughed on southwestwards, gamely trying to shoulder aside the mountainous seas, while deep in her holds her cargo of heavy steelwork was running amok, threatening to destroy her from within. By noon on the 14th, she was 300 miles northwest of Cape Finisterre, and with the barometer steady at 1030 mb, the wind had eased slightly. But the sea and swell showed no signs of going down, and the ship continued to take heavy punishment.

There was at least one man on board not paralysed by fear, and he was the Filipino carpenter A.G. Geollegue. Although he was taking a fearful risk in venturing out on the wave-swept main deck, Geollegue had continued throughout to take his daily soundings of the hold bilges, except at No. 1 hold, where the sounding pipes were covered by the containers on deck. From the time of sailing from Antwerp, all bilges sounded three or four inches of water, a negligible amount, and to be expected in an 11-year-old ship in heavy weather.

It is known that on the morning of the 14th, the morning after the mysterious noises were first heard coming from the holds, Geollegue had found between ten and twelve inches in Nos. 4 and 5 hold bilges. This was very significant, and ominous, but whether it was reported to Chief Mate Jean is not known. Geollegue will almost certainly have entered the readings in the bilge sounding book—that is if one was being kept. In any event, nothing was done. Either Chen and Jean were not aware of the sudden increase in soundings in the after bilges, or they chose to ignore this.

On the morning of the 15th, Geollegue again found only a small amount in the forward hold bilges, but Nos. 4 and 5 holds now showed between twenty inches and two feet of water. Unbelievably, such obvious warning signs were completely ignored; no attempt was made to pump out the bilges, and the cause was not investigated.

The *Antacus* was then 470 miles due west of Finisterre, and although the sea was still rough and the swell heavy, the wind was moderating and veering to the north. The ship continued to roll and pitch, shipping heavy water on deck, but the thumps and bangs in the holds had ceased. It seemed that, by the grace of God, and with no help from those who manned her, the *Antacus* had survived her ordeal by storm without serious damage. With her engines turning over smoothly, and making a steady 12 knots, she continued on course for the Gulf of Mexico.

The blow fell soon after midnight that night, when Second Assistant Engineer Alex Alipis was making his rounds of the engine-room. As was the routine, Alipis opened the watertight door leading to the pipe tunnel running under the holds, and shone his torch inside. The beam of light glinted on water, and a closer examination revealed the tunnel was flooded almost to the top rung of the ladder. Horrified, Alipis slammed the door to and dogged it down. He then ordered his oiler to open the suction and discharge valves to the tunnel, while he ran to start the bilge pump.

When the pump was running, Alipis called Chief Engineer Lee Chang-Jou, who joined him in the engine-room within a few minutes. Both men opened the tunnel door to find that the water level had risen another six inches and was now near the top of the tunnel. The door was slammed quickly and battened down securely. On his own initiative, and without consulting the bridge, Lee then changed over fuel from heavy oil to diesel, to allow easy manoeuvring, and slowed the engine down. Second Mate Ely Zenarosa, who was on watch on the bridge, detected the drop in engine revs, and called Captain Chen. It was now twenty minutes after midnight. When he reached the bridge, Chen telephoned the engine-room and spoke to Lee, who acquainted him with the seriousness of the situation, and advised that all holds and tanks be sounded at once. Chen sent for Chief Officer Jean and Carpenter Geollegue.

Fortunately, by now the wind had gone round astern, and was blowing east-northeasterly force 5-6. The *Antacus* was reasonably steady and no longer shipping water on deck. This gave Jean and Geollegue the opportunity to take soundings. Working from forward to aft, they sounded the wing and hopper tanks, and all cargo holds except No. 1, the sounding pipe of which was not accessible. They found all tanks to be dry, and, as before, the forward hold bilges showed only a few inches. It was only when the two men reached the after deck that the true predicament of the ship was revealed. Geollegue's sounding rod showed three feet of water in No. 4 hold and thirteen feet in No. 5.

Chief Officer Jean immediately returned to the bridge, where he reported to Chen. It was already apparent to Chen by the slope of the deck that the *Antacus* was well down by the stern, but he was not prepared for the news that he had in the region of 2,000 tons of water in his after holds. Only then did he realise that whatever had been adrift in the holds at the height of the storm had done serious damage. His ship was in danger of sinking.

Chen, at last aroused from his apathy, conferred briefly with Chief Engineer Lee, who then put all available pumps, two electric and one steam, onto Nos. 4 and 5 hold bilges. Working in concert, the three powerful pumps spewed water over the side at a rate in excess of 80,000 gallons per hour, but all to no avail. Soundings taken by Geollegue half an hour later showed that although the water in No. 4 hold had increased only slightly, the level in No. 5 had risen by over six feet. The pumps were not coping with the inrush of water, and the ship was going further by the stern.

Soon after receiving the second set of soundings, Chen made the decision to abandon ship. He gave orders for the starboard lifeboat to be swung out and prepared for lowering, and then sent for Radio Officer Lin Hung-Cho. Lin was instructed to send the following distress message over the radio telephone:

MAYDAY. THIS IS MOTOR VESSEL *ANTACUS*. WATER INTO CARGO HOLD. VERY DANGEROUS REQUIRE IMMEDIATE ASSISTANCE.

It may well have been that Chen was under considerable stress when he dictated the message, but it is still difficult to understand how any ship's captain, however troubled, could possibly omit the ship's position from an SOS. Standard practice is always position first, then the text. In this way, should the message be cut short, then at least rescuers will have a position to make for. As it stood, Chen's distress was useless, for all it would to convey to any station receiving it was that a ship called *Antacus* was in trouble. But where was she? In the Atlantic? In the North Sea? In the English Channel? She could be anywhere, and without a position no rescue operation could be set in motion.

But if Captain Chen was amiss, then Radio Officer Lin was doubly so. Being in possession of a Liberian licence, he was judged to be a competent radio operator, and yet he accepted Chen's message as it was, not questioning the need to give the ship's position.

Returning to the radio-room, Lin switched on the main transmitter, and when it had warmed up, tuned to the W/T distress frequency of 500 kHz. He then started the automatic keying device, which began to send a series of morse signals designed to trigger auto-alarms on nearby ships, if any, and shore radio stations within range. Having run the keying device for some one and a half minutes, Lin then changed over to the voice frequency, 2,182 metres, and began to broadcast Chen's message in plain language.

Chen had meanwhile sent Boatswain Morgal to turn out the deck crew, who then, under the supervision of Second Mate Zenarosa, swung out the starboard lifeboat. The boat was lowered to the main deck, where it was stocked with blankets, warm clothing and extra provisions. Zenarosa and his party then stood by the boat to await further orders from the bridge.

Over the next hour Radio Officer Lin frequently made use of the automatic keying device, followed by voice transmission on 2,182 metres to broadcast the distress. He also tried to establish contact with two radio stations in the Azores, but without success. It may be that Lin's very limited knowledge of the English language had something to do with this, but it could also be that his equipment was at fault. However, this seems unlikely, for since leaving Antwerp on the 11th, Lin had on a number of occasions been in touch with stations in Europe and America. Less than two hours before he began the distress routine, he had contacted a British weather station for a forecast, and had also listened in to a Belgian station. Yet, following the first distress broadcast, Lin claimed that throughout the time he was on the air he did not hear a single radio station on any of the frequencies he listened to, which is very strange. The *Antacus* was only 150 miles from the Azores, and less than 700 miles from the coast of Europe. The air should have been alive with voice and morse chatter.

At 0220 on the 16th, with the pumps running hot but not holding the sea at bay, Captain Chen concluded that the *Antacus* was sinking slowly by the stern, and gave the order to abandon ship. At this point he was aware that there had been no response to his distress signal.

On receiving the order to abandon ship, Chief Engineer Lee stopped the main engine and then evacuated the engine-room, which was in accordance with the proper procedure for abandoning ship. Then, for some reason which is hard to explain, before leaving the engine-room himself, he shut down the generator, possibly the worst action he could have taken at that time. The ship was immediately plunged into darkness, and the pumps came to a halt. Lee later explained that he stopped the generator because he feared an explosion should the engine-room become flooded. There was, in fact, no sign of this happening, for when Lee, using a torch to light his way, left his post to go on deck, the door to the pipe tunnel was still dogged tight, and there was no sign of water entering the engine-room.

Abandoning a ship at night in mid-ocean is an operation fraught with many hazards. When that ship is in complete darkness, rolling in a heavy swell, and manned by men who have no common language, then the task is doubly difficult, and inevitably beset by panic. So it was with the *Antacus*, but, somewhat miraculously it must be said, her starboard lifeboat was lowered and all nineteen crew got away without injury. An inflatable life raft was also launched, and made fast astern of the boat. Radio Officer Lin, whom it appears was last to leave the ship, switched the automatic keying device to the emergency transmitter before abandoning the radio-room, so that at least an SOS signal would continue to go out. As soon as the boat was clear of the ship's side, Lin set up the portable lifeboat radio and began transmitting distress signals on 500 kHz. He continued to transmit for some hours, but received no reply. Throughout, he could clearly hear the automatic signals emanating from the *Antacus*, which indicates that the lifeboat receiver was in working order.

When daylight came, the lifeboat was some 5 miles off the *Antacus*, which was still very much afloat. The abandoned ship was, however, heavily by the stern, and around noon that day her bows were seen to rear up, and she slid beneath the waves stern first.

With the *Antacus* gone to her last resting place, to her survivors left riding the Atlantic swells in a small boat, the sea became a very empty and hostile place. Their approximate position they calculated to be some 150 miles north-northeast of the Azores, and so far as they were aware, their distress calls had not been heard by anyone–at least, no one had answered their calls for help. This was a lonely part of the ocean, where few ships passed, and the 28-foot boat, low in freeboard and often out of sight in the troughs was unlikely to be sighted by chance. It could be many days before the *Antacus* was missed, and by then another vicious Atlantic gale might have completed the grim cycle of events begun on the night of the 13th.

After an uncomfortable day spent tossing on the waves, hopes were raised late that afternoon, when Radio Officer Lin reported an acknowledgement of his distress calls. The signal was brief and inconclusive, just, "Regarding your SOS..." then silence. It might not even have been addressed to them, and Lin was unable to identify the station calling. He also heard other stations calling one another, but was unable to establish contact. The outside world was there, but was it aware of their predicament?

In fact, no one ashore or afloat had heard Lin Hung-Cho's distress calls, said to have gone out for over 19 hours, firstly from the radio-room of the *Antacus*, then from her lifeboat. It was just sheer chance that the French yacht *Saint Jean*, inward bound for the Channel, was on a tack that took her close to the drifting lifeboat, which she sighted just after first light on the 17th. The *Saint Jean* was unable to take the survivors on board, but she stood by the boat all day, sending out distress signals on behalf of Captain Chen. These were picked up by the Honduras-registered cargo ship *Olanche*, which arrived on the scene that afternoon. The *Olanche* rescued all nineteen men and later transferred them to the Portuguese warship *Augusto Castilho*. They were landed at Ponta Delgado, in the Azores, early on the morning of the 18th.

A formal investigation into the loss of the *Antacus* was held in Monrovia on 10 March, 1987 by the Liberian Commissioner of Maritime Affairs. The court ruled that: "The probable cause of the casualty was that the fabricated steel cargo stowed in either hold No. 4 or hold No. 5 began to shift during the period July 13-14, 1984, due to improper stowage, and became progressively loosened from its lashings, ultimately causing a crack or larger opening through the side shell plating of the vessel, allowing water into the holds. The water found its way into the pipe tunnel through a loosened manhole cover or a crack or other opening in the floor of one or both of holds Nos. 4 and 5."

This was all supposition, but probably very near to the truth. As to the action—or lack of action—taken to prevent the disaster, the Liberian court was scathing: "Although the noises were first heard from those holds and vibrations felt when the vessel rolled, neither the Master nor the Chief Mate made any effort to ascertain the reason for these noises. If the stowage had been proper, the cargo should not have broken loose in sea and wind conditions no worse that those prevailing during the voyage. Most importantly, the Master took no action to reduce the laboring of the vessel at any time during the two days that this 'very heavy and dull' noise was coming from the vicinity of the cargo holds. The Master could have ordered course changes and/or speed reductions after the noises were heard in an effort to reduce the stress on the vessel, but did not do so. It cannot be dismissed that course changes and/or speed reduction might have reduced the heavy rolling to such an extent that cargo which had broken its stow would have ceased to strike against the shell plating of the vessel.... The failure to explore the possibility of reducing stress on the vessel by taking such action constituted gross negligence on the part of both the Master and Chief Mate."

The court commented on the obvious confusion that reigned on board the *Antacus* in her hour of need: "While there is no testimony upon which to evaluate the level of communication aboard ship prior to the heavy weather encountered before the sinking, there is much remarkable testimony to the effect that no one aboard the vessel spoke with anyone else concerning repeated loud noises coming from the vicinity of the cargo holds—over a two-day period. The only explanation ever offered for this was that of the Third Mate, Mr Realigue: 'Because this is too obvious to discuss with, sir. Everyone can hear the loud noise. It is loud enough and the vibration you can feel.' Yet the Chief Mate, at the end of his testimony, was of the opinion that if the noise had been investigated there might have been some possibility of saving the ship. Of course it is true that such an investigation might have revealed that there was no possibility of saving the ship, but since none was ever made and the matter was never even discussed by the Master with his officers, all possibilities were sacrificed."

The actions of Radio Officer Lin Hung-Cho came in for particular criticism: "The Radio Officer did not perform his duties with the required skill and competence. While the Radio Officer switched transmissions back and forth between the emergency and main transmitters, never once did he transmit the vessel's position as part of his distress message. His failure to transmit the vessel's position as part of any distress message (his explanation being that 'since we are all very, very busy, I just send out the message as the Captain told me') does not meet international standards for conduct under such circumstances."

The reality was that no ship or coast station picked up Lin's distress calls, and it was said by the court: "It was clearly evident from his testimony that his knowledge of the English language was wholly inadequate so that even if his voice transmissions had been received they probably would not have been understood."

Chief Engineer Lee Chang-Jou was similarly damned: "The Chief Engineer, Mr Lee, testified on deposition that when he left the engine-room he shut down all the machinery, including the generators. This is consistent with his earlier written statement in which he declared this to be his own decision, and that he did so because he felt that 'as we were abandoning the vessel everything should be turned off.' Both the Chief Engineer and the Master agree that the Chief Engineer never received an order from the Master to shut down the power plant. His decision to do so on his own was irresponsible and evidence of incompetence."

In his summing up, the President of the Court, Gordon W. Paulsen, concluded: "Under these most demanding conditions, the Master failed to exercise the most basic requirements of command. He did not question why the Chief Engineer had shut down the plant. He did not give the Radio Officer the ship's position, or ask the Radio Officer if the distress call had been acknowledged." The President went on: "It was imprudent and premature for the Master to order the vessel to be abandoned at about 0220, on the rationale that, notwithstanding the pumping with the steam bilge pump, general service pump and fire and bilge pump (with combined capacities of about 350 tons/hr) the vessel's trim had increased to about 15 feet by the stern with the surface of the water about one meter below the main deck at the stern. The fact that the abandonment order was premature is evident from the facts that: (a) at the time of last observation, the water in the pipe tunnel had not reached the threshold of the water-tight door leading from the engine room into the pipe tunnel; and (b) the pumps were operating and capable of operation for an indefinite period; and (c) the vessel could have remained afloat for an additional 15 hours or so if the crew had remained aboard and the pumps continued to operate. She actually sank about 9 to 10 hours after having been abandoned."

And now came a most damning indictment of Captain Chen Ming-Cheng and his crew: "It is clear that the abandonment order was carried out with unseemly and unnecessary haste. All of the vessel's documents went down with her except the deck log book, the chart in use, and the licenses, passports and seamen's books of the individual crew members. The Master testified that he had no time to open the ship's safe, and though he did not take any of his personal belongings off the vessel, other officers and crew members did."

And, finally, the finger of suspicion was pointed: "The evidence of gross fault on the part of those in charge of the vessel during the loading of the cargo and during the voyage is such that there will probably always be a lingering doubt as to whether the sinking might have been intentional."

On reflection, it seems highly unlikely that, had they been involved in some plot to deliberately scuttle the *Antacus*, Chen and his officers would have chosen to perpetrate the deed 700 miles out in the Atlantic. The weather was not good, and given the incompetence of Radio Officer Lin, there was every chance of them perishing after abandoning ship. It seems more likely that this was simply a case of a once-stout ship in the hands of men who were neither qualified to, nor capable of caring for her. They were apparently not aware of their responsibilities regarding the loading and securing of the cargo—even though their own lives might be at risk. Furthermore, when what must have been a heavy piece of cargo broke adrift in the gale, they had no idea of what action they should take. This was an inexcusable state of affairs—a good ship delivered into the hands of a bunch of rank amateurs, and a situation all too common in the shady world of flags of convenience.

As a result of the formal investigation into the loss of the *Antacus*, the following action was taken against her officers: Captain Chen Ming-Cheng's Liberian licence was permanently revoked. He was offered the opportunity to apply for a Liberian licence in the grade of Chief Mate. Chief Mate Jean Jyi-Shyong's Liberian licence was suspended for a period of one year, and he was given a letter of censure and reprimand. He was authorised to apply for a Liberian licence in the next lower grade during the period of the suspension. Chief Engineer Lee Chang-Jou's Liberian licence was also suspended for a period of one year, and he was similarly allowed to apply for a licence in the next lower grade. Radio Officer Lin Hung-Cho was sent a letter of censure and reprimand to be placed in his file. His licence as Radiotelegraph

Operator was suspended until such time as he was able to satisfactorily pass a test of his English language competence. The question that must be asked is how and why these men were granted Liberian licences in the first place.

Arctic Career

The 69,389-ton Panamanian-flag bulk carrier *Arctic Career* sailed from Tubarao, Brazil on 17 June 1985, bound for Cigading, Indonesia. The 19-year-old ship, crewed by twelve Hong Kong Chinese officers and fifteen Filipino ratings, had on board a cargo of 67,051-tons of iron ore. She was owned by Arctic Maritime Carriers Inc. and managed by Prompt Shipping of Hong Kong.

The *Arctic Career* reported her noon position every 48 hours to Hong Kong, until 23 June, when her last message gave her position as 440 miles northwest of Tristan da Cunha. Nothing further was heard from her. In his final message, the Master radioed that he was encountering "boisterous weather," with a force 9 northwesterly wind. He reported damage to shell plating and a hatch coaming caused by the weather. South African aircraft mounted an extensive search covering many thousands of square miles around the *Arctic Career's* last known position. An oil slick and a few empty oil drums were sighted about 300 miles north of Tristan da Cunha, otherwise, there was no trace of the missing ship. She was presumed to have sunk, taking all her crew with her.

6

An Unfortunate Chain of Events

"Ironically, a letter from Lord Brabazon, junior transport minister, stating that there would be no public inquiry into the loss of the *Derbyshire*, was written on Tuesday, the very day the *Kowloon Bridge* ran into trouble."

–Daily Telegraph, 21 November 1986

In the North Atlantic, the winter of 1978 was severe, a not unusual state of affairs in this troubled ocean. On 28 December, the 3,300-ton Greek motor vessel *Tenorga*, on passage from Antwerp to Algeria, having fought a long and punishing battle across the Bay of Biscay, was hove-to off the west coast of Portugal. The wind was gusting force 11, the seas were mountainous, the ship was making water at an alarming rate, and one crew member lay seriously injured. In desperation, the *Tenorga's* master decide to make for the nearest port. This was Leixoes.

The port of Lexioes, lying 3 miles north of the mouth of the River Douro, is exposed to the open Atlantic and difficult to enter in bad weather. When notified of the *Tenorga's* intention to enter, the port authorities advised it was impossible to send out a pilot and urged the Greek ship to stand off an await an improvement in the weather. But by then conditions aboard the *Tenorga* were such that she was forced to seek shelter without further delay. She began her approach. With the wind and sea astern, the ship steered badly, veering from side to side, her engines racing each time her stern lifted on the big following seas. Not surprisingly, she piled up in the entrance to the harbour and sank with the loss of all but three of her crew of twenty-four.

The wreck of the *Tenorga*, lying in the approach channel to Lexioes, constituted a major hazard to shipping, especially to the large tankers using the port. They were too big and too deep to edge past the wreck, and so the port authorities suspended the movement of all large vessels in and out of Lexioes. Thus, quite unintentionally, the sinking of a 23-year-old Greek tramp set in motion a chain of events that would cause considerable havoc in the shipping world for many years to come.

One of the first ships to be affected by the loss of the *Tenorga* was the 121,430-ton French tanker *Betelgeuse*, then inward bound for Lexioes from Saudi Arabia with a cargo of 120,000 tons of crude oil. The Portugeuse terminal being closed, the *Betelgeuse* was re-routed to Bantry Bay, on the southwest coast of Ireland. On arrival there, she was berthed alongside the Gulf Oil terminal at Whiddy Island, at the head of the bay, and the discharge of her cargo commenced.

In the early hours of the morning of 8 January, 1979, just 40,000 tons of oil remained in the tanker, when suddenly a series of massive explosions occurred on board. The *Betelgeuse* was ripped apart and sank at once, spewing burning oil onto the water and setting fire to the shore terminal.

It was said at the time that the force of the explosions aboard the ship shook every house in Bantry, and the flames, which turned night into day, were reported visible 60 miles off. The intense heat, the thick black smoke and gaseous fumes prevented fire crews approaching the conflagration at Whiddy, which burned unchecked for twenty-four hours. Another two weeks elapsed before it was judged safe to approach the area. It was then possible to confirm that all forty-two members of the *Betelgeuse's* crew, the wife of one officer, and seven oil terminal workers had lost their lives in the holocaust. The terminal was a still-smoking ruin, and the *Betelgeuse* had been blown into four separate pieces, which now lay submerged alongside the remains of the jetty. The eventual cost of this disaster to the insurers of the tanker was in the region of £90 million, and it was not until the late summer of 1980 that the devastation caused by the disaster was finally cleared away. And all this because one small Greek ship had sought a port of refuge on a stormy night two years earlier.

In September of that year, the disappearance of the *Derbyshire* ousted the *Betelgeuse* from the headlines, and interest shifted to the Far East. Whereas the French tanker had acted out her last hours in full view of the television cameras, the *Derbyshire* had gone like a will-o'-the-wisp snatched away by the wind. Here was a mystery that, for a while at least, gripped the imagination of the shipping world. The power of the typhoon is well known, but that any storm, no matter how violent, could overwhelm a well-found, well-manned ship of such gigantic proportions was beyond belief. It was not long before probing questions were being asked.

The inquiry into the loss of the *Derbyshire*, held in London in November 1980, was informal and superficial. Its conclusions were predictable. The Court ruled that the oil/bulk/ore carrier had suffered a sudden and catastrophic end, but in the absence of wreckage and survivors, the cause of the loss of the ship could not be established. On the basis of this finding, the Department of Trade recommended that research be carried out to establish, if at all possible, any contributing factors to the loss. Beyond that, no further action was contemplated. The *Derbyshire* was about to join the long list of ships "lost at sea without trace."

The civil servants did not, however, take account the grief-driven anger of those who were left to mourn those lost in the *Derbyshire*. The relatives were not satisfied with the perfunctory way in which a great ship and the forty-four people on board had been laid to rest. They called for a full Public Inquiry, a move strongly resisted by the *Derbyshire's* owners, her builders and the Department of Trade. But the fight for the truth went on. More than a year passed with the campaigners making little progress against the closed ranks of the bureaucrats. Then, in March 1982, the *Tyne Bridge* made the headlines.

The 169,428-ton *Tyne Bridge*, a sister ship of the *Derbyshire* sailing under the Italian flag, ran into trouble in the North Sea while outward bound from Hamburg in ballast. Lashed by storm-force winds and rough seas, the oil/bulk/ore carrier developed serious cracks in her deck plating just forward of the bridge. Fearing his ship might be in danger of breaking up, the master of the *Tyne Bridge* called for help. Helicopters took off twenty-eight of the ship's thirty-five-man crew, while the remainder nursed her back to the Elbe for repairs. When she reached port, an examination showed that cracks in the deck immediately forward of the bridge—the most vulnerable point in the ship's 970-foot long hull—were so serious that she had, as her master had feared, been very close to breaking in two. Prompt action had saved the ship and her crew. Had she been in more distant waters, the story might have ended very differently.

After undergoing extensive repairs, the *Tyne Bridge* returned to sea, but her narrow escape became public knowledge and resulted in renewed calls for a comprehensive inquiry into the loss of the *Derbyshire*. The two ships were identical, and what had so nearly happened to the one could well have been reality for her sister caught in a typhoon in the Pacific. Unable to deny this possibility, the Department of Trade at last agreed to an independent investigation into the design of the Bridge class oil/bulk/ore carriers, with particular reference to the *Derbyshire*. On the subject of a Public Inquiry, however, the DoT stubbornly refused to give way.

The results of the independent investigation were inconclusive, and again, as might be expected, the *Derbyshire* relatives were not satisfied. Backed by the seamen's unions, they kept up the pressure for a full Public Inquiry, but for reasons hard to explain, the British Government continued for another four years to dodge the issue. Finally, on 18 November 1986, Michael Spicer, a Junior Transport Minister, harried in the House of Commons by Opposition MPs, reached the point of exasperation. In a letter to all interested parties, he declared emphatically that there was insufficient evidence to warrant any further inquiries. As far as he and the Government were concerned, Spicer wrote, the matter of the *Derbyshire* and her missing crew was finally and irrevocably closed. Even as he dictated his letter, the Minister's case for doing nothing was about to be blown sky high.

On that grey November day, while the cold drizzle misted the windows of the Houses of Parliament in London, far out in the North Atlantic the storm gods were riding. Fuelled by a series of deep depressions tracking in from the west, a violent storm raged to the west of Ireland and two big ships were in trouble. One was the 89,284-ton Italian tanker *Capo Emma*, two days out of Sullom Voe and bound for Halifax, Nova Scotia with a full cargo of North Sea crude. In riding out the storm, the *Capo Emma* had lost a section of her bow plating on the starboard side, below the waterline, but fortunately in way of an empty ballast tank. The tanker was in no immediate danger of sinking, but she was labouring heavily in the seaway, and there was every possibility that the fracture in the ship's side would spread to the after bulkhead of the ballast tank. If that bulkhead then collapsed, the ship would be in serious trouble, probably at risk of foundering. The *Capo Emma's* master decided to come about and run for the nearest shelter, which was 96 miles away in Bantry Bay.

Hard on the heels of the stricken Italian tanker, and also heading for the shelter of Bantry Bay, was the 169,080-ton oil/bulk/ore carrier *Kowloon Bridge*, yet another sister of the *Derbyshire*. She was bound for the Clyde with a cargo of 160,700 tons of pelletised iron ore from Seven Islands, having left that port eleven days earlier. Running into bad weather in mid-Atlantic, she had endured several days of storm-force winds, with waves up to 50 feet high, and had taken a prolonged and heavy beating.

The *Kowloon Bridge*, once part of Bibby Line's Seabridge consortium, came out of Swan Hunter's Wallsend yard in 1976 as the *English Bridge*. She had then sailed under the Bibby house flag until 1979, when she was sold to the Amroth Investments Corporation of Monrovia, and joined the swelling ranks of flag of convenience ships. Flying the Liberian flag, she plied her trade for a while blessed with the distinctly unnautical name *Sunshine*, before passing to the ownership of Grimaldi Line of Palermo. Renamed *Mercurio* and flying the Italian flag, she regained some of her honour, but resumed the downward path when she was sold to the Far Eastern Navigation Corporation of Taipei. She then became the *Crystal Transporter* and hoisted the Taiwan flag.

In 1985, the *English Bridge*, ex-*Sunshine*, ex-*Mercurio*, ex-*Crystal Transporter*, was sold to Dutch-owned Helinger Ltd of Hong Kong and renamed *Kowloon Bridge*. Managed by for Helinger by Zodiac Maritime Agencies of London, she flew the Hong Kong flag and was commanded by Captain S.T. Rao. Her officers were Indian, her ratings Turkish. She had become, in the end, a typical flag of convenience mongrel, her ownership deliberately confused, her crew bi-national and with built-in communications difficulties.

At midnight on 17 November 1986, the *Kowloon Bridge* was 150 miles west of Ireland, and in storm-force winds with heavy and confused seas. Her decks were continually awash as she rolled and pitched, every plate and frame in her heavily-loaded hull creaking and groaning in protest. The protests proved well-founded, for just before 0100 on the 18th, Captain Rao sent the following urgent radio message to all stations:

I HAVE A CRACK IN NUMBER FIVE HATCH COAM-
ING ON THE STARBOARD SIDE. ALSO HAVE A
CRACK BETWEEN NUMBER NINE AND PUMP-
ROOM. THIS CRACK IS SLOWLY EXPANDING. I AM
MAKING FOR BANTRY BAY.

Rao may, or may not, have been familiar with the
Tyne Bridge incident; if he was, he will have been aware that
his ship was giving out the same warning signals that had
sent the other scurrying for the shelter of the Elbe nearly
four years earlier. The *Kowloon Bridge*, running before an
Atlantic storm, was in the early stages of breaking up.

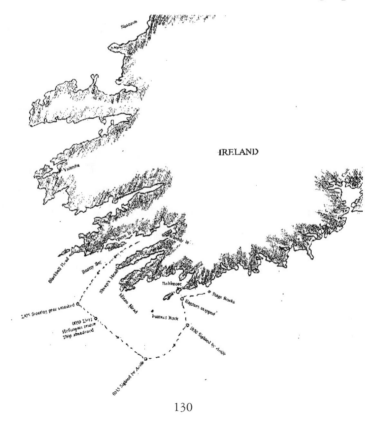

Valentia Radio passed Rao's message to Bantry Bay, where the authorities already had a difficult situation on their hands. The *Capo Emma*, loaded with 80,000 tons of volatile crude oil, and with a large hole in her bows, being then in the approaches to the bay. The first reaction ashore was to tell Captain Rao to take his ship and his troubles elsewhere, but this they could not do.

Seven years had passed since the *Betelgeuse* wreaked her terrible destruction at Whiddy Island, but the memories were still fresh. Acting on instructions from the Irish Department of Communications–then responsible for merchant shipping–the port authorities at Bantry Bay kept quiet about the *Capo Emma's* damage and discreetly ushered her into an anchorage off the ruined jetty at Whiddy Island. Experienced workmen were called in, pollution control and fire-fighting equipment set up, and preparations put in hand for discharging the Italian ship's cargo into other tankers. This would not be an easy operation, for Bantry Bay is open to the southwest, and the wind being in that quarter, the seas were running right up to the head of the bay. And while all the limited resources of Bantry Bay were being directed towards making the *Capo Emma* safe, the *Kowloon Bridge* arrived.

Bantry Bay is a deep, fjord-like indent in the southwest corner of Ireland 18 miles long by 3 miles across at its widest point, with deep water in most places right up to the shore, and good holding ground for anchors. If the mouth of the bay faced any other way but into the prevailing winds of the North Atlantic, it would make an ideal safe haven for shipping. On that wild November morning in 1986 it was perhaps the last place for a ship to seek shelter. However, for

Captain Rao, desperately in need of breathing space to examine his damaged ship, Bantry represented the only possible escape from the wrath of the Atlantic. Pilotage was not compulsory, but Rao had no large scale chart of the area on board, and as soon as he passed Sheep Head, at the entrance to the bay, he called for a pilot. The response from the shore was not encouraging. With the Whiddy Island terminal closed since the *Betelgeuse* explosion, full-time pilots for large vessels were no longer employed, and it was thought it would take some time to find anyone to guide the ore carrier in. This was small comfort to Rao, for if he was to find any shelter at all, he must take the *Kowloon Bridge* as deep into the bay as possible. Yet he had no local knowledge, no chart, and a ship drawing 59 feet of water. It was the kind of nightmarish situation that haunts all men who command ships on the high seas. If Rao stayed out his ship might break up, if he went in he could well run her ashore.

At 1400, the *Kowloon Bridge* was abeam of Bere Island, 7 miles into the bay and nearing the old pilot station off Roancarrigmore Light. At this point Rao, reluctant to continue on, was about to turn his ship around and head back out to sea, when the Harbour Master at Castletown offered his services. The Harbour Master made it plain that he had no experience of piloting anything bigger than a fishing boat, but he was willing to help with the *Kowloon Bridge*. The heavily overcast sky would bring darkness within the hour, and Rao was desperate. He accepted the offer gratefully and made what lee he could for the pilot boat to come alongside, which as his room to manoeuvre was restricted was precious little.

Even this far into Bantry Bay there was a big sea running, and each time the Castletown pilot boat attempted to get alongside the *Kowloon Bridge*, she was in great danger of being smashed against the ship's side. The operation was eventually abandoned, and Rao was obliged to turn his ship around and steam back into a more open part of the bay, where he was able to heave-to head to the wind. As luck would have it, around midnight the wind suddenly eased and veered to the northwest. There was now some shelter from the land, and Rao reversed course and called for a pilot again. The Castletown Harbour Master boarded off Roancarrigmore Light at 0330 on the 19th.

Ideally, the *Kowloon Bridge* should have gone right to the head of Bantry Bay to anchor off Whiddy Island, where there was good shelter, but this anchorage was already occupied by the *Capo Emma*. In the end, the ore carrier was obliged to anchor 4 miles to seaward of the Italian tanker. This was not a good anchorage, for in addition to being exposed, it was within 2 cables of a shoal patch with less than 11 fathoms of water over it. The *Kowloon Bridge* was drawing nearly 10 fathoms.

It was after 0500 before the ore carrier was anchored, by which time Rao and his crew, who had had a long and stress-filled night on top of their ordeal of the previous few days, were near to the point of exhaustion. But they were to be allowed no rest. As soon as it was light, officials from the Department of Communications, perturbed at the unexpected appearance of not one, but two large casualties in their normally untroubled waters, boarded to ask questions. They were closely followed by two representatives of the ship's owners and a Lloyd's surveyor.

Following an examination of the ship, the Lloyd's surveyor reported: "The vessel has been subjected to very severe weather and had sustained impact damage from poop seas. A generator house aft has been destroyed. Other damage sustained which does not, repeat not, affect the structure in way of bulkhead 65 is: (a) distortion of the deck between the line of hatches from frames 67 to 71 together with supporting structure in way—minor cracking occurred in way of distortion (b) fracturing of Nos. 4, 5, 6 and 7 hatch side coamings at their mid-length. These fractures do not penetrate into the deck plating."

On the basis of the surveyor's report, it would appear that the storm damage to the *Kowloon Bridge*, although quite widespread, was not all that threatening. It may be that Captain Rao had been premature in running for shelter, especially in the light of the weather having abated within a few hours of the ship's arrival in Bantry Bay. But that is hindsight. However, by daylight on the 19th, only a light southwesterly was blowing, and now might have been the time to get the ship away to sea and running at all speed for the safety of the Clyde, only a day's steaming away. This was not to be, for the bureaucrats of the Irish Department of Communications ordered Rao to remain at anchor until repairs to his ship were carried out. Rao had no option but to concur.

The *Kowloon Bridge* carried three trained welders in her crew, and these were now set to work welding up cracks in the deck plating under the supervision of the various superintendents and surveyors now on board. The work was slow, and became even slower when, on the night of the 21st, the weather deteriorated. The vessel began to pitch in the rough seas coming into the bay and rolling heavily each time she swung to the tide. The welders had great difficulty in keeping their feet, let alone carry out precision work. Rao requested that his ship be moved to an anchorage deeper in the bay, to the north of Whiddy Island where there appeared to be more shelter, but the Port Authority refused. The reason given for their refusal was that the anchorage Rao suggested was no better than the one he was in. The truth of the matter was that the *Capo Emma*, with her cargo of oil, was off Whiddy Island, and it was feared that having another large, and possibly unmanageable, vessel anchored close by could well lead to another disaster of *Betelgeuse* proportions. Where she was, the *Kowloon Bridge*, with an inert cargo of iron ore, was a danger only to herself.

And so, Rao was left to his own devices. That night Valentia Radio broadcast a storm warning for the area, but Rao chose not to drop his second anchor, which might have been wise, deciding only to pay out more chain on the starboard anchor. During the night, the wind rose to gale force from the southwest, blowing directly into the bay, and accompanied by a rough sea and heavy swell. Rao's response was to pay out to 9 shackles on the starboard anchor and put his engines on stand by. Another long night vigil began.

At 0330 on the morning of the 22nd, while the rain lashed down from a black, heavily overcast sky and the wind roared unchecked in from the Atlantic, the *Kowloon Bridge* began to drag her anchor. Caught in a trap from which there was no easy escape, Rao eased his starboard anchor chain out to 11 shackles, and with men on the forecastle head to tend the anchor, went slowly ahead on his engines to hold the ship in position. By 0700, the wind had increased to hurricane force, and the *Kowloon Bridge*, despite her retaining anchor, was pitching heavily and shipping water over her bows. One wave came clean over the forecastle head, sweeping the anchor party off its feet and injuring one man. The forecastle head was abandoned.

Disaster was then very near, the ship rising and falling on the steep, short seas, and jerking at her anchor cable like a frightened horse. At 0755, the cable parted with a crack clearly audible above the raging of the storm. If anyone had succeeded in reaching the wave-swept forecastle head–and no one was foolish enough to try–it was too late to drop the port anchor. Rao took the only action remaining open to him, ringing for full speed ahead on the engines. He was not a moment too soon, for as the propellor gripped the water and the *Kowloon Bridge* moved slowly ahead, the echo sounder on the bridge was showing only three feet of water under the keel. Those on watch in the engine-room felt several heavy bumps as the ship dragged onto the shoal patch near her anchorage. She actually grounded, but was pulled clear by the power of her engines before any real damage could be done–or so it seemed. By 0827, she was back in the middle of Bantry Bay and steaming full ahead into the wind, just holding her own and no more.

Rao, who still had two company superintendents and the Lloyd's surveyor on board, established contact with the shore by VHF and various possibilities were discussed, but at that stage there was not much more he could do, other than edge slowly seawards, hoping the weather would improve before he cleared the bay. This was a forlorn hope. If anything, the weather deteriorated further, and in order to keep steerage way Rao was forced to increase revolutions.

The whole might of the Atlantic storm was thundering into Bantry Bay unchecked, and into this, her decks awash and her scuppers running white water, the *Kowloon Bridge* moved slowly seawards, urged on by a contrary outgoing current.

At around 1600, having lost her forward inflatable life raft overboard, the ore carrier was off Black Ball Head, at the mouth of the bay. The outgoing current had died, and the ship was all but hove-to in the teeth of the storm. Then, probably because what little shelter the land afforded was being lost, the wind increased in ferocity, and the great ship began to lose ground, slipping slowly back into the bay.

Rao knew he had now reached the point of no return and a decision must be made. If he increased speed further, he would move out to sea into the heart of the storm; if he did not, he might be driven back into Bantry Bay and risk being blown ashore. He was out of VHF range, and in despair, he contacted Valentia Radio on W/T, passing a message for the Department of Communications asking for advice. The reply was short and to the point; as master of the ship, the decision must be his. The Irish had washed their hands of Captain Rao and the *Kowloon Bridge*.

For a while, Rao attempted to keep within the bay, but he was in unfamiliar waters and in danger of being blown onto a lee shore. Before long, he decided it was better to take his chances in the open sea, and by nightfall the *Kowloon Bridge* was 5 miles to the west of Sheep's Head. Now began the fight to break clear of the land.

There was a fine balance to be made, for the ship was meeting the big rollers head-on. With too much way on her, she slammed into the waves with sickening force, sending great arcs of spray flying outwards from her blunt bows; too slow and she came to a halt. As the night went on, the seas became heavier and ever more menacing, until just before 2200, with the last of the land showing up on the radar to starboard, an enormous wave bore down on the *Kowloon Bridge* and lifted her bodily as though she were no more than a dinghy. She was slammed down again with an incredible force that sent an enormous shock wave running throughout her length. A loud bang was heard from aft, and a few seconds later the helmsman reported that the ship was not answering the wheel. Engineers ran aft to find the steering gear smashed and the rudder swinging from side to side, out of control and hammering against the stops. Efforts were made to rig the emergency steering gear, but the damage done was too great.

The *Kowloon Bridge* had by this time reached a position about 10 miles to the west of Mizen Head. She had previously been steering a southwesterly course, but with her rudder not answering, each heavy sea colliding with her bows pushed her head further around to the south. At 2320, having established that the emergency steering gear could not be rigged, Rao sent a Mayday to Valentia Radio, adding a request that his owners be informed of the plight of their ship.

And the plight of the *Kowloon Bridge* could not have been more serious. Lying off a lee shore in mountainous seas with no means of steering, she seemed condemned to early destruction. She was noticeably down by the head, leading Rao to fear that one or more of her forward hatches had been smashed in, and that water was pouring into the holds. The pumps were running, but with waves breaking clean over the decks, there was no means of finding out if they were having any effect.

Fearing that it was only a matter of time before the violent movement of the ship reopened the cracks welded up in Bantry Bay, Rao now began to consider abandoning ship. The decision was postponed when Zodiac Maritime informed him through Valentia Radio that the ocean-going salvage tug *Typhoon*, then on station in Galway, was coming to his aid. Soon afterwards, the *Typhoon* herself established radio contact, advising that she was on her way. Unfortunately, soon after the Dutch tug left the shelter of Galway harbour and ran into the full force of the storm, she suffered major damage. Several of her forward-facing armoured glass windows were stove in, and three crew members injured. The *Typhoon* returned to port for repairs and to land the injured men.

Meanwhile, the situation on board the *Kowloon Bridge* had reached crisis level, and her crew were standing by the lifeboats, ready to abandon ship. Before they could do so—which given the very severe weather conditions was probably just as well—an RAF Nimrod long-range aircraft arrived overhead. At 0021 on the 23rd, the aircraft established radio contact, then circled at low level, using its searchlight to examine the ship's hull. No obvious damage could be seen, in which case Rao decided to keep his men on board to await rescue.

It seemed that the wait might be a long one, for there were no Irish helicopters available which were capable of flying in the weather prevailing. Then it was discovered that two RAF Sea Kings from Brawdy, in West Wales, were refuelling at Cork Airport after answering a distress call from two Spanish trawlers. The helicopter crews were tired, but took off again without hesitation and flew west to join the Nimrod. Within 45 minutes, they were hovering over the *Kowloon Bridge* and fighting to hold their own against a 75-knot wind. Below them, the crippled ore carrier, her foredeck constantly awash, rolled wildly in seas estimated to be 80 feet high. The Sea Kings went in one by one.

Fourteen men were lifted off by the first helicopter in a copybook operation carried out quickly and efficiently under the most hazardous conditions. Then the second Sea King, which had been hovering nearby, went in to complete the rescue. Sergeant Barry Hunter, the 28-year-old winchman, was lowered into the fury of the dark night and was unlucky enough to be going down when the ship took a sudden upward surge on the crest of a wave. He crashed into the side of a hatch cover, suffering severe bruising and breaking bones in his left hand. In spite of his injuries, which left him with only one usable hand, Hunter carried on, and with the *Kowloon Bridge* rising and falling on the waves like a seesaw out of control, began sending survivors up in the rescue harness two at a time.

The whole operation took only 40 minutes; a magnificent piece of work carried out under the most dreadful conditions imaginable. To the helicopter crews it was just another job, but their courage and professionalism were of the highest. It must also be said that Captain Rao and his crew showed great discipline under very harrowing circumstances. It had originally been Rao's intention to stay with the ship with a few men to take a towline if the tug came, but when the helicopters indicated that their time overhead was very limited, he decided to leave.

When she was abandoned, at 0128 on the 23rd, the *Kowloon Bridge* was 8 miles southwest of Mizen Head. Her engines were still ticking over, and she was heading in a southwesterly direction at about 1 knot. All her deck lights were on, casting an eerie glow on the foaming crests on the waves bearing down on her. This was how the Irish Navy patrol ship *Aoife*, commanded by Lieutenant-Commander Rory Costello, found her soon afterwards. Costello had orders to stand by the derelict, and this he did until 0515, when a distress call was received from a Spanish fishing vessel. The *Aoife* could not ignore the distress, and she left the side of the *Kowloon Bridge*, which was then south of the Fastnet Rock, which lies 10 miles southeast of Mizen Head. The ore carrier was still heading out to sea, but was being carried bodily to the southeast by the wind and sea. Ashore, the consensus of opinion was that, as she was drifting away from the land, she was best left alone to sink in her own good time. How such a cavalier decision was arrived at is hard to understand, for the *Kowloon Bridge*, despite her predicament, was still a very valuable ship, having on board a cargo worth nearly £3 million. She also had in her bunker tanks 2,600 tons of fuel oil with the potential to pollute huge tracts of the coastline. Nevertheless, for the second time the Irish authorities washed their hands of this unfortunate ship. From the moment the *Aoife* left on her errand of mercy, no effort was made by the Department of Communications to monitor the progress of the *Kowloon Bridge*.

At around 1230 that day, a light aircraft chartered by the Press located the abandoned ship about 6 miles south-southeast of the Fastnet, indicating she was then drifting in a northeasterly direction, towards the coast. Surprisingly, there was no official reaction to the aircraft's report. When, at around 1830, the *Aoife* returned to the area after standing by the Spanish fisherman, she found the *Kowloon Bridge* about 8 miles south of the small fishing port of Baltimore, which lies 16 miles east of Mizen Head and 11 miles north-east of the Fastnet. The ship appeared to be drifting north at the rate of 3 or 4 knots, and it was plainly obvious that she would soon run ashore. The wind was still blowing force 9 to 10, with a high sea running, ruling out any attempt at boarding from the *Aoife*. Lieutenant-Commander Costello had no choice but to stand off and wait for the inevitable to happen.

At 2220, the *Kowloon Bridge* was within a mile of the entrance to Baltimore harbour and turning in a slow circle to starboard, indicating that her rudder may have jammed hard over. The helpless watchers aboard the *Aoife* suddenly saw flame and smoke erupt from the bulk carrier's funnel, probably as a result of an explosion in her engine-room. Then her engines appeared to stop and her lights flickered twice, then went out. Now only a dark shadow against the land, the crippled ship drifted eastwards close inshore for another four hours, with the *Aoife* keeping pace, but unable to alter the course of events. Finally, at 0257 on 24 November, the *Kowloon Bridge* piled up on the Stags Rocks, 6 miles east of Baltimore.

The sorry tale of the *Kowloon Bridge* did not end there. For four days she lay impaled on the Stags Rocks, her bows firmly held, her stern afloat in deep water, with two Dutch salvage tugs trying in vain to pull her clear. For much of the time the weather was moderate enough for boats filled with reporters and cameramen to venture out from Baltimore to view her. Other interested parties also ventured out, but with less ethical motives. Locals stripped the ship of her radio equipment, sextants, chronometers, clocks, brass fittings–anything removable and of value. Two centuries earlier, this coast had been notorious for its wreckers, and it was clear that their descendants had not lost the art.

On the 28th, Captain Rao returned to the ship to collect his personal belongings–or what was left of them–boarding from the Irish Fishery Protection vessel *Emer*. With him went inspectors for the Department of Communications. An inspection was carried out which revealed the ship was still afloat aft, her engine-room was not flooded, and her pumps and generators were capable of being used. However, the Irish authorities made no decision to attempt to refloat her, neither did they make any effort to empty her bunker tanks. And the opportunity was soon lost, for at the end of the month the weather deteriorated with the return of the winter gales. There was a lull in December, and an oil recovery vessel was put alongside, but the work was abandoned after a few days when it became known that the Irish Government had sold the wreck to a breaker for the nominal sum of £1.

It was only a matter of time before the *Kowloon Bridge* broke her back. Her after section, which contained most of the 2,600 tons of bunker oil, sank in 15 fathoms of water, and the oil began to seep out, adding sheen to the coating of black ore dust floating on the sea around her grave. It was not until the middle of May that the Irish authorities became concerned at the pollution of their waters and began an expensive operation to pump out the remaining oil. By this time it was too late. Thousands of birds and seals were dead, and some of Ireland's finest beaches, from Mizen Head to Ballycotton, were covered with black oil.

Looked at in hindsight, Rao's decision to take the *Kowloon Bridge* into Bantry Bay in the first place is open to question. Confidential reports by surveyors of the British Department of Transport who visited the ship when she was at anchor, suggested that the cracks in her decks were not serious enough to have led to her breaking up at sea. Rather than seek the doubtful shelter of Bantry Bay, which was wide open to the weather, Rao might have been better advised to carry on. Another ten hours at the most would have seen the *Kowloon Bridge* around Tuskar Rock and under the lee of the east coast of Ireland. The fact that the ship was still afloat twenty-four hours after she was abandoned adds credence to this supposition. On the other hand, Rao may have had in mind the *Derbyshire's* sudden end, and more recently, the *Tyne Bridge* incident in the North Sea. There can be no doubt that he feared for his ship and his crew. This is borne out by a radio telephone conversation he had with Zodiac Maritime soon after anchoring in Bantry Bay, and overheard by Captain Tom Byrne, master of an Irish cargo vessel. Byrne reported: "I overheard the *Kowloon Bridge* captain talking to a man in London with a Dutch accent. The Captain said he had done some checks and specified various defects he had found in the ship's holds. He said the ship was unseaworthy, and that the man he was speaking to should come and see for himself. The person from London was trying to stop the Captain talking and eventually got through to him that he did not want him to say anything—telling him: 'Don't speak about the ship being unseaworthy.

Everybody in the world is listening to you.' The man in London told the skipper to contact his office in Morse Code in future."

The question was asked—by those who knew no better, it must be said—why Rao did not stay in Bantry Bay to

Kowloon Bridge ashore on Stags Rocks, Southern Ireland, November 1986. Photo: *Cork Examiner*

ride out the storm of the 22nd; the bay is very large and has deep water, they argued. But then, the *Kowloon Bridge* was a very large ship, and having at the height of the storm lost one of his anchors and touched ground on a shoal patch, Rao was only too happy to escape from the bay, which is what any prudent seaman would have done under similar circumstances. It was unfortunate that in grounding the *Kowloon*

145

Bridge's rudder was partially unshipped or damaged–or so it would appear. The ship was then already doomed.

There are grounds–again in hindsight–for believing the *Kowloon Bridge* was abandoned unnecessarily when she was off Mizen Head in the early hours of the 23rd. She may have been down by the head and unable to steer, but she was not sinking, and her engines were still working, with the wind and waves holding her on a course that would take her out to sea. In the light of this, Rao could have stayed aboard with a skeleton crew, using his engines to best effect until a tug arrived. However, the night was dark, the storm of awesome proportions, and the helicopters were overhead. The temptation to abandon was overwhelming.

In one aspect at least, the *Kowloon Bridge* was not sacrificed in vain. A few months after she was declared a total loss, and insurance totalling £11.1 million paid on her hull and cargo, a new Department of Marine was set up by the Irish Government charged with supervising shipping, and, it was hoped, to react more quickly to any future disasters threatening the coast of the republic. But the *Kowloon Bridge's* greatest legacy was a change of heart by Britain's Department of Transport, which in the light of the circumstances surrounding the Liberian ship's loss at last ordered a full scale inquiry into the disappearance of the *Derbyshire*.

On 30 November 1986, the following report appeared in the Sunday *Times*: "Following an alert to Interpol by the Canadian Mounted Police, Irish Customs officers and police searched the *Kowloon Bridge* on Friday afternoon for drugs. Local fishermen took ten men to the wreck at Stags Rocks," writes Max Prangnell. "They removed two sealed plastic containers, but have so far refused to comment on their contents. However, it is known that members of the Turkish and Indian crew had been under surveillance for several months by the RCMP as part of a big drug smuggling investigation. Scottish drugs squad officers have also confirmed that they were involved."

Alexandros F.

On 7 May 1986, the 116,450-ton, Panamanian-flag oil/bulk/ore carrier *Alexandros F.* was 440 miles southwest of the Cape Verde Islands, bound from Ponta da Madeira, Brazil to Dunkirk with a cargo of 109,000 tons of iron ore. Violent explosions occurred in her No. 3 hold, and she began taking in water. The pumps failed to cope with the ingress, and she was abandoned by her crew of twenty-seven on the 8th. They were picked up from life rafts by the Greek bulk carrier *Eastwind* soon afterwards. The *Alexandros F.*, built in Poland in 1978, and owned by Espartus Investment Trust Inc., sank about one hour after she was abandoned. The underwriters paid insurance of $25 million.

7

Death in the Horse Latitudes

"The time taken to start a search was criticised by Mr
E.H. Farrow, General Secretary of the Merchant Navy
Officers Guild in Hong Kong. 'It is astounding that so
much time could be allowed to elapse with a ship reporting
in this way,' he said. But a Grande Seatrade Agencies
spokesman replied they did not react more swiftly because
they thought at first the storm must have damaged the
ship's radio."

–Lloyd's List

In December 1986, more than six years after the
Derbyshire failed to keep her appointment in Kawasaki,
the Department of Transport in London finally gave in
to demands for a formal investigation into her loss. The role
played in this reluctant change of heart by the ignominious
end of the *Kowloon Bridge* is self-evident, and even the junior
minister charged with defending the Government's position,
Michael Spicer, admitted that the *Kowloon Bridge* had
"tipped the balance." He was, however, at pains to point out
that the damage to the Liberian ship had been inflicted by

storm conditions in the North Atlantic, and that there was no evidence of structural damage in the region of bulkhead 65, the bridge front bulkhead. His opinion was supported by Lloyd's Register of Shipping. The minister concluded: "It's difficult to see what new information will be forthcoming. There will be great difficulties trying to investigate events which took place six years ago." This did not indicate any great enthusiasm on the part of the Government for a new inquiry, but the relatives of those lost and others who had campaigned so long for a full airing of the *Derbyshire* case, were delighted.

By this time, Bibby Line, disillusioned by the heavy blow inflicted by the untimely end of the *Derbyshire*, had dropped out of the iron ore trade, preferring to operate a fleet of six liquefied petroleum gas tankers. These were high-risk ships requiring expert handling, but they were more predictable than the OBOs. In any case, the carriage of iron ore by sea had become a highly competitive trade, no longer the prerequisite of the big, mainly European bulk carrier operators. More and more flags of convenience and so-called second registers were opening up, the latest—and probably the most bizarre to date—the frozen archipelago of Spitsbergen, deep in the Arctic Ocean. The point had been reached where the national flag had little meaning, and anyone with access to a bank could set up as a ship owner. A big bulk carrier was the best proposition, preferably one nearing the end of its useful life, and manned by a bunch semi-literate fishermen culled from the backwaters of South East Asia. Few questions were asked, and only one or two good cargoes were needed to make a fortune for any sharp entrepreneur. Insurance coverage was relatively easy to obtain, and if in her subsequent voyaging the ship went missing, then a very handsome bonus was forthcoming.

Sigval Bergesen, unlike Bibby Line, had stayed with the bulk carriers, and having recovered from the loss of the *Berge Istra* and *Berge Vanga*, were prepared to fight off the threat of the freight-cutting flag of convenience ships. Their answer was to build bigger and better, and in January 1987 the *Berge Stahl* came into service.

Built at the Ulsan yard of Hyundai Heavy Industries in South Korea, the *Berge Stahl* was a monster ship of 365,000 tons deadweight, 1,132 feet long, 210 feet in the beam, and with a loaded draught of 76 feet. She was hailed as the world's largest ever dry cargo carrier—which indeed she was. Thirty-four thousand tons of high tensile steel were used in her construction, and she was equipped with every conceivable technological aid to increase her efficiency of operation, which was just as well. This great powered barge—for she could not be otherwise described—carried a crew of only 14, representing perhaps the ultimate in any ship owner's dream of cost-effective manning. The *Berge Stahl's* employment was ensured for a number of years by a long-term charter to carry iron ore from the Brazilian port of Ponta da Madeira to Rotterdam for the West German steel industry.

If the *Berge Stahl* represented the very best of bulk carriers afloat at the dawn of 1987, then the *Cathay Seatrade* was at the other end of the scale. A medium-sized bulk carrier of 63,600 tons, she was then fourteen years old, having been launched in 1973 in Sweden for Kjell Billner of Gothenburg and originally named *Lili Billner*. In 1978, she went the way of so many of her kind, being sold to a one-ship operator, Perry Shipping of Monrovia. Renamed *Cathay Seatrade* and flying the Liberian flag, she was managed from a safe distance by Grand Seatrade Shipping Agencies of Hong Kong.

Manned by a Taiwanese crew of twenty-five, the *Cathay Seatrade* was sadly typical of her day. She was a ship born into the aristocracy of the sea, but after fourteen years in a hard, cut-throat trade, reduced in circumstances and operating in a shadowy world where everything is sacrificed in the pursuit of profit. Carrying ten to twelve cargoes a year, with little time between voyages for maintenance–even supposing such an extravagance was contemplated–she was a tired old ship. Her hull was stressed and strained by uneven loading and heavy rolling, battered by massive grabs and bulldozers at work in her holds when discharging, and weakened by corrosion. She was still in class with Norske Veritas, and therefore insurable, but she had been reported to the International Maritime Organisation, the shipping watchdog, as "deficient," with many faults long overdue to be put right. In January 1987, the *Cathay Seatrade* found herself in "home" waters, loading iron ore in the Liberian port of Buchanan.

Buchanan, 60 miles to the southeast of Monrovia, lies at the seaward end of the 170-mile long railway running northeastwards into the Nimba mountains, source of the iron ore to which the port owes its existence. There are several small factories, a cluster of houses and a hospital of sorts in Buchanan. The port, once only a fishing village, is dominated by a tall conveyor standing on the 800-foot long loading quay, which is seldom without a large ore carrier alongside, and on this occasion it was the *Cathay Seatrade*.

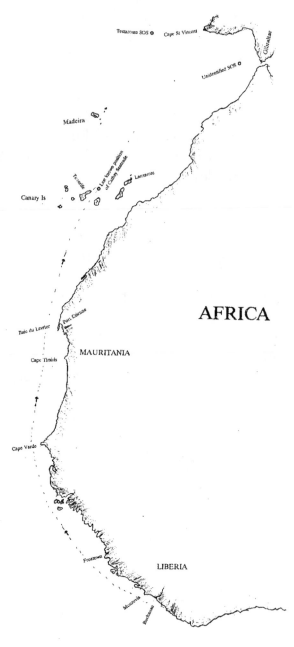

Testarossa SOS ⊙   Cape St Vincent

Gibraltar

Unidentified SOS ⊙

Madeira

Tenerife

Last known position
of Calma Sestrade

Lanzarote

Canary Is

AFRICA

Baie du Levrier

Port Etienne

MAURITANIA

Cape Timiris

Cape Verde

Freetown

LIBERIA

Monrovia

Buchanan

When she sailed from Buchanan, at 1030 on the morning of 6 January 1987, the *Cathay Seatrade* was under the command of Captain Chow Horng-Huei, and she had on board a total complement of 27, all Taiwanese, which included two officers' wives. Her cargo of 59,020 tons of iron ore for Emden, North Germany, was loaded in five holds, Nos 2 and 6 holds being left empty, and No. 4 hold containing only 5,200 tons. In that it helped to raise the ship's centre of gravity and would thus ease her rolling in heavy seas, this was a good distribution of the cargo, but it did impose stress levels on the hull that were very near to the prudent maximum. This was evidenced by the fact that the *Cathay Seatrade* with a sailing draught of 41 feet 4 inches, was "hogged" three inches amidships, her bow and stern being that much deeper in the water than her midships section. It is also recorded that the iron ore in her holds had been left as it was loaded by the conveyor—that is in the shape of a pyramid, and not trimmed level. Had she been loading the same cargo in, say, Canada or South Africa, then this would have been perfectly acceptable. However, Liberian iron ore is finer and drier than other ores, and has an angle of repose—the maximum angle to the horizontal at which it will remain without sliding—of only 35 degrees. With regard to such cargoes, the IMO Code of Safe Practice for Solid Bulk Cargoes states: "Such material should be trimmed reasonably level and cargo spaces in which they are loaded should be filled as fully as is practicable without resulting in an excessive material mass on the supporting bottom structure or deck."

This was the *Cathay Seatrade's* first visit to Liberia, and it may be that Captain Chow was not familiar with the sliding tendencies of Liberian iron ore–although as master of a bulk carrier he should have been. And if he was not, then the terminal should have advised him of the necessity to trim his cargo. It could have been, however, that Chow knew the rules and had just not bothered to implement them. He was perhaps anticipating that on the 13-day passage to Germany, the *Cathay Seatrade* was unlikely to encounter weather bad enough to cause her to roll excessively, even when crossing the Bay of Biscay. Whether through ignorance or calculated risk taking–it will never be known–the *Cathay Seatrade* left Buchanan on 6 January not fully prepared to meet all the perils of the sea. There was, of course, no hint of this deficiency in the radio message Captain Chow sent to Grand Seatrade in Hong Kong after clearing Buchanan.

SAILED BUCHANAN 6TH/1024 FO/578MT DO/54.6MT DRAFT 41FT4IN EVEN KEEL LOADED IRON ORE 59020MT ETA/EMDEN JAN/19TH.

The weather on the west coast of Africa is normally benign all year round, with high temperatures and high humidity. Strong winds are rare, except in the thundery squalls known locally as "tornadoes," and these are short-lived, seldom lasting more than an hour. November to April is the dry season, when the winds are their lightest, and calm blue seas, disturbed only by the lazy plop of the dolphin predominate. Given such favourable conditions, so rarely experienced by the seafarer in other waters, the *Cathay Seatrade* made excellent progress northwards, her 17,000 horse power diesel urging her through the water at 11 knots. Under the circumstances–she was a 14-year-old ship, not in the best of condition, and displacing over 70,000 tons–she was giving a satisfactory return for the money invested in her.

Freetown was passed at noon on the 7th, and the deep-laden ship slid through the mirror-calm, shark-infested waters off the Guinea coast for the next 48 hours, reaching a position abeam of Cape Verde around noon on the 9th. Chow then sent his second message to Hong Kong, wasting none of the company's money on superfluous words.

9TH/NOON 14.9N 17.9W 10.78/354 ETA/191500

In plain language, this spelled out that the *Cathay Seatrade* was 30 miles west-northwest of Cape Verde, on a course of 354 degrees and making a speed of 10.78 knots. Her estimated time of arrival Emden was 1500 on 19 January. The drop in speed from 11.5 to 10.78 knots indicated she was feeling the first of the North-East Trades, blowing a steady force 4 to 5 at this time of the year. In this area the wind, known locally by the coast Arabs as the "harmattan," carries a gritty sand haze blown off the inland deserts of Africa. It is likely that the visibility was down to less than 2 miles, making the already hot and humid atmosphere more uncomfortable than ever.

Twenty-four hours later, the *Cathay Seatrade* was off the coast of Mauritania and abeam of Cape Timiris, a peninsular of sandhills too low to show up on the bulk carrier's radar screen. At the same time, 120 miles to the north, at Port Étienne, another ship was preparing for sea. The 115,721-ton *Testarossa*, deep-loaded with a full cargo of iron ore from the mines at Fort Gourand, 325 miles inland, would soon be jousting with the fleets of fishing boats clogging the entrance to the Baie du Levrier, heading for the open sea. The 17-year-old bulk carrier, flying the flag of the Philippines, was bound for Antwerp, and would preceed the *Cathay Seatrade* on the passage north.

In another twelve hours, with the African coast falling away to starboard, the effect of the harmattan was lost, and the *Cathay Seatrade* moved into clearer weather. She was now feeling the effect of a weak south-flowing current, but the strength had gone out of the trades, and she was picking up speed again. With the horizon sharp, and few low clouds around, Pico del Teide, the 12,000-foot high peak off of the island of Tenerife was visible soon after dawn on the 12th, and when Chow sent in his positional report at noon, the ship was 20 miles east of the port of Santa Cruz, and making 11.65 knots. Chow gave his ETA Antwerp as 1200 on the 19th. Sailing northwards under a clear blue sky with the sun warm on their backs North Europe, then in the grip of a mini-ice age, must have seemed a world away. The grey skies and biting winds would come soon enough, but meanwhile the *Cathay Seatrade* was working up to 12 knots and putting the miles behind her with an ease that surprised even her chief engineer.

The Liberian bulk carrier had by now entered the "horse latitudes," which lie between the trade winds and the prevailing westerly winds of higher latitudes. Here gales are a rare occurrence, but not entirely unknown. Occasionally in winter, an eastbound North Atlantic depression takes a more southerly course and presses up against the Azores High. The low pressure system cannot break through the high, which maintains an average pressure of 1030 mb. The end result is a squeezing together of the isobars, creating a very steep wind gradient and giving rise to a "high pressure gale." Hurricane force winds may result, and as such a gale is usually totally unexpected, it poses a great danger to the unwary mariner.

It may be that this is what the *Cathay Seatrade* experienced, for at 0905 GMT on the 13th, Grand Seatrade Shipping received an unscheduled message through Portishead Radio. It read:

ETA/RVTG DUE/GALE FORCE/ WIND

No position was given, and the message appeared to be incomplete, almost garbled, but its import was clear. The *Cathay Seatrade* had run into bad weather. Captain Chow's ETA/RVTG (reverting) was a warning that the ship would almost certainly be delayed in arriving at Antwerp. How bad the weather had become, and by how long she would be delayed, Chow did not say, but weather reports then coming in from ships to the north of the Canaries indicated "severe storm" conditions. Weather charts later in the day showed that a rogue depression had slammed into the northern side of the Azores High. Ships to the east of Madeira were reporting northwesterly winds between 50 and 60 knots, with swells running up to 20 feet high. The Spanish Naval base at Las Palmas warned of "high winds lashing the Atlantic waters of the Canaries."

It was not long before the first dramatic SOS came in, and from a most unlikely source. Early in the afternoon, the 116,000-ton *Testarossa* radioed that she was in serious trouble in position 36° 32,–N 12° 10,–W, some 180 miles west of Cape St. Vincent.

The master of the *Testarossa* reported that she was making water in her No. 1 hold, and required immediate assistance. Later in the day, the radio station on Porto Santo, Madeira heard a faint distress call in Spanish on 2182 kHz, the radio telephone distress frequency. The ship was not identified, but the position given was 34° 32,–N 07° 00,–W, which transferred to the chart showed her to be in the approaches to the Straits of Gibraltar and 270 miles east-southeastwards from the position reported by the *Testarrosa*. Was this another ship calling for help?

Several more transmissions of the SOS were picked up by Porto Santo during the day, the final one very faint, and fading away altogether at 0048 on the 14th. In the dreadful chaos that often attends a sinking ship, radio messages are sometimes wrongly sent or received, and it might well be that the distress calls did come from the *Testarossa*, her exact position being confused in the trauma of the moment. The truth will never be known, for the *Testarossa* and her crew of thirty were not seen again. Two merchant vessels searched the area for survivors for some time, but without success. A Portugeuse Navy frigate joined the search and found three empty life rafts and two lifeboats, also empty, but saw no wreckage and found no survivors or bodies. The search was called off after three days, and the *Testarossa* joined the growing list of bulk carriers lost at sea without trace. Insurance of $7.2 million on her hull and machinery was paid in full.

Seven thousand miles away in Hong Kong, Grande Seatrade were unaware of the dramatic events in the eastern Atlantic, and following the receipt of the rather vague message from the *Cathay Seatrade* on the morning of the 13th, did not become concerned for the safety of their ship. They were, however, anxious to learn the revised ETA at the discharging port, for here money was involved. Over the course of the next three days, Seatrade sent six radio messages to Captain Chow, one on the 13th, one on the 14th, two on the 15th and two on the 16th, each urging him to clarify his ETA Emden. The final message, sent on the 16th, read:

STILL NOT/RCVD YOUR/ETA PLS/ADVISE
NOON/POSITION.

It had been the agreed routine for the *Cathay Seatrade* to keep Hong Kong informed of her progress by sending in her noon position every three days, a practice common in many shipping companies. This enabled Grand Seatrade to advise the consignees of the cargo of any expected delay in delivery, at the same time reassuring themselves that their ship was still afloat and heading in the right direction. When Chow's routine message, expected soon after noon on the 16th, was not received in Hong Kong, Grande Seatrade contacted Portishead Radio, through which their message to the *Cathay Seatrade* were being sent. Portishead came back with the disturbing news that they had been trying to contact the *Cathay Seatrade* for three days without response. Grande Seatrade's six messages of the 13th, 14th, 15th and 16th were still awaiting transmission.

Had Grande Seatrade been aware of the severe storm that hit the Canaries on the 13th, or heard of the disappearance of the *Testarossa,* then the Hong Kong office would surely have been stirred into activity. As it was, they knew of neither event and no one in Europe had seen fit to enlighten them. It was therefore assumed in Hong Kong the lack of news from the *Cathay Seatrade* was due to her radio being out of action. This assumption, to say the least, showed crass naivety.

Cathay Seatrade
Photo: Skyfotos

On the 17th, the consignees of the *Cathay Seatrade's* cargo of iron ore decided they now required delivery at Rotterdam, and not Emden, and it was vital that the ship be contacted without delay. If on schedule, she should by then have been somewhere off Ushant and about to enter the English Channel. Grande Seatrade now at last became seriously worried, and asked their Rotterdam agent to attempt to contact the ship by VHF, at the same time asking other ships for news of her. All to no avail. The silence was deafening.

At long last, on 19 January, six days after the last message was received from the *Cathay Seatrade*, someone in Hong Kong woke up to the fact that something catastrophic might have happened to their ship. Grande Seatrade then asked Portishead to transmit an urgent message alerting all passing vessels in the vicinity of the Canary Islands to search for any signs of the *Cathay Seatrade*. A little later on that same day, a telex was sent to the Maritime Rescue Co-ordinating Centre at Falmouth, requesting that a Search and Rescue operation be set up for the missing ship.

Once apprised of the situation, Falmouth Coast Guard moved quickly, passing the following message to Portishead and Land's End radios to be broadcast on all frequencies:

PAN PAN, LIBERIAN MOTOR BULK CARRIER CATHAY SEATRADE, D5IU: INFORMATION IS REQUESTED OF CATHAY SEATRADE UNREPORTED SINCE JAN 13. LAST KNOWN POSITION OF VESSEL WAS LAT 28.7N LONG 15.7W AT 1200 GMT JAN 12 BOUND FOR EMDEN. DESCRIPTION; BULK CARRIER, ACCOMMODATION AFT. BLACK HULL. WHITE FUNNEL WITH GREEN TRIANGLE. ANY SHIP WITH INFORMATION CONTACT FALMOUTH COAST GUARD. FALMOUTH COAST GUARD CO-ORDINATING. ENDS FALMOUTH MRCC MAKING SAME BROADCAST ON IMARSAT. TO RCC BREMEN, REQUEST CHECK GERMAN PORTS AND COASTAL RADIO STATIONS FOR VESSEL. VESSEL HAS BEEN CALLED BY FOLLOWING COASTAL STATIONS: POR-

TISHEAD SINCE JAN 15, NO CONTACT. SCHEVENINGEN SINCE JAN 15, NO CONTACT. NORDDEICH SINCE JAN 14, NO CONTACT. VESSEL'S ORIGINAL ETA AT EMDEN WAS JAN 19, BUT ETA WAS REVERTED DUE TO GALE FORCE WINDS ON JAN 13.

Ominously, on the 19th Lloyd's Intelligence reported that the Salvage Association had received the following:

MOTOR BULK CARRIER CATHAY SEATRADE: MAN-AGERS REPORTED VESSEL LOADED ABOUT 59,000 TONNES IRON ORE BUCHANAN AND SAILED JAN 6 FOR EMDEN, SUBSEQUENTLY CHANGED TO ROTTERDAM JAN 15. JAN 12 RECEIVED VESSEL'S NOON POSITION LAT 28.7N LONG 15.7W, ETA EMDEN JAN 19. JAN 13 VESSEL ADVISED ETA REVERTING DUE GALE FORCE WIND. SINCE THEN SIX RADIOGRAMS SENT TO VESSEL THROUGH PORTISHEAD JAN 13-16 BUT NO ACKNOWLEDGE-MENT AND REPLY FROM VESSEL. PORTISHEAD RADIO ADVISE MESSAGES STILL NOT DELIVERED TO VESSEL DUE NO CONTACT BY VESSEL.

The search was now on for the *Cathay Seatrade*, but it had begun too late. Within hours of the Falmouth-originated PAN broadcast, the 14,275-ton Nigerian motor vessel *Yinka Folawiyo* reported sighting a badly damaged and waterlogged lifeboat 180 miles north of Lanzarote. Identification was positive, the boat being clearly marked CATHAY SEATRADE MONROVIA. The *Yinka Folawiyo* found no sign of life aboard the lifeboat, or in the vicinity. That something terrible had happened to the *Cathay Seatrade* was now beyond any doubt.

In the Canaries, meanwhile, the Commanding General of the Spanish Maritime Zone of the Canaries had initiated a Search and Rescue operation, with Spanish and Portuguese aircraft cooperating with the Spanish Navy patrol boat *Grossa*. Working on the assumption that the *Cathay Seatrade* had made good a speed of 11.5 knots from her last broadcast position at noon on the 12th, it was calculated that she would have covered 414 miles by midnight on 13/14 January. This put her in latitude 34° 32,–N, the same latitude given by the unidentified ship–then believed to be the *Testarrosa*–when she transmitted an SOS at 0048 on the 14th. On the basis of this, it seemed highly likely to the Canaries SAR Centre that the distress transmissions heard by Porto Santo Radio could well have come from the *Cathay Seatrade* and not the *Testarrosa*. The initial search was therefore centred on the Liberian ship's estimated position at midnight on 13/14 January, and that was 34° 32,–N 13° 07,–W.

This proved to be a miscalculation which sent the searching aircraft off on a wild goose chase, patrolling–although they were not aware of it–more than 200 miles further north than was necessary. It was only when the *Yinka Folawiyo* reported finding the *Cathay Seatrade's* lifeboat that the search area was moved southwards. By this time, the *Grossa* had sighted and identified the *Cathay Seatrade's* lifeboat drifting 96 miles southeast of Madeira, in position 31° 24,–N 15° 00,–W. Three miles south of the boat, the naval ship came across what appeared to be two inflatable life rafts still in their containers. For reasons not recorded, the *Grossa* made no attempt to recover the life rafts or the lifeboat, and she was in fact ordered by the Commanding General of the Maritime Zone to sink the lifeboat. This, after expending a great deal of ammunition, she failed to do, leaving the boat floating on its buoyancy tanks.

The discovery of the lifeboat and rafts only 180 miles north of the Canaries indicated that whatever calamity had overwhelmed the *Cathay Seatrade* must have occurred at some time on the morning of 13 January, possibly soon after she sent her brief message to Grand Seatrade. In the light of this, on the 20th the Commanding General decided it would be pointless to prolong the search. The *Grossa* and the aircraft were recalled that evening, having covered an area in excess of 8,500 square miles without sighting the ship, her wreckage, or even an oil film that would indicate she had sunk.

Although it was now assumed that the *Cathay Seatrade* must have gone down with all hands, there was always hope that some of her crew may have survived. All ships passing through the waters off the Canaries were asked to keep a sharp lookout, and Grande Seatrade chartered a private aircraft to continue the search. The aircraft flew daylight search patterns on 21, 22, 24, 27 and 30 January, and finally on 4 February, but nothing was seen. Bearing in mind survivors may have come ashore unnoticed on one of the uninhabited islands of the Canary group, search parties were landed on 29 and 30 January, but again nothing was found.

On 16 February, Jose Quintero Perez, a fisherman, was making his way home along a beach on the west coast of Lanzarote when he saw a half-sunken boat drifting offshore. No doubt with an eye to salvage, Perez swam out to the boat, attached a line to it, and at high water dragged it ashore. It was the *Cathay Seatrade's* lifeboat, riddled with holes as a result of the *Grossa's* gunfire. The naval authorities were called in, and on examination it was found that the boat's engine was still intact, and the starting handle was in place. As the starting handle of a ship's lifeboat engine is normally unshipped at sea, this suggested to the Spanish inspectors that an attempt might have been made to start the boat's engine, possibly by a survivor. On the basis of this somewhat doubtful hypothesis, Grande Seatrade, who were by now clutching at straws, made an appeal through the Las Palmas newspaper *La Provincia* for news of survivors. On 28 February, *La Provincia* published photographs of all crew members of the *Cathay Seatrade*, but no information was ever forthcoming.

And so, as spring came again to the North Atlantic the last faint hope of finding the *Cathay Seatrade* and her crew faded. As modern bulk carriers go, the ship was not of the largest by any means, but at 715 feet long and 106 feet in the beam, she was still a big ship; too big, one would think, to disappear in these busy waters without a trace, other than the lifeboat that came ashore on Lanzarote. It was later revealed that she was a lapsed AMVER reporting ship, US Coast guard records showing she had not taken part in the scheme since December 1984. Had she, on this her final voyage, been sending in regular reports to New York, while the AMVER plot would not have influenced her ultimate fate, it might have provided valuable clues to the reason for her disappearance.

The Court of Inquiry into the loss of the *Cathay Seatrade*, held by the Commissioner of Maritime Affairs in Monrovia in November 1988, had little hard evidence on which to base its findings. The court did, however, reach the following verdict: "In consideration of all the available facts, the conclusion is made that the bulk carrier *Cathay Seatrade*, and all the officers, crew, and the two wives on board, were most probably lost due to the entry of sea water into at least one cargo hold, which caused the iron ore cargo of Nimba Washed Fines to liquify, resulting in the shift of cargo in that hold, and causing such an angle of heel as would be adequate to cause a shift of cargo in all holds. This last possible cause case places the responsibility of the loss in part on an assumed failure of the Master to seek the most favourable course and speed to minimise the possible damage from the internal and external conditions that were imposed on the bulk carrier Cathay Seatrade. Contributory responsibility under this possible cause is assigned to the failure to correctly trim the iron ore cargo.

"The fact that the Cathay Seatrade lifeboat was discovered along the extended track of the vessel lends some credibility to the assumption that the Master had maintained his course at about 020° in order to minimise lost time, in spite of the pounding by heavy seas."

In the complete absence of distress signals of any kind, and with no survivors, bodies or wreckage being found, it is clear that the *Cathay Seatrade* came to a sudden and violent end. It is known that, like all bulk carriers loaded with iron ore stowing at no more than 15 cubic feet to the ton, she had a very low centre of gravity. The end result of this is invariably a "stiff" ship, having a quick, spasmodic roll in a seaway. At the time it is thought the ship might have been lost, in the early hours of 13 January, there were reports of wind speeds of up to 50 knots, the wind being between west and northwest. If the *Cathay Seatrade* was then on a heading of 020°, the usual course steered from the Canaries to Cape Finisterre, she will have had the wind and sea on the beam, and must have been rolling very heavily, imposing a tremendous strain on the hull each time she whipped back and forth. The prudent, seaman-like action to take under such circumstances is to slow down and put the wind and sea fine on the bow. The ship should then ride the waves without inflicting damage on herself. This, of course, also means she is more or less hove-to, making little forward progress.

From the evidence available, it seems likely that Captain Chow ignored the basic rules of good seamanship and pressed on at full speed, with the weather on the beam. The *Cathay Seatrade* was deep in the water, with not a great deal of freeboard, and in addition to the heavy rolling, seas will have been breaking over her decks. It is quite possible—in fact probable—that the tortured working of the ship opened up a crack in her hull or main deck, and water entered a hold. It must be borne in mind that this ship was fourteen years old, and by all accounts not in the best of condition. Liberian iron ore is like a fine black sand, and liquifies when water is added. In the case of the *Cathay Seatrade*, one good roll and the 13,000 tons, or so of ore in the hold could have slid to one side like so much wet mud, giving her a heavy list. The ore in the other holds, not being properly trimmed, would probably follow suit, resulting in an immediate capsize. There would have been no time to send out an SOS, and the ship, with 59,000 tons of iron ore in her, going to the bottom like a stone, taking her crew with her. The lifeboat and rafts seen by the *Grossa* may have come to the surface later.

The freak storm that swept across the Canaries and into the Straits of Gibraltar on 13 January 1987 left a trail of death and destruction behind it out of all proportion to its size. Having been responsible for the sinking of the *Cathay Seatrade* and the *Testarossa*, it roared into the Mediterranean, where it caught up with the 3,163-ton *Kythera Star* on the 17th. This 21-year-old Maltese-flag ship was on voyage from Corruna to the Lebanon with a cargo of iron bars. She was 63 miles southeast of Barcelona when a big wave hit her and her cargo shifted. The *Kythera Star* went down in five minutes, leaving only two survivors in the water. They were picked up by the Russian tanker *Josip Broz Tito*, which, fortunately, happened to be close by.

In all, a relatively insignificant Atlantic storm had in the course of four days been responsible for the loss of over 184,000 tons of shipping, 170,000 tons of cargo, and seventy-five lives. Such is the power of the sea, which is ignored only by the ignorant and unwary.

Topkapi S.

In October 1987, the 68,000-ton Turkish-flag bulk carrier *Topkapi S.* was on passage from Rio de Janeiro to Eregli, Turkey with a cargo of 60,000 tons of iron ore fines. Shortly after entering the Black Sea on the 29th, she ran into storm-force weather conditions and sank within sight of her destination. Only six of the bulk carrier's crew of twenty-four were rescued, the survivors reporting that the ship went down in six to eight minutes. The cause of her sinking remains unknown. The *Topkapi S.*, owned by Cevhertas Deniz Nakliyati SA., was built in Japan in 1966.

8

In the Wake of the Bounty

"Some of the vessels on which the brokers have
secured insurance will be the colour of rust inside. That rust
may be no thin veneer of oxidisation but wastage so great as
to render the ship unseaworthy."
                                        –Douglas Foy FNI, MRIN

Pitcairn Island, one-and-three-quarter square miles of
rock covered with trees, shows as only a tiny speck on
the chart of the South Pacific Ocean. Situated halfway
between New Zealand and South America, the island offers,
even to this day, the ultimate in isolation–which explains
why Fletcher Christian and the *Bounty* mutineers made it
their home in January 1790.

Fletcher Christian, Edward Young, Matthew Quintal
and the others are long gone to account for their actions in
another place, but their descendants, some fifty strong, still
cling to lonely Pitcairn. The island has no airport, no harbour, and ships call only very occasionally. For much of the
time, Pitcairn's only link with the outside world is through
its powerful radio station at Adamstown. It was here, on the

morning of 12 June 1987, that Tom Christian, a direct descendant of Fletcher and his Tahitian woman Mauatua, heard a desperate cry for help. Christian, the island's radio operator, was idly trawling the wavelengths when he heard the bulk carrier *Cumberlande* calling Sydney, requesting immediate assistance. Sydney was not answering. The 37,570-ton *Cumberlande*, on passage from Newcastle, NSW to the Panama Canal, gave her position as some 180 miles east-northeast of Pitcairn. Her message was brief and to the point, telling of a critical situation on board. Her two forward holds were flooded, and she was making all possible speed for the nearest land, the uninhabited Henderson Island, 120 miles northeast of Pitcairn. Later in the day, Christian established contact with the *Cumberlande* by radio telephone and received the following message:

MAYDAY. CUMBERLANDE POSITION AT 2250 GMT LAT 2350S LONG 12750W COURSE 242 TRUE SPEED 11.5 KNOTS. TRYING MAKE HENDERSON ISLAND. POSSIBILITY ABANDON SHIP. REQUEST IMMEDI-ATE ASSISTANCE.

Pitcairn, unlike other more populated parts of the world, has no air/sea rescue service. There were no lifeboats or helicopters for Tom Christian to alert and send racing to the *Cumberlande's* aid. Alone in his radio shack, Christian had only words of comfort to offer his unseen opposite number on the stricken ship. This done, he warmed up his main transmitter and called Sydney, 4,000 miles away, the nearest station capable of handling the emergency.

Half an hour or so later, when he had finished talking to Sydney on W/T, Christian picked up the radio telephone and called the *Cumberlande* again. He learned that she was beyond help and her crew was taking to the boats.

The *Cumberlande* began her life in the Hellenic Shipyard at Skaramanga, Greece in April 1973. She was a medium-sized bulk carrier, 647 feet long, and equipped with six electric cranes which allowed her to be self-sustaining in cargo handling. Her seven holds were hopper-shaped to avoid any need for trimming the ore, and were flanked by seven saddle ballast tanks. Her Polish-built Sulzer diesel engine gave her a service speed of 16 knots. She was first registered in Piraeus under the name *World Achilles*, and served her original owners for only twenty months, before being sold to the Broken Hill Proprietary Company of Australia.

Renamed *Iron Cumberlande*, she was then re-registered under the Hong Kong flag in the ownership of the County Shipping Company, a wholly owned subsidiary of Broken Hill–a flagged-out Australian ship, in other words. Manned by a full Australian crew, she plied the Australian coastal trade for the next twelve years, much of the time carrying iron ore from Yampi Sound, West Australia to Port Kembla and Newcastle, NSW. Being a handy size and having her own cranes, the *Iron Cumberlande* was ideally suited to this run, but she was inevitably pushed to her utmost limits. The passage between ports was only eight days, the turnround times fast, and there was little time to spare for maintenance, which gradually assumed a very low priority. The *Iron Cumberlande* grew old and battered in the service of Broken Hill.

In December 1986, then nearing the end of her useful life, she was sold to a third owner, Glenara Ltd., and became plain *Cumberlande*, retaining her Hong Kong registry. Manned by an Indian crew, she was then immediately taken on long term charter by none other than her previous owners, Broken Hill Proprietary. The phoenix had risen from the ashes, with a new name, a new insignia on her funnel, but otherwise, apart from a few essential repairs, the *Cumberlande* was still her tired old self.

The *Cumberlande's* chief officer, the first of her new all-Indian crew, joined her in Hakata, Japan on 16 November 1986, just nine days before she was handed over to Glenara. He was not impressed with the state of his new ship, which in his stated opinion had suffered years of neglect, particularly on deck. He found the hull and deck plating to be badly corroded in many areas, while below decks bulkheads, tank tops and the ship's side plates were covered with loose rust. The maindeck he reported as covered with a thick coating of fish oil mixed with ore dust, below which was thick rust. Quite obviously, the *Cumberlande* was a victim of the modern approach to ship operation, which spurns anything that might be construed as cosmetic maintenance. Only the bare minimum of work required to keep the insurance in force is carried out, all else being looked upon as making unwarranted inroads into profit.

At fourteen years old, the *Cumberlande* was due for a special hull survey, and if she was to remain in class, and therefore insurable, this could not be avoided. She entered dry dock at Ulsan, South Korea on 9 January 1987, and nine days later emerged with all her certificates in force. But nothing could disguise the fact that the long years on a punishing, non-stop schedule had taken their toll. She was long overdue for the breaker's yard, but before she went, Glenara intended to put her to the ultimate test on the long-haul Pacific run. Over the following five months, she made three round voyages in quick succession from Australia to Japan. It was when she was returning from Japan in ballast for the third time that her newly joined Indian chief officer, when making a routine inspection of the holds, discovered a six foot-long crack in the watertight bulkhead separating Nos. 1 and 2 holds. This crack was welded up at sea by the ship's engineers.

The *Cumberlande* arrived at Bell Bay, Tasmania, where she was to commence loading, on 12 May 1987. Here Captain W.G. Kaisar assumed command. With regard to the state of the bulk carrier's holds, he noted her general condition as poor, with much superficial damage to the hull and holds, neither of which had seen paint in a long while. Her tank tops and hoppers were battered, and the corrugated bulkhead between holds No. 1 and 2 was wasted and welded up in places.

An independent surveyor, carrying out an "on hire" survey at Bell Bay for the charterers, BHP, reported in a similar vein, but appeared not to notice the faults in the forward watertight bulkhead, as reported by Captain Kaisar. However, after being advised by Kaisar, the *Cumberlande's* owners agreed to the employment of shore welders to re-weld the fracture in the bulkhead on both sides. There was nothing that could be done about the obvious wastage of the steel in the bulkhead.

Unexpectedly, the *Cumberlande* was delayed awaiting a berth at Bell Bay, and it was not until 23 May that she sailed, having loaded 21,285 tons of Manganese Sinter and 4,419 tons of Ferro Manganese Fines. The latter, being an exceptionally dense cargo, stowing at only 9 cubic feet to the ton, was placed amidships in No. 4 hold, while the Sinter, a coke-like ore stowing at 20 cubic feet to the ton, was distributed between Nos. 1, 3, 5 and 7 holds.

The passage to Newcastle, where the *Cumberlande* was to complete loading, was uneventful. The weather on passage was not good, force 6 north-northwesterly winds, with a moderate sea and swell prevailing. A reasonable speed was maintained, the ship reaching Newcastle on the evening of the 25th. Here she loaded 10,278 tons of Elura Lead Concentrate, split equally between her Nos. 2 and 5 holds. Lead Concentrate is another very heavy cargo, stowing at around 12 cubic feet to the ton, and has a tendency to form a slurry if mixed with water.

When the *Cumberlande* sailed from Newcastle, on the evening of 27 May, her draught was 38 feet, and she had on board a total cargo of 35,942 tons. This was as evenly distributed between her seven holds as was possible. Before sailing, the Chief Officer calculated the shearing force and bending moment at each bulkhead between the holds, and confirmed to Captain Kaisar that the stresses on the ship were well within the permissible limits. The calculated metacentric height of ship and cargo was just over 18 feet, giving the ship great stability, but as is usual with a loaded ore carrier, an uncomfortable stiffness in any sort of a sea.

The declared destination of the *Cumberlande's* cargo was Burnside, near New Orleans, in the Gulf of Mexico. She was small enough to transit the Panama Canal, but even so, she faced a passage of over 9,000 miles. The weather on

route was expected to be favourable, however, the *Cumberlande* was heavy, and her engine had seen its best days. She was unlikely to average much more than 12 knots, at which rate she would expect to reach Balbao, at the Pacific end of the canal, in around twenty-five days. It would be the end of June before she arrived off New Orleans.

On the long ocean passage between Newcastle and Balbao, across the vast emptiness of the South Pacific, the *Cumberlande* was to be weather-routed by Navitech, New York. She would follow the great circle track south of the islands of Polynesia, and then direct to Panama, participating throughout in the AMVER reporting scheme. It was anticipated that the passage would be leisurely and uneventful.

Things began to go wrong for the *Cumberlande* from the moment she cleared the breakwaters at the mouth of the Hunter River. She immediately ran into a force 8 south-southwesterly, with rough seas and a heavy swell, and beam-on to this began to roll her gunwales under. For those on board who were experiencing their first ocean passage in the bulker this was not a happy introduction. Mercifully, the gale did not linger, and by noon on the 29th, when the *Cumberlande* was south of Lord Howe Island, the weather became more friendly. The wind eased, the sun broke through, and the ship was soon putting the miles behind her at a steady 11 knots, although she had now acquired a long, lazy roll as she rode the big swells bearing down on her from the south.

On the afternoon of 31st, the *Cumberlande* was in the 30-mile-wide channel between Three Kings Islands and the northern point of New Zealand. The weather continued to improve, the wind having dropped away to no more than a moderate breeze from the southeast. This was the first of the South-East Trades, which brought with them blue skies dotted with fair weather cumulus, and a discernable lifting of spirits aboard the *Cumberlande*. The news from New York was also good, Navitech indicating that a large area of high pressure covered much of the ship's intended route. West to northwest winds force 4 to 6 were forecast up to longitude 170° W. Thereafter, it was predicted that the wind would ease and go round to the northeast before backing and settling down between southeast and southwest. At no time was the wind expected to exceed force 6.

By noon on 2 June, the bulker had reached a position 230 miles south of the Kermadec Islands, and was logging a very respectable 12 knots, but as forecast by Navitech, the wind was beginning to come ahead. The International Date Line was crossed at about 1600 on the 3rd and the clocks were retarded one whole day, the third day of the month becoming the second, much to the bewilderment of some crew members. The wind was now due east, blowing from right ahead, and bringing with it a rising sea that sent spray soaring over the *Cumberlande's* blunt bows.

The futility of attempting to read the weather from an office 6,500 miles removed from the scene was now becoming evident. Navitech's forecast had gone badly wrong, and by noon on the 4th the *Cumberlande*, then south of the Cook Islands, was experiencing a near gale from the east and labouring in rough seas. As the days passed, the weather grew steadily worse, and by the time the deep-laden carrier was south of Iles Gambier, on the morning of the 9th, she was battling against a full gale and shipping green seas on deck. Navitech continued to talk of winds force 4 to 6, although they did concede that there might be a brief, but only brief, increase to force 7.

As per ship's routine, the *Cumberlande's* hold bilges were being sounded twice a day by the carpenter. It was on the 9th that he first reported water in No. 1 hold bilges. His rod showed 3 inches port and starboard, not a great deal of water; it might be moisture draining off the cargo, or water shipped through a leaking hatch. In a ship as old and ill-used as the *Cumberlande*, the latter would not be surprising. The pumps were started and the bilges showed dry within a very short time.

Pitcairn Island was passed at a distance of 35 miles to the north on the afternoon of the 10th. The weather had eased somewhat, but it was still blowing east-northeast force 7, with very rough seas. The *Cumberlande* was riding the weather comfortably enough, rolling and pitching moderately, and making 10.3 knots. Navitech was now predicting a further improvement, forecasting the wind to drop to force 5.

The night went well, and on the morning of the 11th the carrier was to the south of Ducie Island, the easternmost of the Pitcairn Group. The wind had veered to east-southeast, bringing it on the starboard bow, but it continued to blow force 7, although the sea seemed to be flattening out. Speed was up to a little in excess of 11 knots. At 1130, the Second Engineer, making his rounds of the engine-room, sounded the lubricating oil drain tank, and found it to be 1.5 inches below the normal level. He examined the tank for signs of leakage, but found none. Given that this tank when full contained only 19.5 tons, the loss was not significant, but there was something about it that worried the Second Engineer. He checked the sounding again, and then for a third time. The discrepancy was still there.

That afternoon, at around 1600, the Second Engineer again went below to check the lubricating oil tank. The sounding was down by another 1.5 inches, but, as before, there was no visible sign of a leak. Fortunately, the engineer was a shrewd man with a good knowledge of his ship. He concluded that, as the tank sounding pipe was at its after end, the unexplained reduction of 3 inches in the sounding must indicate the *Cumberlande* was trimming by the head, whereas she should have been slightly by the stern. He rang the bridge, suggesting to the Chief Officer, who was then on watch, that the forward holds and tanks be sounded.

Captain Kaisar was called and at once took a grasp of the situation. The *Cumberlande* was at the time pitching heavily and shipping water on the foredeck, so Kaisar brought her round onto a northerly course, putting the sea abaft the starboard beam. This left the port side of the deck dry, and a cadet was sent forward to take soundings. He came aft again fifteen minutes later with the devastating news that No. 1 port bilge was showing 20 feet of water.

Kaisar then sent the Chief Officer on deck, who, armed with a torch, entered No. 1 hold through the forward access hatch. As he descended, he heard the unmistakeable swish of water below him. The beam of his torch revealed that the cargo in the hold was completely submerged. The water level was, in fact, only five steps below him on the ladder; at a rough estimate 30 feet deep.

Regaining the deck, the Chief Officer then checked No. 2 hold in the same manner, and he found a similar state of affairs, the water being at about half height of the hold, again around 30 feet deep. There was a strong and obnoxious smell in the hold, and the atmosphere was misty. This was probably due to the water turning the lead concentrates in the hold to a slurry.

It was with some trepidation that the Chief Officer, now thoroughly alarmed, moved aft to No. 3 hold, and shone his torch down through the access hatch. He was relieved when the beam showed only a mound of dry ore. If there was any water in the hold, then it was below the level of the cargo. The Chief Officer returned to the bridge and reported his findings to Captain Kaisar, who instructed the engine-room to put its most powerful pumps on No. 1 hold bilges. Both ballast pumps were brought into use, and by 1830 were pumping water over the side at the rate of 300 tons per hour. After two hours, the pumps were changed over to No. 2 hold bilges.

Kaisar was faced with a nightmarish situation. It seemed certain that his ship had somehow been holed below the waterline–how badly he could not tell, but she had taken in several thousand tons of water since soundings that morning. She was already sluggish in answering the helm, a sure sign that she was down by the head. It could be that the pumps would be able to hold the water at bay, allowing the *Cumberlande* to reach Balboa. On the other hand, the ship was now at the point of no return in her passage, about to leave the Polynesian islands behind her and launch out into 3,000 miles of empty ocean. Once committed, there would be no going back. Kaisar deliberated only for a short while, then decided to reverse course and make for Pitcairn Island, which although it had no harbour or beach shelving enough to run the ship ashore, was at least inhabited. Course was altered to 280° and speed increased as much as the weather would allow.

At 2200, the *Cumberlande's* second engineer, accompanied by a cadet, made his way up the foredeck, which was now dry, to inspect the forward holds. No. 3 still appeared to be dry, but in Nos. 1 and 2 the water had risen to within about 3 feet or so of the top platform of the ladder. It was the Second Engineer's opinion that either the bulkhead between the holds was breached, or the ship's hull was holed in both holds. Whatever had transpired, it was plain that the pumps were losing the battle with the sea.

A further inspection of the holds was made at 2300, this time by the Chief Officer and a cadet. They found the water level in both Nos. 1 and 2 holds had risen another two feet. The message could not have been clearer—the *Cumberlande* was slowly sinking. Curiously enough, it was not until 0221 on the 12th, more than three hours later, that Kaisar decided to inform the outside world of his plight, and this he did not do so with any sense of urgency. In an AMVER message sent to the US Coast Guard Station on Hawaii, via Sydney Radio, he gave the *Cumberlande's* position , and mentioned—almost as an afterthought—that two of his holds were flooded.

At daylight on the 12th, when the Chief Officer again checked the forward holds, he found the water was now over the top platform of the ladder in Nos. 1 and 2. These holds were in fact all but full. Again, there was no sign of water in No. 3 hold, and the forepeak tank, immediately forward of No. 1, was also dry. A glance over the side showed the waves to be lapping just 3 feet below the main deck bulwarks.

By this time, the wind had dropped away to no more than a moderate breeze, with a slight sea running, but the ship now had so little freeboard the seas were lapping over the bulwarks onto the deck. By 0900, the *Cumberlande's* forecastle head was awash. It was only then that Kaisar decided to call Sydney asking for assistance. This was the message picked up Tom Christian on Pitcairn.

An hour later, Kaisar mustered his crew and advised them of the situation, for the first time mentioning the possibility of abandoning ship. Anxious to avoid panic, he assured his men that help was at hand from Pitcairn, the Radio Officer being in constant touch with the island. He did not, however, tell them that Pitcairn had no rescue services. Both lifeboats were then lowered to the embarkation deck and stocked with extra provisions, fuel, pyrotechnics and blankets.

Throughout that morning, the *Cumberlande's* freeboard continued to decrease, and it became obvious that she must sink within the next few hours. At noon, all crew members were mustered on the boat deck wearing lifejackets, as they had done so often at their regular boat drills. On this occasion, however, the usual air of bored indifference was replaced by a nervous fear of the unknown. To practice abandoning ship was one thing; to be faced with the finality of taking to the boats in earnest was something else. Providentially, the wind and sea had by now gone down completely, but the swell was still formidable, and the horizon was empty as far as the eye could see. This was a very lonely and still potentially hostile ocean.

At 1320, Kaisar instructed the Radio Officer to contact Pitcairn and pass the following message to the ship's managers, Anglo Eastern Management Services in Hong Kong:

NO IMPROVEMENT IN DRAUGHT PUMPING OUT CONTINUOUSLY SHIPPING MORE SEAS ON FOCSLE: FOCSLE REMAINING UNDER WATER FOR LONG PERIOD CONTINUING TOWARDS PITCAIRN ISL. SHIP POSITION 12TH 2100 HRS GMT (1300 HRS SMT) 23° 40,–S 127° 29,–W SPEED 11.4 KNOTS COURSE 242° ON WAY PASSING HENDERSON ISLAND 13TH 0200 HRS GMT (12TH 1800 HRS SMT) WHERE MIGHT HAVE TO WAIT ANCHOR DEPENDING ON SITUATION. IN CASE SITUATION WORSE MIGHT HAVE TO ABANDON VESSEL. CONTACT WITH PITCAIRN RADIO UNABLE CONTACT SYDNEY RADIO.

In his message to Hong Kong, Kaisar appeared to be presenting the situation in its best possible light. It was in fact far worse. The *Cumberlande* was heavily down by the head with the sea washing over her foredeck, and her time was fast running out. Kaisar's only hope now lay in getting as near as possible to Henderson Island, then 65 miles to the southwest, before taking to the boats.

It was an hour and a half later that Tom Christian, listening on 2182 kHz, picked up the *Cumberlande's* Mayday, which was also repeated at 1522 on 500 kHz, the W/T distress frequency.

Meanwhile, on board the sinking bulk carrier, the engine-room had been evacuated and the main engine and all auxiliaries shut down by remote control from the deck. At 1524, Kaisar, judging the end to be near, gave the order to abandon ship. Apart from the swell, weather conditions were ideal, and the ship being upright, both lifeboats were lowered without difficulty. The only man to suffer any real discomfort was the Second Officer, who was left behind, having gone to the bridge to collect the deck log book and a chart of the area. When he returned to the boat deck, both boats had moved clear of the ship's side to avoid damage by the swell. With the log book and chart tied to his body, the unfortunate officer was clinging to a ladder, waiting for one of the boats to come in and pick him up, when the *Cumberlande*, her bulkheads collapsing with the weight of water in her holds, began to slide under. He was obliged to jump into the sea to save himself, losing both log book and chart in the progress of swimming clear of the sinking ship. He was picked up by No. 2 lifeboat, by which time the *Cumberlande* had sunk. Only seven minutes had elapsed from the time the order was given to abandon ship.

While this drama was being enacted at sea, ashore on Pitcairn, Tom Christian had passed the *Cumberlande's* Mayday to the US Coast Guard on Hawaii. The Coast Guard immediately initiated a search and rescue operation. The French Air Base on Tahiti was nominated as the Rescue Coordination Centre, but the distances involved were great, and the resources available meagre. The nearest long-range aircraft, a French naval plane, was at Mururoa Atoll, 650 miles to the west of Pitcairn, while the nearest ship, the British container vessel *ACT 5*, was 460 miles to the east.

The only thing the *Cumberlande's* survivors had on their side was the weather, which had now become a flat calm.

The *Cumberlande's* radio officer, using a portable lifeboat radio, remained in contact with Tom Christian, who kept the survivors advised of the progress of the rescue operation. At 1830, just as the short tropical twilight was turning to night, the French naval aircraft from Mururoa arrived overhead and dropped flares, followed by a package containing food and water. The package was lost in the darkness, but as, thanks to the foresight of Captain Kaisar the boats were well stocked, this was of no real consequence. That the aircraft had found them was encouragement enough for those in tiny boats rising and falling on the long Pacific swells. For many of them, afflicted with the curse of seasickness, the night had been long and miserable. Radio contact was maintained with Pitcairn throughout the night, and at 0736 on the 13th Tom Christian passed the good news that the containership *ACT 5* was making all speed towards them, and would arrive that evening, at around 1840.

The day was long and hot, with the constant sea-saw motion of the boats a torment to those inflicted with sea sickness. But they were never alone. The radio link with Pitcairn was kept open, and the aircraft reappeared overhead, flying in wide circles while it directed the rescue ship towards them. It was fully dark, when at 1900 the lights of the *ACT 5* were seen approaching from the east. Perversely, as so often happens on such occasions at sea, the weather now took a turn for the worse. The sky clouded over, the wind freshened from the northwest, and heavy rain lashed down. Conditions were the worst possible for a sea rescue, but the master of the 27,000-ton *ACT 5* manoeuvred his great, slab-sided ship with consummate skill, making a good lee for the lifeboats to come alongside. All twenty-nine crew members of the *Cumberlande* were safely aboard the containership by 2030.

The *ACT 5* set course for Pitcairn, then 135 miles away, with the empty lifeboats in tow, having in mind the desperate need of boats on the island. Unfortunately, the motor lifeboat was lost in the early hours of the 14th. The other boat also broke adrift soon after daylight, but by this time the *ACT 5* was close to Pitcairn, and the delighted descendants of the Bounty mutineers put to sea to claim their reward for their part in the rescue. After heaving-to off Pitcairn for about 40 minutes, the rescue ship continued on to Auckland, where she landed the *Cumberlande* survivors on 22 June.

The Court of Inquiry held in Hong Kong in October 1988 to investigate the loss of the *Cumberlande* looked at all possibilities, including the deliberate sinking of the ship by her crew for insurance purposes. However, apart from the use of explosives, there is no easy way to scuttle a ship of her size. The "sea cocks" so often opened up in nautical fiction are mythical, existing only in the imagination of the author totally ignorant of the construction of a ship. In the case of the *Cumberlande*, the two forward holds could have been deliberately flooded only by filling them with fire hoses through the access hatches, or by removing the non-return valves in the engine-room and flooding through the bilge lines. The use of either method is long and laborious, and could not have been done without most of the crew being aware of what was going on. The truth would then surely have been revealed at the inquiry. It must also be borne in mind that there are far more convenient places to scuttle the ship than in the middle of the South Pacific, where the chances of a speedy rescue were not good. As it was, the *Cumberlande's* crew spent a very uncomfortable 28 hours in the boats, and if Tom Christian had not been scanning the air waves on the 12th, the outcome of the matter might have been very different.

After examining all the evidence, the Court of Inquiry concluded that the *Cumberlande* was lost through a crack in the ship's side plating which resulted in the flooding of her Nos. 1 and 2 holds. The recorded weak state of the bulkhead between the two holds was held to be a contributory factor, it being implied that this bulkhead probably collapsed.

The discovery of water in No. 1 bilges on the 9th, and again on the 11th morning, indicates that the crack in the ship's side plating–if there was one–almost certainly first appeared below the waterline in that hold. But what could have caused the crack remains a matter for debate. The most likely causes of a ship being holed below the waterline are through collision with another ship, a rock, or a shoal, violent, traumatic occurrences unlikely to go unnoticed. It is certain that no other ship was involved with the *Cumberlande*, and evidence given by her officers was to the effect that she did not strike any underwater obstruction. Their evidence was supported by the courses reportedly steered, which when plotted on the charts were clear of any known shoal or rock.

That leaves only metal fatigue as a possible cause of any fracture in the ship's side. When this was considered by the Court of Inquiry, it came to light that the *Cumberlande* had a history of cracks in her hull plating. In May 1982, following a passage in particularly rough weather, water was found in No. 1 hold, which was traced to two significant cracks in the port side shell plating low down in the hold. These were gouged out and welded up. Eight months later, in January 1983, No. 1 hold was again found to be making water, and an inspection of the hold revealed a 16 inch-long crack on the port side near the previous repair. In April of that year, yet another crack opened up in the same area. When the ship went for a Special Survey in December 1983, a detailed examination was made of her hull in No. 1 hold, this time a small fracture being reported. A permanent repair was made by cropping and renewing part of the shell plating in the area.

Although up until the time of foundering no further hull cracking was reported, it seems clear that there was some inherent weakness in the *Cumberlande's* plating on the port side of No. 1 hold. This weakness was probably aggravated by the pounding of the vessel in heavy weather, leading to cracking. However, on her final voyage the weather does not appear to have been exceptionally bad, and at no time did her officers report heavy pounding. It may be, that after fourteen years of carrying ore cargoes, and with little or no internal maintenance, the ship's shell plating in this area could have worn thin and been severely fatigued.

The *Cumberlande's* construction was such that, when fully loaded, she was capable of floating with one hold flooded. And she may well have done so, if the bulkhead between Nos. 1 and 2 holds had held. But this bulkhead was known to be weak. During the Special Survey carried out at Ulsan in January 1987, ultrasonic testing of the bulkhead showed a weardown or wastage of 40 percent on average, and in at least one area in excess of 60 percent. In accordance with the Classification Society's guidelines, plates which average a weardown of 30 percent or more of the original thickness should be renewed. In this case, only a small section of the bulkhead near the starboard lower corner of the bulkhead was renewed.

There can be no doubt that the bulkhead between the *Cumberlande's* Nos. 1 and 2 holds was highly suspect. The 6 foot-long crack that appeared in this bulkhead on the ballast passage from Japan to Tasmania is evidence enough of that. When the water rose in No. 1 hold, the bulkhead was subjected to immense pressures, which it eventually could not withstand. It is highly likely that it collapsed, leading to the flooding of No. 2 hold. From then on the *Cumberlande* began to sink.

Age, metal fatigue and a chronic lack of proper maintenance must all have contributed to the eventual loss of the *Cumberlande*. She was a ship that had been hard run over the years in the pursuit of maximum profit. Her days were ended under a rented flag and with a master and senior officers, who although fully aware of her shortcomings, were prepared to turn a blind eye in the interests of their own continued employment.

Singa Sea

In July 1988, the 26,586-ton bulk carrier *Singa Sea*, loaded with a cargo of mineral sands, broke in two and sank in heavy seas off Western Australia. Six survivors from her crew of twenty-five were picked up twenty-nine days later by the bulk carrier *Standard Virtue*. The men, in a 16-foot fibreglass lifeboat, had survived on biscuits and rain water collected in a small sail. They reported their ship had gone down within minutes after breaking up.

The *Singa Sea*, built on the Clyde in 1976 as the *Dona Magdalena* for Northern Lines Inc. of the Philippines, was owned by Singa Ship Holdings Ltd. and flew the Singapore flag.

9

The Friday Ship

"The crew agree by signing articles to serve, obey and be diligent in carrying out their duties, and in a time of danger to do everything possible to save the ship."

—Edward F. Stevens, *Shipping Practice*

The superstitions of the sea die hard, and none harder than the seaman's aversion to leaving port on a Friday. In the heyday of sail, many a mutiny was born out of a master's insistence on casting off the ropes on this day which will forever be associated with the Crucifixion. Nowadays, it is more likely the thought of losing an idle weekend in port that produces reluctant sailors, but the suspicion that no good will come of sailing on a Friday still lingers on.

There is no record of any unrest on board the oil/bulk/ore carrier *Yarrawonga* when she sailed from the Swedish port of Oxelösund on Friday 23 December 1988, bound in ballast for Seven Islands. However, it being then so near to Christmas and the Atlantic in its usual winter ferment, it is certain that few, if any, on board showed any enthusiasm for putting to sea.

The 85,150-ton *Yarrawonga*, owned by the Bionicserve Shipping Company, flew the convenience flag of Cyprus. She had begun her days in Yugoslavia, built in 1971 as one of a class of three, and over the years had suffered the indignity of being passed from owner to owner while performing her dual roll on the oceans. Her original owners were J.C. Carras of London, who for reasons best known to themselves, masqueraded as the Propellor Shipping Company of Monrovia. They registered her under the Greek flag as the *Capetan Carras*. Classed as 100A1 at Lloyd's for the carriage of bulk cargoes and oil, she was a double-hulled ship, in that she had side ballast tanks running the length of the ship, port and starboard. Her cargo was carried in nine holds, each of which was closed by two steel hatch covers secured by fifty-two locking cleats. On trials, the *Capetan Carras's* two MAN diesels geared to one propellor gave her a speed of 16 knots.

The first change of owner came in the mid-1970s, when she was sold to Alfarmar Cia Naviera. She then hoisted the flag of Panama, but retained her original name. In July 1979, she moved to the Singapore flag with Equatorial Navigation Ltd., being renamed *Norman Pacific*. Equatorial Navigation, which evolved into Singa Ship Management, changed her name to *Singa Pacific* in 1984. Two years later, still under the Singapore flag, she went to Astranor Shipping, becoming the *Astranor*. In April 1988, she was lying in Marseilles, when Bionicserve, acting for Chemikalien See Transport of Hamburg, bought her and registered her in Limassol as the *Yarrawonga*. By this time, she was seventeen years old, and bore the marks of her punishing trade. Bionicserve dry-docked her in Rotterdam, where she was inspected by the classification society Norske Veritas, whose surveyors reported badly rusted bulkheads in the top wing tanks and the afterpeak tank, and recommended extensive repairs. Three weeks later, although extra welders had been brought in, the repairs were still not complete, but the ogre of lost freights was rearing its ugly head. Under pressure, Norske Veritas declared the ship seaworthy, and the *Yarrawonga* was rushed into service to earn her keep for her German owners. She was commanded by a German master, Captain Klaas Petersen, carried a German chief engineer and stewardess, with the remainder of her crew of thirty-two being from the Philippines.

In winter, night comes early to the Baltic Sea, and darkness was complete when, at 1700 on the 23 December, the *Yarrawonga* sailed from Oxelösund, an ore and timber port 60 miles south of Stockholm. Ice breakers had swept the approach channel free of ice, but with the air temperature down to minus 10° C., a brittle crust was already forming on the surface of the water. Accompanying the muted thump of her diesels, the progress of the ship was marked by an audible crackling as she pushed her way through the glistening rind. Slowly, the lights of the port faded astern, and the night closed in around the *Yarrawonga*, until she became just a long, dark shadow gliding across the frost-bound sea.

Working up to 13 knots, the empty ship was off the island of Gotland by midnight. She passed Bornholm at noon on the 24th, rounded the southwestern tip of Sweden soon after dark, and then set course to the north for the Öresund. To port lay the Danish island of Zeeland, to starboard the Swedish mainland, both sides a fairyland of twinkling lights, beckoning on this cold, crisp Christmas Eve. Ahead, to be navigated in the dead of night, lay 50 miles of narrow channel alive with criss-crossing ferries. Captain Klaas Petersen, already tired from long hours on the bridge of the *Yarrawonga*, would have been more than pleased to be otherwise engaged. His crew, many of whom were on deck watching the shore lights go by, shared his sentiments. For all of them, Christmas was a time for home and family.

It was midnight on the 24th before the *Yarrawonga* ran clear of the Öresund, and with Kronborg Castle, setting for Shakespeare's Hamlet, silhouetted by the shore lights to port, entered the Kattegat. She then doubled back, heading south into Danish waters and reaching the bunkering port of Spodsberg, on Langeland Island, just as Christmas Day dawned. Here, she took on 1,351 tons of heavy fuel oil, 151 tons of diesel, 82 tons of gas oil for her generators, and 622 tons of fresh water. At the same time, her ballast tanks were filled with 31,484 tons of sea water. Late that night, considerably lower in the water, the *Yarrawonga* put to sea again. It had not been a good Christmas for Petersen and his crew, and there was worse to come.

The Kattegat was re-entered before dawn on the 26th, and at around noon that day the *Yarrawonga* rounded the Skaw and headed westwards into the Skagerrak. Beyond that lay the North Sea, from which the precursors of winter were already advancing. The sky was grey and leaden, lowering fast to keep pace with a falling barometer. By the time the lighthouse on Lindesnes, southern point of Norway, was abeam, at around 2200, the wind was freshening purposefully from the southwest, building up white horses on a dark, forbidding sea. A long swell rolling in from the west confirmed for Petersen that a depression was moving in from the Atlantic.

The shortest route to the *Yarrawonga's* port of loading, Seven Islands, lay via the north of Scotland, first passing either between the Shetlands and Orkney, or through the Pentland Firth. Using the latter would save a few miles, but the dangers were considerable. The Pentland Firth, the 14-mile-long channel between Orkney and the north coast of Scotland, is 8 miles across at its widest, narrowing to 2 miles, and contains some of the strongest tidal streams known to the navigator, reaching a rate of 12 knots at spring tides. In places, owing to inequalities in the bottom, shoals, islands and intervening headlands, fast-running eddies abound. And, of course, the channel acts as a funnel for the winds that blow on these wild northern shores of Britain. Except in calm, clear weather, the Pentland Firth is best left to the fishermen who make their living there.

It is not known whether Captain Petersen was familiar with the hazards of Pentland, but for some reason, perhaps to save time, he chose to take his ship through the firth. When he arrived off Duncansby Head, at the eastern end of the channel, it was nearing midnight on the 27th; a black, threatening night, with the wind already blowing a full gale from the west. Conditions could not have been worse for a east to west passage, but by this time the *Yarrawonga* was committed. She was equipped with satellite navigator and good radars, but—and Petersen was only too well aware of this—her engines had seen their best days and were none too reliable. If they faltered, big as she was, her end would be swift, swept bodily by the raging tides onto the jagged rocks

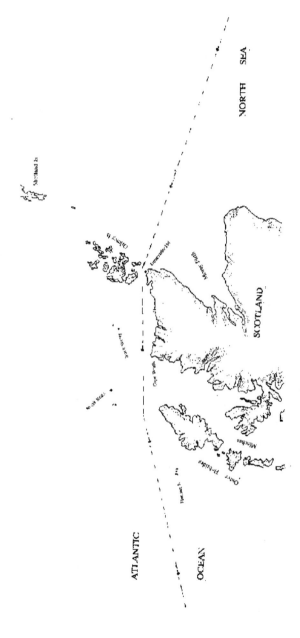

that lie in wait off the steep-sided cliffs fronting these bleak shores.

The gods were watching over the *Yarrawonga* that night, for she emerged from the western end of the Pentland Firth unscathed. But, it would seem, her ordeal was only just beginning. Out in the open sea again and heading for the aptly-named Cape Wrath, she met the full force of the gathering storm. The wind quickly climbed to force 10, swinging wildly from south to west and back again, and gusting to hurricane force 12. Fortunately, the ship, being in ballast, was high out of the water, but the seas became steep and menacing, and she began to slam into them, each one dealing her a blow like a sledgehammer and sending spray flying high over her bows. To carry on at full speed was to risk serious damage, and Petersen had little choice but to slow down. At reduced speed, it was well into the morning of the 28th before the brooding Cape Wrath was abeam to port. The coming of daylight–if it could be called that–was only transient; a brief lightening of the low, ragged clouds at around noon. Then it was dark again, and the *Yarrawonga* left Scotland behind, the long flash of the world's most powerful lighthouse on Cape Wrath following her out into the untamed reaches of the North Atlantic.

The old year went out and the new came in without a glass being raised aboard the *Yarrawonga*. In the nightmare world of flying spray and spume she inhabited, plunging awkwardly from crest to trough, and at times coming to a juddering halt as she hit what appeared to be a brick wall, there could be no cause for celebration. Meals were chaotic and sleep impossible.

On 2 January 1989, the *Yarrawonga* had reached a point 160 miles west of Rockall, having made good an average speed of just 4 knots over the previous five days. There was no let-up in the weather, the wind being still ahead and blowing force 9 to 10, with gusts to force 12. Petersen knew his groaning ship was paying a heavy price in this continuing battle with the sea, but he had a charter to honour, a date to keep in Seven Islands, and he must push on. And all the time at the back of his mind was the need to get men down below to clean holds ready to receive the next cargo. In half-reasonable weather, the job was not difficult, a couple of days' hard work with brooms and hoses for all the crew. But in the current weather conditions, with the ship seeming at times to stand on her head, it would be impossible to persuade men to risk their lives in the holds. Petersen made several alterations of course, until he found a heading on which the *Yarrawonga's* motion was less violent. Speed was reduced to the bare minimum to give steerage way, and over the next 48 hours hold cleaning went ahead, although it was, at best, a half-hearted effort. Course and speed were resumed on the 4th.

In the small hours of the 6th, the *Yarrawonga* was in mid-Atlantic, 640 miles west of Newfoundland, and in the ninth day of her endless battle with the elements. There had been no improvement in the weather, this night being a repetition of all the others gone; filled with the incessant howl of the wind and the crash of the waves. The only noticeable change since leaving Scotland astern had been a slow, but steady, rise in the temperature as the ship fought her way southwestwards and into the warmer waters of the Gulf Stream. She still rolled and pitched violently, taking occasional waves on deck, but with the bitter chill gone out of the wind, the misery of the storm was easier to bear. Then, without warning, disaster struck.

Soon after the change of the watch at 0400, those on the bridge of the *Yarrawonga* heard a loud crash, and a shudder went through the ship. It was as though she had hit something solid, but the radar showed nothing. Petersen suspected that a bigger than usual wave shipped forward was responsible, but when the deck lights were switched on no damage could be seen. He took a party of seamen on deck to investigate, but they were forced back almost as soon as they left the shelter of the bridge. In the dark, with seas sweeping the deck, it was too dangerous to venture forward.

The dawn on the 7th was slow to come, and it was 0600 before there was enough light to venture out on deck in comparative safety. The inspection confirmed Petersen's worst fears. The freak wave that struck at 0400–and it was assumed this was what had happened–had dislodged one of the steel hatch covers of No. 4 hold, and the hold was wide open, water pouring in with every wave that broke on deck. Before going aft again, Petersen leaned out over the starboard bulkwark and was horrified to see a large jagged hole in the ship's side near the waterline. An inspection of the wing ballast tank showed that it too was breached. No. 4 hold was wide open to the sea.

Petersen ran aft to the bridge, and altered course to bring the wind and sea on the port side, thus giving some protection to the breached starboard plating. After instructing the engine-room to put the pumps on No. 4 hold, he attempted to contact Bionicserve in Hamburg, only to find that his wireless aerials were down.

An emergency aerial was rigged, and contact was established with Hamburg by radiotelephone, Petersen informing Bionicserve of the situation. Meanwhile, the pumps appeared to be holding the water at bay in No. 4 hold. The *Yarrawonga* remained upright, but she was hove-to with the weather on the port bow, and virtually helpless. Petersen was satisfied he had contained the emergency–for the time being at least–but his Filipino crew did not share his confidence. There was panic in the air, and seventeen of the twenty-nine Filipinos stormed the bridge, demanding to be taken off the ship there and then. The *Yarrawonga* then being over 600 miles from the nearest land, and in the middle of a raging storm, early rescue was clearly out of the question, although this was not easy to explain to the agitated Filipinos.

The situation became critical that night, when as a result of the failure of the hydraulics, the ship's steering gear ceased to function. This was a severe blow, for without her rudder the *Yarrawonga* could not be held up into the wind. She fell off and broached-to, rolling heavily in the trough. Within a few hours she had taken on a list to port of between 20 and 30 degrees. Ballast tanks on the starboard side were filled using hoses, but this was a slow process, and it was not until noon on the 7th that the ship came upright again. It was also around this time that the weather at last relented, and the *Yarrawonga* was able to make progress towards Newfoundland at 7 knots, a speed she had not achieved for ten days past. Her good fortune was, however, very short lived. Later that day the engines, hard-run over so many days and nights, finally faltered and ground to a halt. It was while the engineers were struggling to restart the engines it was discovered the ship was running short of boiler water. Badly corroded tubes in the boiler were leaking water so fast that the feed tanks were running dry. Without the boiler the pumps would not run, and more importantly, the heavy fuel oil used in the main engines could not be pre-heated. All that night, the *Yarrawonga* lay stopped and drifting while her engineers grappled with the chaos below.

Ashore in Hamburg, Bionicserve, kept informed by Petersen of the deteriorating situation in their ship, now decided to take action. They first notified the Charterer, as required by the Charter Party, and the ship was put "off hire"–meaning that the *Yarrawonga* once more became the sole responsibility of her owners. Having in mind firstly the state of near mutiny on board, Bionicserve made contact with the Canadian Coast Guard and asked for a cutter to be sent out to stand by the ship. It was then agreed with the insurers of the *Yarrawonga* that a tow would probably be needed. Before dark, a Coast Guard cutter and the powerful rig supply vessel *Triumph Sea* were on their way out from Halifax, Nova Scotia.

Repairs on the *Yarrawonga's* main engines were completed by 0900 on the 8th, by which time she had drifted a considerable distance. Her boiler was still shut down, and heavy fuel oil could not be used. Lighter diesel oil was used to restart the engines, but as the *Yarrawonga* carried only a relatively small supply of diesel, this could only a temporary arrangement. All efforts in the engine-room were now concentrated on replacing the leaking boiler tubes.

In keeping with the erratic behaviour of the North Atlantic in winter, soon after the *Yarrawonga* got under way again the weather deteriorated rapidly and it was soon blowing a strong gale from the west with a high swell and very rough seas. The disabled ship resumed her fight for survival, hove-to with the wind and sea on the port bow. Her sluggish movements indicated she had taken on a considerable amount of water, but with her pumps out of action, nothing could be done to hold the sea at bay. To make matters worse, the temperature had dropped until it was hovering around freezing, and with the boiler shut down, there was no heating in the accommodation. The Filipinos, used to warmer climes, became even more unhappy.

The Canadian Coast Guard cutter and the *Triumph Sea* arrived in the vicinity on the 9th, by which time the weather was considerably worse. Neither ship dared approach the *Yarrawonga* for fear of being thrown against the side of the huge bulk carrier. They stood off, helpless to intervene, watching as she struggled to avoid broaching to.

Working under the most difficult of conditions–the ship was never still–the *Yarrawonga's* engineers completed repairs to her boiler and hydraulic system late on the 10th. This gave Petersen considerably more control over his ship, but she was making little progress westwards, and although the pumps were running again, they were not coping with the water in No. 4 hold. The wind was climbing again towards hurricane force, and during the night Petersen decided the only hope of survival lay in turning the ship around to run before the storm. He consulted with Hamburg, who agreed the ship would have more chance of survival in European waters, and late on the afternoon of the 11th, in a temporary slackening of the wind, he brought the ship around using helm and engines. The *Yarrawonga* rolled wildly when she came beam-on to the sea and her battered hull groaned in agony, but she survived the ordeal. By 1700, she had the wind and sea astern and was on course for the English Channel, over a thousand miles to the east. The tiny Coast Guard cutter, which had suffered severe punishment at the hands of the sea, then gratefully set off to return to Halifax.

With the *Triumph Sea* still in attendance, the *Yarrawonga* continued on her way, rolling and yawing in the following sea, but making good a speed of 11 knots, which the supply ship found hard to match. Speed was now of the essence, for soundings taken by the bulk carrier's carpenter showed No. 2 hold was also taking in water, either through a hole in the ship's side or a displaced hatch cover. The bad news was passed to Bionicserve, who informed Petersen they had contracted the deep sea salvage tug *Typhoon* to come to his aid. The *Typhoon*, which two years earlier had failed to reach the troubled *Kowloon Bridge*, was then already on her way from La Corruna. The *Triumph Sea* was ordered to return to Halifax, no doubt much to the relief of her crew.

In the late afternoon, the weather showed a gradual improvement, and it seemed to those aboard the *Yarrawonga* that the worst of their frightening experience was past. Then, just as another grey winter's day was drawing to a close, the situation deteriorated again. First, the boiler began to leak and it was necessary to shut it down for emergency repairs, then the wind suddenly backed to the southeast and strengthened. Within a few hours, the *Yarrawonga* was battling against a force 12 head wind, yet still running before a high westerly swell. She caught in a trap between two powerful and opposing forces, from which there was no escape. Petersen did what he could, heaving to with the wind on the port bow, but with at least two of her holds open to the sea, and her pumps out of action, the *Yarrawonga* was again facing disaster. Most of her Filipino crew, paralysed by fear, refused to take any further part in the fight to save the ship. On the morning of the 13th, when 500 miles from the Irish coast, Petersen ceased talking to Bionicserve and used his radiotelephone to broadcast a PAN message to all stations.

A message broadcast by voice radio and prefixed by the code word PAN, is only one step short of an SOS, and indicates that the safety of a ship or those on board is threatened. The Maritime Rescue Coordination Centre at Falmouth picked up Petersen's cry for help and acted without delay. RAF St. Mawgan was notified, and within the hour a long-range Nimrod reconnaisance aircraft had taken off and was heading out into the Atlantic.

In the meantime, the *Yarrawonga*, hove-to in hurricane force winds, was gradually destroying herself. At least two of her holds were awash, and the compression of the air in the holds, caused by thousands of tons of water swirling from side to side as she rolled, was acting like a giant hammer, dislodging hatch covers and punching holes in bulkheads and ship's side plates. The sea poured in, and the bulk carrier began to list heavily. With the majority of his crew overcome by fear and apathy, Petersen could do no more. He uprated his PAN call to a MAYDAY, indicating that his ship was in grave danger, and required immediate assistance. This resulted in a full-scale rescue operation being mounted.

The Search and Rescue Headquarters in Plymouth took charge, first despatching two more Nimrods from St. Mawgan to locate the *Yarrawonga*. The US Army Air Force

Rescue and Recovery Squadron, based at Woodbridge, Suffolk, was then contacted, and immediately offered the services of two Chinook long-range helicopters. As the stricken ship was beyond the reach of even these twin-rotored helicopters, three C-130 Hercules air tankers were called in to refuel the Chinooks in flight. This would be the longest range air rescue ever attempted.

Shortly before dark on the 13th, the first Nimrod from St. Mawgan found the *Yarrawonga* 430 miles off the Irish coast, under way again and heading east. Weather conditions were very bad, with winds up to 70 mph, but the big aircraft went in low and began to circle the ship. The pilots reported huge 200-metre square holes torn in the *Yarrawonga's* side at the waterline, one to port and one to starboard. The ship's plight was even worse than Captain Petersen had reported.

SAR HQ Plymouth decided that, in the weather prevailing, a night rescue operation would be impossible, so plans were made for the attempt to begin at first light on the 14th. The Chinooks and the Hercules tankers had meanwhile been flown to Shannon Airport, where they were standing by. Throughout the night, the *Yarrawonga* was watched over by a relay of Nimrods. The aircraft had been joined by the British bulk carrier *Ravenscraig*, the Canadian timber carrier *Irving Forest* and a Russian fishing vessel, all of whom had come in answer to Petersen's Mayday.

During the course of the night, the wind out in the Atlantic backed to the west, and the *Yarrawonga* was once more able to forge ahead. Her fresh water tanks were by now empty, and her boiler was using sea water to produce steam to heat the fuel and drive the pumps. This would destroy the boiler, but this was no time for niceties to be observed. The ship was taking on water at an accelerating rate, the hole in the port side of the hull having become larger, and cracks were opening up in the fore peak tank and No. 1 ballast tank. There was little time left and Petersen was driving his ship eastwards as fast as she would go.

At 1000 on the 14th, the *Yarrawonga* was only 260 miles off the Irish coast and making 11 knots. Two hours later, Petersen received word from one of the patrolling Nimrods that the first helicopter would be overhead in another hour. He altered course 10 degrees to starboard to ease the rolling, and waited, praying that the wait would not be long. The sounds now coming from forward were frightening.

The Chinooks were on time, arriving overhead together at 1300, accompanied by a Hercules. The helicopters were then on the extreme limit of their range, and first had to refuel. Although the wind had eased somewhat, it was still blowing force 10, and refuelling in mid-air required a high decree of skill that did great credit to the American pilots. By 1400, it was done, and while Petersen held his ship stern to the wind, the first Chinook dropped down and hovered over the *Yarrawonga's* foredeck. The rescue operation was swift and professional, all thirty-two men being lifted off the ship in less than an hour. Petersen and his chief engineer were last to leave. Two hours later, the survivors, unharmed but bearing the mental scars of their long battle against the sea, were landed at Shannon.

The abandoned *Yarrawonga*, her engines shut down, was left to fend for herself, and as the darkness of night closed in to hide her shame, she lay rolling helplessly in the trough of the waves. And that was how the 1,216-ton Wijsmuller salvage tug *Typhoon* found her on the 15th. The weather was still too rough to attempt boarding the derelict, but the wind was slackening. On the 16th, with the help of the Irish Navy vessel *Eithne*, the *Typhoon* put a line and a salvage crew aboard the *Yarrawonga* and began the tow. It was at first planned to tow the ship into calmer waters and there anchor her, but as the weather improved dramatically it was decided to carry on up the English Channel. The *Typhoon* and her tow reached Rotterdam on 22 January.

The *Yarrawonga* entered dry dock in Rotterdam on the 23rd, and all tanks and holds were opened up for inspection. Although the ship had been abandoned at sea, and now belonged to her insurers, Bionicserve's superintendents, inspectors from Norske Veritas, and her late commander, Captain Klaas Petersen were invited to attend on board while a survey was carried out by experts appointed by the German Ministry of Shipping. The survey showed very severe corrosion throughout the ship, particularly inside the side tanks, which constituted the double hull of the bulk carrier. Some plates, originally 18 mm thick, had only 2 or 3 mm of steel left, and in some places were rusted right through. The cross members between the inner and outer hull were all extremely badly rusted. It was obvious that for much of her long life the inside of the *Yarrawonga's* double hull had been totally neglected. Her steel hatch covers, an integral part of her watertightness, could be closed but not properly secured. Many of the fifty-two cleats used to secure each cover were either missing or bent. The survey also found that the *Yarrawonga's* engines were in poor condition.

The conclusion reached by the German Ministry of Shipping, not surprisingly, was that the *Yarrawonga* could not be considered seaworthy, and that, furthermore, all her many faults must have been evident before she sailed from Oxelösund on 23 December. And, if she was not seaworthy then, the same must have been the case when she was inspected by Norske Veritas in the previous April, shortly before she was taken over by Bionicserve. Yet Norske Veritas had at that time classified the ship as 100A1, which indicates the highest standard of seaworthiness awarded to merchant ships.

A seaworthy ship is defined as "one that is in every way fit to cope with the perils likely to be encountered on the voyage. Not only must the hull and machinery be in good working order and condition but she must be manned with a full complement of competent officers and crew; equipped with the bunkers, stores, water and provisions required for the voyage and in possession of the necessary charts and documentation." That the *Yarrawonga* was well stocked with fuel, water and stores when she sailed from Oxelösund cannot be disputed, but she was clearly not fit to cope with the perils of the North Atlantic in winter. Of the latter, it is clear that her master, owners and classification society were all well aware. In which case, this ship should not have put to sea, and as she did so, there must have been collusion between all three parties to cover up her dangerous shortcomings. Doubts must also be cast on the competency of her officers and crew.

To further cloud the issue, the Hamburg Ocean Weather Bureau stated that most of the weather reports sent in by the *Yarrawonga* on her Atlantic passage could not be substantiated. The Bureau was of the opinion that Captain Petersen was at times exaggerating the wind by up to three points on the Beaufort Scale. This is a practice not unknown in merchant ships; bad weather in the log book can be held to account for all manner of damage and delays, and it is difficult for underwriters and charterers to dispute this. However, on this occasion it does seem that Captain Petersen was weighting the scales a bit too much. On the other hand, the alleged exaggeration might not have been deliberate, but could have been due to the stress Petersen was under at the time. Things always seem much worse in the dead of night, and more so in mid-Atlantic when your ship is apparently breaking up under you.

Although the *Yarrawonga* flew the flag of Cyprus, she was German-owned and carried a German captain. It was therefore fitting that when a Court of Inquiry was convened in February 1990 to investigate the incident, it took place in Emden, and under the auspices of the German Seeamt. However, notwithstanding that all the evidence pointed that way, the Court would not go as far as to rule that the poor state of the ship was responsible for her near-loss. It did, however, conclude that the *Yarrawonga* was unseaworthy due to corrosion in the double hull, the cross members between the inner and outer hull being badly wasted. Bionicserve Shipping of Limassol, which was really Chemikalien See Transport of Hamburg, was held responsible for not maintaining the ship properly, while Norske Veritas, being the classification society, was condemned for colluding with Bionicserve to cover up the state of the ship. Captain Klaas Petersen was found guilty of endangering the lives of his crew by taking an unseaworthy ship to sea. As

Petersen was in command of the *Yarrawonga*, and in law had the ultimate say in whether the ship went to sea or not, the whole sorry business was laid at his door. Seeamt at first considered cancelling his certificate of competency, then relented and issued only a reprimand.

When the final reckoning was made, it showed that the saving of the *Yarrawonga* and her crew was a very costly business. The charter of the Canadian supply vessel *Triumph Sea* and the deep sea tug *Typhoon* alone ran into many millions of dollars. To that must be added the salvage award to Wijsmuller for bringing the ship in. And then there was the huge expense involved in rescuing the crew in mid-Atlantic. Just to put one Nimrod in the air costs around £4,000, and this operation involved three Nimrods, two Chinooks and three C-130 tankers, all airborne for many hours. British and American taxpayers paid very dear for the years of neglect that led to the abandonment of the *Yarrawonga* in mid-Atlantic.

It might be thought that that was the end of the *Yarrawonga*, for she was declared a total loss by her insurers, who then paid Bionicserve her value. By all accounts, this ship should now have gone to the breaker's yard, but market forces were at work. There was then a shortage of large bulk carriers, and after repairs, the *Yarrawonga* was sold to a Greek concern, the Maritime Ship Trading Company, for $6.9 million and renamed *Cape North*. In February 1990, she changed hands again, going to the Palembros Shipping Company for a reported $7.5 million. Palembros, a Greek company trading from London, retained the name *Cape North*, and although no classification society would accept the ship, she was somehow allowed to register under the British flag, probably on a bareboat charter.

In June 1990, the *Yarrawonga/Cape North* was again reported to be in trouble, putting into Algeciras with heavy weather damage while on a voyage from West Africa to Bremerhaven. Temporary repairs were carried out at the Spanish port, then she went on to Gdansk for further repairs. It is hardly necessary to ask what form the damage took this time.

The career of this infamous ship finally came to an end when, in February 1993, she went to her last resting place, a breaker's yard in China. It is said that even for scrap she fetched $2.6 million. In her long life of 22 years, during which she served five owners under five different flags, the *Yarrawonga* made fortunes for many, but caused untold anguish for all who sailed in her.

Walter Leonhardt

The 42,805-ton bulk carrier *Walter Leonhardt* sailed from Tampa, Florida on 15 February 1990 with a cargo of rock phosphate for Antwerp. Three days later, she sank in mid-Atlantic from an unknown cause, but believed to be the rupture of ship's side plating in No. 2 hold. The weather at the time was reported to be wind force 5 with a heavy swell. Her crew were picked up by the Polish bulk carrier *Kopainia Zolfiowka* and landed in the Azores.

The *Walter Leonhardt*, owned by Leonhardt & Blumberg of Hamburg, and managed by the Silver Stream Company of Limassol, sailed under the Cypriot flag. She was built in Emden in 1966 as the *Bornheim* for Unterweser Reederei. In 1968 she was stretched by 72 feet to give one extra hold.

10

A Decade On

"A joint meeting of the London Maritime Association and City Master Mariners was called to consider bulker losses which led to the loss of more than 200 lives in less than 12 months."

–Lloyd's List February 1991

September 1990, being the tenth anniversary of the disappearance of the *Derbyshire*, brought renewed calls for a public inquiry into her loss. Coincidentally, the month also saw the end of another big ship, which went down in very similar circumstances. The 169,623-ton Liberian-flag oil/bulk/ore carrier *Algarrobo* was, like the *Derbyshire*, bound for Kawasaki with a full cargo of iron ore when, on or about 19 September, she disappeared in the Pacific with her crew of thirty-two. A court of inquiry into the loss of this 17-year-old ship held by the Liberian Deputy Commissioner of Maritime Affairs concluded that: "There are no findings of fact that would lead to any conclusion of a positive proximate cause of the unique, sudden and apparent catastrophic condition(s) that led to the unexplained loss of the ore/oil carrier *Algarrobo* and her entire crew."

Eloquent words to explain away a sudden, but most certainly not unique catastrophe. Disappearing bulk carriers were by now quite commonplace. In the twelve months ending December 1990, a total of twenty-one of these ships went down, taking with them over 200 men. It all began with the *Orient Pioneer*.

On the morning of 7 January 1990, the 152,835-ton Liberian-flag motor tanker *Golar Coleen* was in mid-Indian Ocean, five days out of the Sunda Strait and bound for St. Croix in the US Virgin Islands. The weather was fair, with the South-East Trades blowing fresh, the sky partly clouded and the odd shower bringing relief from the hot tropical sun. The Swedish-owned tanker was commanded by Captain Miguel A. Azcueta, who now surveyed the empty horizon with a less than enthusiastic eye. A long, undulating swell was coming out of the southwest which, combined with a steadily falling barometer, indicated to Azcueta that he was chasing a cyclone.

The cyclones of the South Indian Ocean, close cousins of the Pacific typhoons, are said to originate in about 10° South 70° East, in the vicinity of the Chagos Archipelago–possibly triggered off by the rising air over these islands. Once formed, the cyclones travel in a west-southwesterly direction towards Mauritius. Occasionally, one of these vicious storms strikes the island, destroying its precious sugar cane crop, but the majority haul to the southward before reaching Mauritius, eventually to merge with the mayhem of the Roaring Forties.

Late that night, Captain Azcueta was paying his last visit to the bridge before turning in, when the radio officer handed him and urgent message received from Mauritius Radio. It read:

SOS NR 001/076 FOLLOWING SOS RECEIVED FROM ORIENT PIONEER/D5ZB ON RADIO TELEX AT 07/1141Z POSN 1921S 07612E NOW BADLY CONDITION HATCH LEAKAGE INCOMING WATER PLS HELICOPTER SAIL TUBARAO BRAZIL DESTINATION KAOSHIUNG NOW CYCLONE.

The message was jumbled, but the gist was clear to Azcueta. This was a vessel in serious trouble and requiring assistance. The position given by the *Orient Pioneer* put her nearly 1,000 miles east of Mauritius and 700 miles south of Diego Garcia. In which case, her request for a helicopter would go unanswered. The *Golar Coleen*, however, was well placed to help, being then only 183 miles northeast of the *Orient Pioneer*. Azcueta altered course to the southwest and increased speed.

One hour later, Azcueta contacted the *Orient Pioneer* on radiotelephone, and learned that the first position given by the ship in distress was wildly in error. She was, in fact, then only 80 miles southwest of the *Golar Coleen*.

During the course of the night, the two ships maintained radio contact as the distance between them narrowed. The master of the *Orient Pioneer* reported the water was rising rapidly in her holds, the situation on board worsening by the hour. It was his intention to abandon ship as soon as the *Golar Coleen* was close, if he was not forced to do so

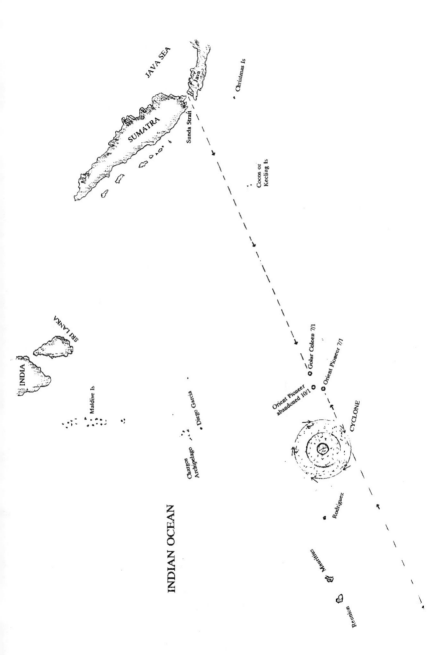

before. He agreed to use his own boats to transfer his crew to the rescue ship.

At 0145 on the 8th, the two ships were in sight of each other, but as the *Orient Pioneer* seemed to be in no immediate danger of sinking, it was judged safer to wait until daylight before taking her crew off.

First light, which was around 0500, revealed the *Orient Pioneer* to be dangerously low in the water. She was close to starboard of the *Golar Coleen* and rolling sluggishly in the heavy swell. Her story was a familiar one. The 108,504-ton bulk carrier, built in 1971 for Ropner Management of the UK, was sailing under the Liberian flag, her declared owners being the Conduit Shipping Company of Monrovia. Manned by a Korean crew, she had been on passage from Brazil to Taiwan with a cargo of 103,700 tons of iron ore when she ran into the cyclone. At the height of the storm, heavy seas had smashed her hatch coamings, resulting in the unshipping and subsequent loss of most of her hatch covers. From then on her fate was sealed. Water poured into her half-empty holds, and as she wallowed in the swell, she was battered by the sea from both inside and out. The ship was 19 years old, her hull plating worn paper-thin through lack of maintenance, and she soon had gaping holes in her side in way of three holds. More water poured in. It was fortunate for the *Orient Pioneer* that the Indian Ocean cyclone, although fierce, is small in diameter and passes relatively quickly. Had the storm held her in its grip for much longer, she would most certainly have broken up and gone to the bottom before help reached her.

With the coming of full daylight, the *Golar Coleen* was in position close to the *Orient Pioneer* and Azcueta signalled her to lower her boats and begin the transfer of her crew. At this late point, the master of the disabled ore carrier discovered–conveniently it might seem–that his lifeboats were "out of service," and requested the *Golar Coleen* to carry out the rescue using her own boats. As the two very large ships were by then in dangerously close proximity to each other, Azcueta was obliged to lower his boats and get on with the job before there was a collision. By 0730, with no thanks to their own efforts, the *Orient Pioneer's* crew, including her master, were safely on board the tanker.

The bulk carrier, although very low in the water, showed no signs of sinking, and when his boats had been hoisted inboard, Azcueta's thoughts, quite naturally, turned to salvage. The loaded ship was too valuable a prize to be abandoned. Azcueta stood by until the morning of the 9th, and finding the *Orient Pioneer* to be still very much afloat, attempted to take her in tow using mooring ropes. The attempt ended in failure, for the ore carrier, then probably displacing in excess of 120,000 tons, was dead in the water. The *Golar Coleen's* ropes were not strong enough to take the strain.

The two ships lay stopped and joined together for another 24 hours, until, in the afternoon of the 10th, Captain Azcueta cut his ropes and set course for Mauritius to land the survivors. When last seen, the *Orient Pioneer* was drifting to the west at a speed of about 1 knot. Left to her own devices, she may well have drifted for days, perhaps weeks, before finally slipping beneath the waves. She was never seen again, and was later declared a total loss; another sad statistic to add to the lengthening list of disappearing ore carriers. Her flag, her age, and her crew must all have had a bearing on her eventual loss.

As the *Orient Pioneer* set off on her last lonely voyage, on the other side of the world in the Gulf of St. Lawrence, the British bulk carrier *Tribulus* was nearing completion of her loading in the ore port of Seven Islands. The 127,907-ton *Tribulus*, owned by Shell Tankers Ltd., was manned by a British crew of twenty-one, commanded by Captain Alan Willy. Also on board were three officers' wives. The 9-year-old ship sailed under the second register flag of the Isle of Man.

The *Tribulus* left Seven Islands on the morning of 29 January 1990 with a full cargo of iron ore for Rotterdam. Soon after clearing the Gulf of St. Lawrence, not unexpectedly, she ran into the full fury of a North Atlantic storm. The winter of 1989-90 was a severe one, with a seemingly endless succession of deep depressions sweeping across the ocean from west to east. One of these had hit the British Isles four days earlier, causing widespread damage and killing forty-six people. Winds gusting to 90 mph lashed southern England, uprooting trees, blowing down power lines and causing chaos on roads and railways. Motorways in the South and West were clogged by overturned lorries, the Severn Bridge was completely closed to traffic, and seven out of the nine London underground lines were shut down by falling trees and masonry. In the English Channel, westbound shipping came to a standstill in the teeth of the wind, while eastbound ships, with and 85-knot wind behind them, flew up Channel at unprecedented speeds. All cross-Channel ferries in the Straits of Dover were confined to port, being unable to manoeuvre out of harbour in the high winds. On the con-

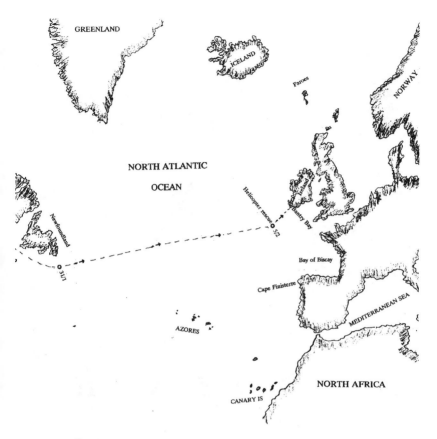

tinent of Europe, another twenty-two people died in the worst storm experienced in over ten years. The violent winds knocked out a number of nuclear power stations in France; in the Netherlands, people were crushed in their cars by falling trees, 70 mph winds shattered hundreds of green-houses, Schipol Airport was closed and most trains were suspended. Next day, the storm crossed the German border and created havoc as far inland as Frankfurt and Hanover.

By the time the *Tribulus* cleared Newfoundland on the evening of the 31st, she was running before a force 9

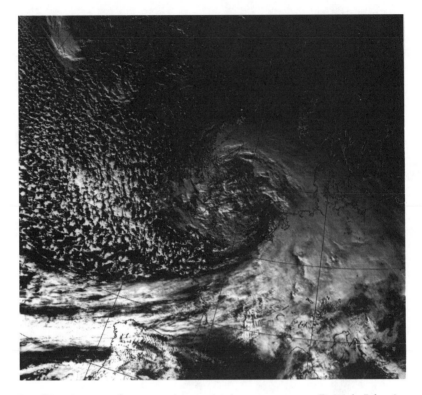

Satellite image of severe storm which swept across British Isles in January 1990. Bulk carrier *Tribulus* was following in its wake.
Photo: University of Dundee

westerly, with driving rain squalls chasing her eastwards under a ragged sky. Mountainous following seas foamed and roared at her stern rails, and she rolled and pitched heavily, sometimes sheering wildly when a sea caught her on the quarter. Five days later, she was 300 miles west of Land's End, and still running before the storm, the ship and all on board her showing clear signs of fatigue.

At 1000 that morning, there was a loud bang that did not match the rhythmical crash of the waves against the ship's side and a tall geyser of dirty water was seen to shoot up from No. 8 hatchway. Then each time the *Tribulus* dipped into the trough there was a loud rush of air and the water column again climbed skywards. A hurried inspection of the deck revealed hatch covers missing from No. 8 hold, and that the starboard side of the ship in the vicinity of the hold was laid open to the sea. This hold, which was empty of cargo, was full to the waterline, hence the water erupting from the hatch each time the pressure was increased by the sea coming in through the hole in the side.

Having taken stock of the situation, Captain Willy sent out a radio call for assistance. This was answered by the Search and Rescue Centre at Falmouth, and the German bulk carrier *Crystal B.*, which was nearby. The *Crystal B.* altered course for the *Tribulus*, and the Dutch salvage tug *Solano*, on station off Land's End, was ordered to sea. Two Sea King helicopters flew in to Cork to stand by in case they were needed.

At last, the weather showed signs of easing, and Willy found that by slowing her down to 7 knots the *Tribulus* rode the waves comfortably. He now decided to make for the nearest shelter, Bantry Bay, then some 230 miles to the northeast. But first he called for a helicopter to take off all non-essential personnel.

One of the RAF Sea Kings from Cork arrived overhead at 2130, and with the wind having dropped to no more than a fresh breeze, the rescue operation was completed in an hour, seven men and three wives being lifted off. Willy, with his reduced crew of three mates, four engineers, a radio officer, five sailors and a cook, then began to coax the waterlogged *Tribulus* towards Bantry Bay. A very fraught situation had been handled expertly and with the minimum of fuss.

Ashore in Bantry Bay, the mood was far from relaxed. For some days the area had been lashed by storm-force winds and torrential rains, which combined with unusually high tides had caused widespread flooding. And now here was news that another *Kowloon Bridge*, in the form of the *Tribulus*, was heading their way. The threat of yet another ecological disaster galvanised into action the Irish Department of the Marine, a body formed as a direct result of the *Kowloon Bridge* fiasco. A major red anti-pollution alert was issued, warning fishermen and mussel farmers, the latter operating a multi-million pound enterprise in Bantry Bay, to be on their guard. Booms and oil dispersant equipment were flown in, and the Irish Lights ship *Grey Seal* was ordered from Waterford to Bantry. Meanwhile, the naval vessel *Eithne* had already left Cork and was heading west to meet the *Tribulus*. Shell Oil also reacted quickly, flying senior managers into Cork by chartered jet with instructions to cooperate fully with the Irish authorities. Scenting a big story, the media, notebooks and cameras at the ready, were arriving in force.

It was just after midnight on the 6 February when the *Tribulus* limped in to Bantry Bay escorted by the *Eithne* and the tug *Solano*. At 0200 on the 7th, the damaged bulk carrier was anchored 6 miles to seaward of the old Whiddy Island terminal. Willy had asked for the ship to be taken deeper into the bay, but the opposition from the local fishermen was so strong that no one seemed prepared to make the decision to take her further in. The Irish authorities were dithering again.

British bulk carrier *Tribulus* at anchor Bantry Bay, February 1990.
Photo: *Cork Examiner*

That night, winter made a savage return, with storm-force westerly winds sweeping into the bay. This led to the suspension of all activity around the *Tribulus*, and for the next five days Willy and his crew fought to hold the ship in position. The weather finally relented on the 12th, whereupon the harbour authorities made a belated decision to take the ship further into the bay. When she was anchored in sheltered waters less than a mile off Whiddy Island, divers were able to go down and inspect the hull. They reported the *Tribulus* had lost a section of her plating measuring 60 feet by 30 feet, meaning that virtually the whole of the ship's side in way of the empty No. 8 hold had gone, as if ripped open by a giant hand.

After temporary repairs in Bantry Bay, the *Tribulus* sailed, and finally reached Rotterdam in mid-March with her cargo still intact. That she survived at all was a great tribute to the professionalism of Captain Alan Willy and his crew, showing the extent to which great adversity can be overcome by competent and dedicated seamen. What actually befell the ship on that storm-wracked February morning far out in the Atlantic no one can say with certainty. It is most probable, however, that her No. 8 hatch covers were first unshipped by a big sea, leading to the hold becoming partially flooded, creating a destructive free surface of water that sloshed from side to side with the rolling. Eventually, although the *Tribulus* was apparently a well-maintained ship, her ship's side plates gave way under the onslaught of the sea. Had her transverse bulkheads not held, she could well have broken up before help reached her.

As the spring of 1990 moved into summer, and the *Tribulus* licked her wounds in dry dock, another link in the *Derbyshire* chain was about to capture the headlines. She was the 80,580-ton bulk carrier *Petingo*, ex-*Pacific Bridge*. This early antecedent of the *Derbyshire* was built in Japan in 1967 for Bibby Line's Seabridge consortium. She passed into Greek hands in February 1974 and went under the Liberian flag. Five years later, she was sold to Hong Kong Chinese owners, a one-ship company, which then began trading under the name Petingo Maritime. The *Petingo*, then at the very advanced age of twenty-three, was re-registered in the Republic of Vanuatu, a newcomer to the world of commercial shipping. She was manned by a Chinese crew of forty commanded by Captain Cheung Kam Yui.

On 25 June 1990, the *Petingo* lay in the South African ore port of Saldanha Bay, 80 miles north of the Cape of Good Hope. She was chartered to take 72,000 tons of lump iron ore for Shanghai, which at the terminal's loading rate of 5,000 tons an hour should have been on board in under sixteen hours. However, having experienced heavy weather on passage, the *Petingo* had arrived in port with all her ballast tanks still full. The depth of water alongside the Saldanha Bay terminal was restricted, and in order to avoid the ship taking ground, the rate of loading was slowed to keep pace with the water ballast being pumped out. This delay will not have been to Captain Cheung's liking, for the 61-year-old Chinese master was on his last voyage before retiring after twenty-two years in command. Shanghai and a new life ashore beckoned.

Despite Cheung's impatience, it was not until late on the evening of the 26th that the last dusty lumps of ore cascaded into the *Petingo's* holds and her crew began to prepare the ship for sea. This was a major operation, involving the securing of the bulk carrier's nine hatches with over 1,000 cleats. It was an operation carried out under pressure, for another ore carrier was already anchored off the port waiting to go alongside the ore berth. One and a half hours after completion of loading, the *Petingo*, then drawing 50 feet of water, sailed from Saldanha Bay.

Within a few hours of leaving the shelter of the bay, the *Petingo* ran into a strong westerly gale. Steering a southerly course for the Cape, she was beam-on to wind and sea and soon rolling so heavily that Cheung feared her cargo might shift. It was not long before he was forced to haul around to the west and heave-to with the wind on the bow.

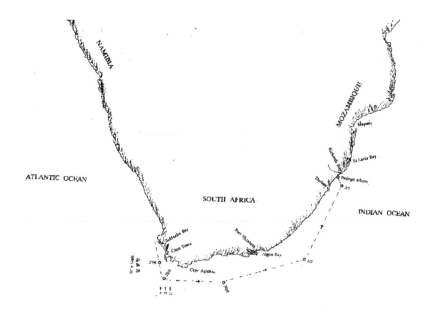

Resuming course and speed whenever the weather would allow, the *Petingo* clawed her way slowly to the south, reaching the latitude of the Cape of Good Hope by late afternoon on the 27th. Next morning, the wind dropped and the sun shone, but this was only a temporary respite. Before noon, the wind was back blowing force 10 and great 40-foot seas were breaking clean over the bulk carrier's decks as she lurched her way southwards. Cheung was pushing her hard, anxious to run well clear of the land before altering to the east. His task was not made any easier when, later in the day, the wind backed until it was in the southwest. Now the *Petingo* was riding the roller coaster of the waves, pounding heavily as she fought her way through the storm.

On the evening of the 29th, when he judged he was sufficiently far south to avoid the powerful, west-flowing Agulhas current, Cheung brought the ship around onto an easterly course, heading out into the Indian Ocean. In doing so, he put her directly across the path of the long Cape Rollers. The heavily laden ship took on a pendulum-like motion, swinging rhythmically from side to side, burying her weather rails every time she rolled to starboard. It was a dangerous movement, for there were times when the *Petingo's* roll synchronised with the waves, and she went progressively further over with each successive roll. When this happened, a temporary change of course was required to break the sequence.

Dawn was slow to come on the 30th, and with it came indications that all was not well. The *Petingo* was noticeably slow to answer the helm, and her rolling was becoming more and more ponderous. Each time she went over, she seemed reluctant to return to the upright. Cheung suspected water in the holds. His fears were confirmed at first light, when it could be seen from the bridge that No. 3 hold had lost three hatch covers. Course and speed were adjusted to hold the ship steady while the Chief Officer took a party on deck. He returned with the devastating news that No. 3 hold was awash and open to the sea on both sides. At some time during the *Petingo's* long battle to round the Cape, she had lost hatch covers at No. 3, resulting in the now familiar breaching of her side plating.

Cheung decided to make for the nearest accessible port in the hope that he might find refuge before his twenty-three-year-old ship sank under him. A look at the chart showed the only reasonable option open being Port Elizabeth, which lies at the western end of Algoa Bay in the shelter of Cape Receife. When the port was contacted by radio, the *Petingo* was refused entrance to the harbour, but

Cheung was given directions for a safe anchorage in Algoa Bay. Grateful for small mercies, Cheung was about to bring his ship round to make for Algoa Bay, then 210 miles to the northwest, when his owners stepped in. Petingo Maritime radioed they were sending a tug, and that meanwhile Cheung should make all possible speed for Durban, where a berth alongside was available.

Petingo underway off the east coast of South Africa and making for Richards Bay, July 1990. No. 3 hold open to the sea.
Photo: Dept. of Transport Shipping Directorate, Marine Division, Republic of South Africa

It was against Cheung's better judgement to carry on, for Durban lay two and a half day's steaming to the northeast, but the offer of a berth alongside was tempting. With her pumps working at full capacity, the *Petingo* struggled on, sinking ever lower in the water as she went.

Twenty-four hours later, Durban radioed that the ship was considered too deep to enter the port—the *Petingo's* draught was then estimated to be about 53 feet. Cheung was advised to continue on to Richards Bay, the ore port 70 miles north of Durban, where there was more water. With the growing realisation that his ship was not welcome in South African waters, Cheung agreed to carry on, not that there was much else he could do.

For the first time since leaving Saldanha Bay five days earlier, fortune now smiled on the *Petingo*. As the day went on, so the weather moderated, the wind falling away to no more than a fresh breeze and the sea flattening out. The decks were dry once more, and bilges were sounded, showing No. 3 hold to be half full, while Nos. 1, 2 and 4 holds had over a foot of water in them. The situation was serious enough, but the *Petingo* was not yet in danger of foundering.

Another gale blew up, but was fortunately short-lived, and by 0600 on 3 July the *Petingo* was off Richards Bay awaiting a pilot to take her in. At this point, it seemed someone ashore was having second thoughts about berthing the ship, and Cheung spent the next hour fighting to hold his shhp in position while minds were made up. When the pilot launch fhnally came alongside, it was found that the *Petingo's* forward draught had increased to 63 feet. Consequently, she was refused entry into Richards Bay, and the pilot left again. Cheung `sked for an anchorage, but by now the port authorities were concerned that this large and threatened ship might sink and block the approaches to the port. After some heated exchanges between ship and shore, Cheung was told to take the *Petingo* out into deep water 50 miles offshore, and there abandon her.

This was really too much to ask of a ship's captain, not least one who was on his last voyage to sea. Not surprisingly, Cheung refused to go away. He was determined to save his ship and so moved in towards the coast, intending to anchor off Durnford Point, where he hoped to take on high-capacity pumps to empty the *Petingo's* holds. He took the utmost care in approaching the anchorage, but failed to make allowance for a current setting inshore. The *Petingo* drove hard aground on the rocky bank that stretches seawards from Durnford Point, and nothing would shift her.

The furore began when it became known ashore that the *Petingo* had on board 1,450 tons of heavy fuel oil, all of which was likely to be spilled when she broke her back—and event that was now inevitable. Salvage teams used explosives to blow open her fuel tanks with the object of shortening the clean-up period, but even though rough weather dispersed most of the oil released, holiday beaches along a 15-mile stretch of the coast were polluted. The subsequent clean-up operation, which involved up to 300 people, including eight divers, required the services of three anti-pollution ships, a light aircraft, a helicopter, nearly 4 miles of booms, bulldozers, tons of heavy machinery and 30,000 gallons of dispersant, cost nearly two million rand. As might be expected, Captain Cheung, the man least able to defend himself, was held responsible for the disaster. He was hauled before the Durban Regional Court charged with contravening the Prevention and Combating of Pollution of the Sea by Oil Act and fined R30,000. Petingo Maritime was handed the bill for the clean-up operation.

The unfortunate *Petingo*, for all her advanced age, did not surrender to the sea easily. For fifteen days she endured

Petingo ashore off Durnford Point, July 1990.
Oil slick spreading from breached fuel tanks.
Photo: Dept. of Transport Shipping Directorate, Marine Division,
Republic of South Africa

the onslaught of the waves until, on 18 July, she finally broke in three pieces, spilling much of her cargo of iron ore onto the sea bed. Her loss was a major blow to the fledgling Vanuatu register, for she had been the biggest ship by far sailing under that flag.

In today's world of high-speed loading and quick turnrounds in port, pressure is always on the ship to sail as quickly as possible after completion of her cargo. The age-old cry "Oh, you can finish battening down the hatches when you get to sea" is all too often used, and many ship-masters, already under pressure from their owners to speed up the voyage, give way. Ore carriers are particularly susceptible, for the number of deep draught berths in any port is restricted, and the demand for these berths is great. It is not recorded whether undue pressure was brought to bear on Captain Cheung by the Saldanha Bay port authorities, but this is not beyond the bounds of possibility. If it was so, it could well be that the bulk carrier's hatches were not properly secured before she sailed, and this was suggested by the Court of Inquiry held into her loss. Perhaps Cheung was satisfied that the work could be finished at sea, but within an hour or two of clearing Saldanha Bay, the *Petingo* was beamon to a full gale, and having little freeboard, the seas will have been sweeping her decks. The opportunity to make her hatches watertight–if they were not already so–was gone.

Whatever was left undone that contributed to the eventual loss of the *Petingo*, it cannot be denied that Captain Cheung Kam Yui and his crew, having found themselves in a desperate situation, did well to bring their crippled ship through seven days of very severe weather to Richards Bay. That she was then lost in sight of her promised port of refuge was due in part to the uncooperative attitude of the South African authorities. Having decided not to allow the ship into the port, they made no attempt to guide Cheung into a safe anchorage. Their advice to take the *Petingo* out to sea and allow her to sink in deep water showed an unacceptable lack of concern for the ship and those on board.

At the end of July, as watchers ashore on the Zululand coast anxiously monitored the *Petingo's* spilled oil drifting in towards their pristine beaches, the typhoons were on the march again in the North Pacific. On the 30th, the Greek-owned oil/bulk/ore carrier *Pasithea* passed south of the Daito Islands, bound from Western Australia for Kashima, a small port 160 miles north of Tokyo Bay. Already that morning the ship had received a warning from Hong Kong Radio that the storm clouds were gathering around her. The signs were ominous, for the *Pasithea* was near the spot where the *Derbyshire* had disappeared in a typhoon ten years earlier, an unhappy coincidence not lost on the Greek ship's master, Captain Constandinos Vardakostas.

The 155,407-ton *Pasithea*, built in Japan in 1971, and owned by Sao Financing and Trading, a company registered in Monrovia, flew the Greek flag and was manned by a crew of thirty-one. Like most of her class, although designed to carry both oil and ores, she had long since dropped her dual role, not having carried a cargo of oil for six years. On the current voyage, she had on board 150,000 tons of iron ore.

Hong Kong came up with more bad news as the *Pasithea* put the Daito Islands astern:

TROPICAL STORM VERNON IN LAT 19.3N 137.2E AT 0001 GMT JULY 30. MOVEMENT PAST SIX HOURS 045 DEGREES AT FOUR KNOTS. POSITION ACCURATE TO WITHIN 45 NAUTICAL MILES BASED ON CENTRE LOCATED BY SATELLITE. MAXIMUM SUSTAINED WINDS 40 KNOTS WITH GUSTS TO 50 KNOTS. RADIUS OF OVER-30 KNOTS WINDS 40 NAUTICAL MILES. AT 0300 GMT JULY 30 POSITION LAT 19.6N LONG 137.4E. VERNON CONTINUES TO DRIFT NORTH EASTWARD.

Vernon presented a very real threat to the *Pasithea*. The storm was to the west of the Marianas, and only 360

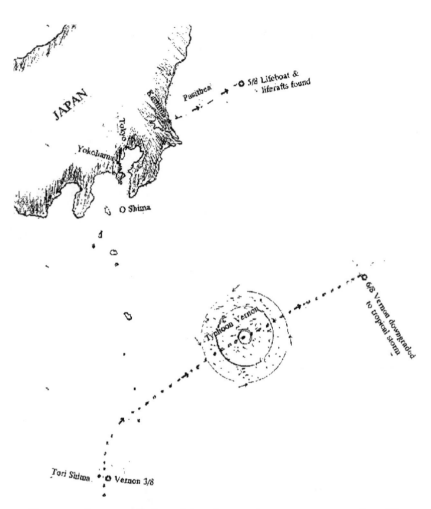

miles southeast of the ship, but what was more significant was that storm and ship were on roughly parallel courses. This left Captain Vardakostas with little choice but to try to outrun Vernon, which was then moving very slowly, and so might be on the point of recurving to the north or northeast. Vardakostas held his course and increased speed to get ahead of the storm.

236

The *Pasithea*, rising and falling on the long, oily swells emanating from the centre of the storm, passed ahead of Vernon during the night and began to increase the distance between them. Vardakostas was beginning to breathe easily again when, on the morning of the 31st, Hong Kong issued another warning:

TYPHOON VERNON, UPGRADED FROM TROPICAL STORM, IN LAT 20.5N LONG 138.1E AT 0001 GMT JULY 31. MOVEMENT PAST SIX HOURS 030 DEGREES AT FOUR KNOTS. POSITION ACCURATE TO WITHIN 30 NAUTICAL MILES BASED ON EYE FIXED BY SATELLITE. MAXIMUM SUSTAINED WINDS 65 KNOTS WITH GUSTS TO 80 KNOTS. RADIUS OF OVER-50 KNOT WINDS 75 NAUTICAL MILES SOUTH SEMICIRCLE AND 50 NAUTICAL MILES ELSEWHERE. RADIUS OF OVER-30 KNOT WINDS 125 NAUTICAL MILES SOUTH SEMICIRCLE AND 100 NAUTICAL MILES ELSEWHERE. AT 0300 GMT JULY 31 POSITION LAT 20.7N LONG 138.2E. LATEST SATELLITE IMAGERY INDICATES VERNON HAS DEVELOPED AN EYE DURING THE PAST SIX HOURS.

Vernon was gathering strength by the hour, and showing only a very gradual–and possibly temporary–swing to the north.

When, 36 hours later, the *Pasithea* arrived off Kashima, Vernon was 680 miles to the south and moving northwest at 5 knots. Maximum sustained winds of 80 knots were being reported, with gusts up to 100 knots. This was now a very dangerous storm. The indications were, however, that Vernon was heading for the Chinese mainland, possibly brushing the southern tip of Japan in passing. The *Pasithea*, then anchored off Kashima queuing for a berth, seemed safe enough.

But Vernon was playing a waiting game, hovering under the influence of the barometric pressure surrounding it, uncertain of which way to move. On the morning of 3 August, the *Pasithea* being still at anchor off Kashima, Hong Kong reported an unwelcome development. Vernon had decided to go north, and was then over the tiny island of Tori Shima, 320 miles south-southwest of Kashima. The typhoon, which had lost some of its strength, was moving due north at speed, on a collision course with Tokyo. Only a slight change of direction was needed to bring Vernon ashore directly over Kashima. Even if the typhoon did hold its course, the very least the port could expect was winds in excess of 50 knots., which is approaching hurricane force on the Beaufort Scale.

The land around Kashima is low-lying and affords little protection from strong winds of any direction. Local harbour regulations advise that, on the approach of a typhoon all ships should put to sea. It may have been that with two anchors down and a good scope of cable on each, the *Pasithea* would have been able to ride out the storm with the help of her engines. However, assuming the eye of Vernon passed close to Kashima–and this now seemed most likely–it would bring with it torrential rains, reducing the visibility to nil, and blanking out the radar screens. Should the ship then drag her anchors, there would be no means of detecting this. Captain Vardakostas decided–wisely it would seem at the time–to take his ship out into the open sea, and there ride out the typhoon without the added danger of being blown ashore.

It is thought that the *Pasithea* left her anchorage off Kashima on the afternoon of the 4th and headed eastwards. The 155,407-ton bulk carrier and her crew of thirty-one were not seen again. Concerns for her safety were first raised on the 5th, when one of her inflatable life rafts was found drifting and empty about 70 miles northeast of Kashima. Naval patrol vessels and aircraft searched the area, discovering an oil slick, an empty lifeboat, two lifebuoys and one lifejacket. The lifeboat was clearly marked with the

Pasithea
Photo: Skyfotos

Pasithea's name and port of registry. The search continued for five days, but nothing further was found.

On the afternoon of 6 August, Typhoon Vernon, by then downgraded to a tropical storm, was reported 230 miles southeast of Kashima, having maximum winds of 45 knots with gust to 55 knots. The storm had not come ashore near Tokyo Bay as forecast, but had veered sharply to the east. In which case, Vernon approached no nearer to Kashima than about 250 miles. The *Pasithea* put to sea on the 4th and was presumably steering to the east, supposedly away from the path of the typhoon. This being so, it is most unlikely that the ship will have come closer than within 150 miles of the eye. At the very worst, she will have experienced gale force winds, which to a ship of her size should have presented no danger. The passing disturbance will however have created a very big and lasting swell, and the *Pasithea* must have experienced heavy rolling.

On 4 December 1990, a line was finally drawn under the *Pasithea* story when she was declared a total loss at Lloyd's and her insurance settled. The reason for her disappearance in weather that should not really have threatened her has never been established. It was suggested that her cargo may have shifted in the heavy rolling and she capsized, or that she was the victim of a massive explosion caused by "the regeneration of gas from rust and waxy deposits in the tanks." The latter is possible, but most unlikely, for the *Pasithea* had not carried an oil cargo for six years before her final voyage. As in the case of the *Derbyshire*—for there were many similarities in the two ships—it was also suggested, and this by the Greek Ministry of Merchant Marine, that the *Pasithea* broke in two forward of the bridge, and the two halves of the ship sank before she could be abandoned or a distress signal sent. Without a proper examination of the wreck–and no one knows where the *Pasithea* lies–this is a theory which will be difficult to prove.

Alexandre P.

In March 1990, the 94,531-ton Panamanian-flag oil/bulk/ore carrier *Alexandre P.* sailed from Dampier, Western Australian, bound for Gijon, Spain with a full cargo of iron ore. She was last heard from on the 14th, when she was 180 miles due west of Dampier. An extensive air and sea search led to the discovery of an oil slick, floating debris and a life raft containing two bodies. It was assumed that sudden structural failure or a massive explosion had been responsible for the loss of the ship and her crew of twenty-five.

The *Alexandre P.* was built at Hiroshima in 1967 for Nippon Yusen Kaisha as the *Tsurusaki Maru*. She was sold to South Korean interests in 1980, and became the *Acacia*. Her owners at the time of her loss were not known.

11

Ad Infinitum

By any account, 1994 was a disastrous year for merchant shipping, with the loss of 103 vessels worldwide, totalling nearly 900,000 tons gross. The human toll exacted was exceptionally heavy, for among the casualties were no fewer than eighteen passenger liners—a new and frightening trend. These included the 21,794-ton Estonian-flag ferry *Estonia*, which went down in a violent equinoctial storm in the Baltic in late September taking 910 people with her. This was the worst maritime disaster in European waters since the Second World War. When 1994 drew to a close, a total of 1,463 lives had been claimed by the sea.

Not unexpectedly, bulk carriers figured high in the 1994 casualty league, sixteen of their number going down along with 147 crew. Once again, the majority were ageing flag of convenience ships.

News of the first bulker loss came in when the New Year was only a few hours old, the 169,147-ton oil/bulk/ore carrier *Marika* sinking in heavy seas some 930 miles east of Newfoundland. The 21-year-old, Liberian-flag *Marika* was on passage from Seven Islands to Ymuiden with 140,000 tons of iron ore when she radioed that she had cracks in her hull. Then there was silence—until her float-free emergency beacon began transmitting. Searchers found no trace of the *Marika* and her 36-man Greek and Filipino crew. The first day of January 1994 had still not come to a close when the 15,000-ton *Nichol* became a total loss after piling up on rocks near Vera Cruz, Mexico. The 19-year-old Cyprus-flag bulk carrier was inward bound for Vera Cruz with a cargo of steel from Venezuela. Fortunately, all her crew were taken off before she broke up.

The next bulker casualty, also occurring in the Gulf of Mexico, followed hard on the heels of the first two. On 5 January, while approaching the New Orleans pilot, inward bound with a cargo of alumina from Jamaica, the 22,076-ton bulk carrier *Golden Crown* was rammed by the outward bound Liberian-flag tanker *Hellespoint Faith*. The 23-year-old *Golden Crown*, registered in Panama, was seriously damaged but reached a berth up-river, where her cargo was discharged. All to no avail. The ship was later judged to be beyond repair and sold to Indian shipbreakers. No loss of life was involved in the collision.

The same good fortune did not attend 1994's fourth bulker loss. On 3 February, while on passage from Liverpool to Vera Cruz with a cargo of scrap, the 27,000-ton *Christinaki* was hit by a severe gale when 240 miles west of Ireland. Heavy seas breaking on board the 21-year-old Maltese-flag ship carried away her hatches and she radioed that her holds were flooding. A large-scale search operation was mounted, but the ship and her crew of twenty-seven Greeks and Filipinos were never found.

On 25 February, the 110,000-ton Cyprus-flag *Kamari* reported serious hull damage sustained in heavy weather in the South Atlantic. This was an all too familiar tale; a 21-year-old flag of convenience bulk carrier loaded to her marks with 120,000 tons of iron ore. Water entered her holds–probably due to hatch covers being lost or unshipped–and punched holes in her hull plating, leading to more flooding.

In this case, the ship, which was on a voyage from Venezuela to China, stayed afloat long enough to reach a sheltered anchorage in the River Plate. Examination of her hull revealed that she required extensive repairs involving the replacement of an estimated 150 tons of steel plating.

The *Kamari* remained at anchor for over a month while her owners and insurers debated her future, her condition deteriorating all the time. By early April she was said to be in danger of sinking, this giving rise to fears that the 2,500 tons of fuel oil still on board might cause massive pollution in the Plate estuary.

Having obviously outstayed her welcome in Uraguayan waters, the *Kamari* sailed north to a new anchorage, off Rio Grande, Brazil. There she remained, with a skeleton crew of eight on board, sluggishly swinging to her anchor and sinking ever lower in the water. Finally, realising that this ship had to all intents and purposes been abandoned by her owners, on 4 June, the Brazilian authorities took matters into their own hands and towed the *Kamari* out into deep water 75 miles off Rio Grande. Two days later, the unfortunate ship obliged everyone concerned by quietly sinking.

Meanwhile, the toll had continued to mount relentlessly. On 13 March, the 25,000-ton Cyprus-flag *Shipbroker* was passing through the Bosporus, inbound in ballast to Novorossisk, when her generators failed. With her rudder jammed hard over, the 14-year-old bulk carrier collided with the outward bound tanker *Nassia*–also under the Cyprus flag. The 132,517-ton *Nassia* was loaded with 98,500 tons of Russian crude oil, which burst into flames setting fire to both ships. The *Shipbroker*, out of control and blazing fiercely, piled up on the eastern shore of the strait, where she quickly became a burnt-out wreck. Only five of her crew of twenty-nine survived.

The *Nassia*, spewing oil from three ruptured tanks and enveloped in flames, ran aground on the opposite shore. She was later refloated and towed into the Black Sea, where she continued to burn at anchor for another four days. The fire was finally extinguished on 17 March. Eighteen of the tanker's crew of twenty-nine lost their lives and nearly 20,000 tons of oil spilled into the sea, causing widespread pollution.

Following the *Shipbroker/Nassia* collision, the Bosporus was closed to all shipping for five days, resulting in a huge backlog of vessels building up. The consequent loss of revenue for owners and charterers was enormous. The only beneficiaries of this major disaster were the Turkish owners of the breaker's yard at Aliaga, where both ships ended their days.

There was a lull for two months, then on 25 May, the 32,336-ton Chinese bulker *Wei Hai* collided in fog with the container ship *Tao He*–also Chinese flag–in the Taiwan Strait. The *Wei Hai*, a 30-year-old ship, was loaded with

26,646 tons of coal. She sank quickly, but all thirty-seven crew members were rescued unharmed.

Three days later, in another ocean, the 22-year-old Indian-flag bulk carrier *Jag Shanti* began taking in water in her engine-room. The 26,646-ton *Jag Shanti* was on a voyage from the west coast of India to Turkey with a full cargo of iron ore pellets. Her crew of forty-five abandoned her on 28 May when only a few hours out from Mangalore. All were picked up. The ship was towed back to an anchorage off Mangalore, but sank a few days later.

On that same day, 5 June, an intense cyclonic depression swept in from the Arabian Sea to hit the west coast of India. At Marmagoa, 160 miles north of Mangalore, hurricane force winds caused extensive damage ashore. The 50,000-ton Cypriot bulk carrier *Sea Transporter*, lying at anchor off the port, caught the full blast of the storm. Having pumped out all her ballast in preparation for loading a cargo of iron ore, she was riding high out of the water, and it was not long before her anchors carried away and she was thrown ashore.

All efforts to refloat the *Sea Transporter* failed, and her crew of thirty-one were taken off by helicopter. The 21-year-old ship, which was eventually declared a total loss, was cut in two by salvors and towed to an Indian breaker's yard for scrap.

The next victim was the 124,000-ton Chinese-owned bulk carrier *Apollo Sea*. Flying the Panama flag, this 21-year-old ship loaded 124,410 tons of iron ore at Saldanha Bay for China, sailing on 20 June. The weather on the Atlantic coast of South Africa was very severe at the time, and it is believed that the *Apollo Sea* went down some four hours after sailing.

The South African authorities did not become aware of the loss of the ship until almost a week after she sank, and then only through belated reports from her owners in China. It was revealed that the Master of the *Apollo Sea* had radioed a distress call on 20 June, but for some inexplicable reason had directed this to his owners, and not to all stations, as is international practice. Consequently, no help was on hand, and thirty-six men who might have been saved by helicopter died.

Wreckage was washed ashore, and 2,400 tons of fuel oil leaking from the bulk carrier's tanks inflicted massive pollution on the pristine beaches of the Cape. This led a salvage vessel to locate the wreck of the *Apollo Sea* some 30 miles northwest of Robben Island in 60 fathoms of water. Sonar scans indicated that the ship had broken in two "in the area of the accommodation section." To date, this is the only known corroboration of the popular theory that the *Derbyshire* might have split at Frame 65.

The 38,000-ton *Forum Chemist*, loaded with 36,000 tons of pig iron from Ponta da Madeira, Brazil, for New Orleans, was almost within sight of her destination when disaster overtook her. On 1 July, this 13-year-old, Cyprus-flag bulk carrier was approaching the Mississippi River pilot when fire broke out in her engine-room. The blaze was so fierce that twenty-seven crew members took to the boats, leaving only the master and three others on board.

Shore-based fire-fighting units eventually brought the fire under control and extinguished it. The *Forum Chemist* was then towed into New Orleans, where her cargo was discharged. The ship herself, however, was declared a total constructive loss, and her underwriters were faced with

22-year-old oil/bulk/ore carrier *Trade Daring* broke her back while
loading at Ponta da Madeira in November 1994.
Photo: Salvage Association

a bill for £6.45 million, which they duly paid. After lying in
New Orleans for nearly six months, the *Forum Chemist* was
finally towed to the Yugoslav port of Rijeka for repairs,
emerging some time later with a new identity.

Heavy weather in the Indian Ocean claimed another
victim in August. On the 5th, the 23,000-ton *Wellborn*
limped into an anchorage off Port Dauphin, on Madagascar's
southeast coast with serious cracks in her hull plating. The
23-year-old, Liberian-flag bulker, loaded with a full cargo of
manganese ore, lay at anchor for a full month while her fate
was debated. Before any decision regarding repairs was
reached, she resolved the issue by dragging her anchor and
running aground on a coral reef. Within days, the *Wellborn*

had broken her back and was a total loss. Oil from her fuel tanks caused massive pollution on nearby beaches.

Another large, Cyprus-registered, bulk carrier came to grief in September. While on passage from Tubarao to China with a cargo of iron ore, the 90,000-ton *Iron Antonis* ran into heavy seas when some 600 miles north of Tristan da Cunha. On 5 September, she was reported to be making water through a crack in her starboard side hull plating. The leak must have been a major one, for her crew of three Greek officers and twenty-one Filipino ratings abandoned her a few hours later. They were never seen again.

It subsequently emerged—too late for her crew—that the 26-year-old *Iron Antonis* had been operating on the wrong side of the law for a number of years. In 1991, her crew made a complaint to a Missions to Seamen chaplain—it seems there was no one else they could turn to—of a 30-foot long split in the ship's side plating, of frequent fires on board and inadequate lifeboats. Her engine room was said to be in a dilapidated state, with only one of her two generators operational. The *Iron Antonis* was uninsured at the time of her loss, having been de-classed by Bureau Veritas some months earlier. The question that must be asked is how a ship in such an apparently deplorable state was ever allowed to go to sea.

The next casualty, the 22-year-old oil/bulk/ore carrier *Trade Daring*, failed even to reach the open sea before she came to grief. On 11 November, the 145,053-ton Cyprus-flag ship, with 139,700 tons of iron and manganese ores on board, was nearing completion of loading in the Brazilian port of Ponta da Madeira when she suddenly broke her back and sank alongside the berth. Age, lack of maintenance and an excessive loading rate were said to be responsible. The *Trade Daring* was eventually salvaged and towed clear of the ore terminal, but such was the damage to her hull that she was judged to be not worth repairing. She was scuttled in deep water off Brazil on 10 January 1995.

Five days after the *Trade Daring* broke her back, on 15 November, another 22-year-old, the 22,076-ton Panama-registered bulk carrier *Golden Chariot*, was lost. She was on her way from Galveston, in the Gulf of Mexico, to West Africa with a cargo of bulk grain when she began to sink off the coast of French Guiana. Her crew of twenty-five took to the boats and all were saved.

And so, mercifully for the bulk carriers, 1994 came to an end. Sixteen of their number had been lost, 147 seamen had died, and the blight of oil pollution had spread far and wide over the seas. For those who had been foolish enough to gamble their money on insuring these rust buckets—and rust buckets they were in the main—the cost was high, over £60 million being paid out on the ships alone. The cargoes lost were to another account as yet unspecified. It is significant that no fewer than seven of the sixteen of the bulk carriers written off sailed under the convenience flag of Cyprus.

As a result of pressure from the underwriters, who had suffered these grievous losses in 1994, the classification societies at last began to pay more attention to the state of the ships they were blithely continuing to class as "seaworthy." Stricter standards were recommended for bulk carriers, with the result that their losses fell off dramatically in 1995, reaching the lowest level for six years. In all, just six bulkers were lost, and only one of these, the 17-year-old, Georgian-flag *Memed Abashidze*—one of the new breed of rust buckets coming out of the ex-Soviet empire—was lost as a result of cracks developing in heavy weather. Of the others, one was due to collision and four ran ashore. A total of eighty-four lives were lost.

Perhaps the most bizarre incident of the year was that involving the 54,615-ton *Mount Olympus*. In early December, this 17-year-old bulk carrier, owned by Rumanian-based Denarius Shipping and flying the Maltese flag, was sailing empty between Ravenna, Italy, and Norfolk, Virginia, when she ran into a force 9 gale in mid-Atlantic. The ship began to break up, and with her holds partly flooded, her Rumanian crew of thirty abandoned ship.

Luckily, the Bulgarian bulker *Rodopi* was nearby, and the Rumanians were all picked up. It would appear, however, that they had taken to the boats in a great hurry, not even bothering to shut down the engine-room before leaving. Two days later, the unmanned *Mount Olympus* was sighted steering southeast at 6 knots, and with all her lights still burning.

It is indeed an ill wind that benefits no one, and on this occasion good fortune came the way of the ocean-going salvage tug *Anglian Earl*, stationed in the Azores. Four days after putting to sea, she found the *Mount Olympus* still very much afloat, although by this time—presumably because the fuel in her engine-room tanks had been used up—she was dead in the water. In improving weather, the *Anglian Earl* took the derelict in tow and headed for Europe.

It was only to be expected that some bulk carrier owners—and it is hardly necessary to specify under which flags they sailed their ships—were strenuously opposed to the higher standards called for by the classification societies.

They particularly resented a proposal to strengthen the holds of existing ships. New ships were one thing, but to suggest that a 20-year-old bulker—most probably only a voyage or two away from the knacker's yard—should be reinforced was, in their opinion, to invite the expenditure of huge amounts of money for no good reason.

The argument raged long and hot throughout 1996, with the International Association of Classification Societies pushing for stricter inspections and structural reinforcement where required. The ship owners fought a fierce rearguard action, but the I.A.C.S eventually won the day. Meanwhile, another eleven bulk carriers had gone down.

Ironically, the first bulk carrier to be lost in 1997 was a ship which had supposedly been subjected to the tougher survey standards imposed by the I.C.A.S.

The 22,021-ton *Leros Strength*, ex-*Benetnasch*, ex-*Delena*, ex-*Ena*, was the archetypal flag of convenience bulk carrier. Built in 1976, she was owned by the Lambda Sea Shipping Company of Limassol, flew the Cypriot flag, was managed by Leros Management of Greece and on long-term charter to August Bolten of Hamburg, who had in turn subchartered her for one voyage to another company. She sailed under the command of Captain Eugeniusz Arciszewski, and carried a total crew of twenty, all of Polish nationality.

How such an obviously Greek ship came to be crewed by Poles must be open to question. The answer is simple. Poland once operated a large merchant fleet, and her seamen were among the best in the world. However, in line with communist doctrine, her ships were shielded from international competition by generous government subsidies. These came to an end when the Iron Curtain of Eastern

Europe began to draw aside in the autumn of 1989. In the ensuing economic melt-down, Polish shipping all but disappeared, leaving a large pool of trained and experienced seamen looking for jobs. These men, desperate for the means to support their families, are prepared to work for small wages and turn a blind eye to the deficiencies of the ships they sail in. Today, Poland has become the new source of cheap labour for European shipping.

The *Leros Strength* arrived in Murmansk on 3 January 1997, having crossed the Atlantic in ballast from Corpus Christi, in the Gulf of Mexico. As might be expected in the depths of winter, the crossing had not been an easy one. Flying light and running before an endless succession of strong westerly gales, the ship rolled and pitched her way across the troubled ocean, her ageing engine straining and her hull plates groaning in protest. Ominous thumps and rattles issuing from her empty holds added to the discomfort of her crew. She survived the stormy passage, but so traumatic had been the ordeal, that soon after berthing in Murmansk four crew members walked down the gangway refusing to sail any further in her—even though her next port was Gdynia. The men later claimed that the ship was in a dangerous condition, her forward watertight bulkheads being so badly corroded that they had broken away from the hull in places.

How valid were the claims of the deserting seamen will now never be known, but the *Leros Strength* certainly had suffered some structural problems in her recent past—which is not surprising. In the summer of 1996, when she was 20 years old, and due for a major hull and engine survey, Leros Management had applied to have the survey postponed. The classification society involved, American Bureau of Shipping, had refused the request, with the result that the ship was switched to another classification society, Registro Italiano Navale, based in Genoa. In July 1996, the Italian society claimed to have implemented all American Bureau's outstanding recommendations, and also said it had put the *Leros Strength* through the enhanced special survey called for by the I.A.C.S.

It would appear that Registro Italiano had been–to say the least–less than thorough in its work. In August 1996, just one month after the *Leros Strength* had supposedly gone through her enhanced survey, she was inspected by Port State Control in Rotterdam and detained on eleven counts. Her lifesaving and fire fighting equipment were found to be below standard, and there were "structural problems" with her hatch covers. She was allowed to sail from Rotterdam only on condition that she proceeded direct to Greece for repairs.

Having made good her safety equipment and completed the required repairs to her hatches in a Greek port, the *Leros Strength* was again inspected by Registro Italiano Navale and passed as seaworthy in all respects. However, Alfred Peda, one of the men who left the ship in Murmansk, stated that only two months later, prior to arrival in Corpus Christi, it was necessary to carry out emergency repairs in the holds involving extensive welding. Some three tons of steel were used to strengthen wasted frames and bulkheads. Peda claimed that the repairs were so well painted over that US Coast Guard officers who inspected the ship on arrival in Corpus Christi failed to spot any defects. When she sailed from America in early December, the *Leros Strength* once again had a clean bill of health.

The Russian port of Murmansk, 50 miles inland from the Barents Sea and 150 miles north of the Arctic Circle, even in high summer, is a bleak industrial sprawl offering little attraction to the visiting seafarer. In winter, when almost perpetual darkness prevails and temperatures dip to -20° C., it is a place of unrelieved misery. Ice covers every exposed part of a ship's superstructure and decks, and the bone-chilling cold destroys all incentive to activity, other than that necessary to maintain life. The only inducement Murmansk has to offer is that in winter the warm North Atlantic Drift flowing past the mouth of the Kola Inlet keeps the port free of ice.

The *Leros Strength* spent a month in Murmansk, much of the time lying idle awaiting cargo. For Captain Arciszewski, fifty-eight years old and thirty-eight years at sea, the long delay was something to be endured philosophically; his less stoical crew did not see it that way. By the time frigid January drew to a close and the *Leros Strength* was down to her winter marks with 18,000 tons of apatite ore—a chalk-like substance used in fertilisers—the seeds of discontent sown by the state of the ship and the rough Atlantic crossing were beginning to sprout. It was time to go home.

The heavily loaded bulk carrier finally cast off her frozen mooring ropes on the morning of 2 February. As she made her way down the Kola Inlet in the Arctic darkness, the shiny crust of ice rind on the water crackling under her bow, a fresh easterly wind was blowing, depressing the thermometer even further. When she entered the Barents Sea in the brief period of grey twilight around noon and headed westwards, the barometer had begun a downward plunge that was all too familiar to the weatherwise Captain Arciszewski. A depression was moving in from the Atlantic.

The progression of the *Leros Strength's* voyage after she dropped her pilot off at Guba Tyuva must be largely reconstruction. It is believed that she passed the North Cape, the northernmost point of Norway, on the afternoon of the 3rd. Weather reports at the time indicated a deepening low was then situated in the Norwegian Sea and tracking northeast, directly into the path of the bulk carrier. Off the west coast of Norway ships were already reporting gale force south-southwesterly winds and rough seas.

Three days later, the *Leros Strength* was believed to be off the Lofoten Islands and steering southwest, having made good a speed of only 8 knots since rounding the North Cape. Meteorological Office charts showed that she would then have been passing between two depressions, one to the east of Iceland and the other over north Denmark. The weather was undoubtedly foul, but no worse than might be expected in the area at the time of the year. Certainly, Captain Arciszewski gave no indication to the outside world that he was experiencing any undue difficulties. However, it is claimed that his radio officer, in a radiotelephone call to his home in Poland, reported that water was entering the ship's holds. The officer did not go into any great detail about the leak, but he was clearly concerned for the safety of the ship. To anyone acquainted with the record of the bulk carriers this lone cry from a storm-wracked sea would have had an all too familiar and ominous ring.

Weather reports on the morning of the 8th indicated a deep low stationary over the Lofoten Islands. Norwegian coast stations were reporting gale force westerly winds accompanied by squalls of sleet and hail. Out at sea, conditions were as bad as they get in this wretched corner of the oceans. Dark racing clouds brushed the foaming crests of mountainous seas rolling in from the Atlantic, flying spray froze in the air and the howling wind carried flurries of spiteful hail sharp enough to draw blood on unprotected skin. At 0650 GMT, the *Leros Strength's* radio burst into life with a Mayday call. The ship was then 30 miles west of Stavanger, Captain Arciszewski reporting severe damage to the bow. He said the ship was listing heavily, the pumps being unable to cope with water entering the holds. The message lasted just three minutes–then there was silence.

Rescue services were alerted, and at 0750 a helicopter arrived over the *Leros Strength's* last known position, where a cold, grey dawn was just breaking. The searchers found only scattered debris and an oil slick spreading on the heaving waters.

What happened to the *Leros Strength* and her crew of twenty is likely to remain forever a matter for conjecture. But, having regard to the known fate of so many bulk carriers of similar age and state of maintenance, it can be assumed that she broke up after battling against heavy seas from the time she rounded the North Cape. With 18,000 tons of ore on board, she must have gone to the bottom very suddenly, perhaps minutes or even seconds after she sent out a call for help. Any of her crew who succeeded in abandoning ship will have perished in the icy waters of the Norwegian Sea in an equally short space of time. The only clue to the mystery of the *Leros Strength's* disappearance is the radio officer's call home on the 5th. If his report that water was entering the ship's holds was correct, then it must be that the water level in the holds rose steadily over the following three days, until the ship either broke up, or became completely waterlogged. Leros Management strongly disputed the radio officer's claim—but then it would be in their interest to do so.

The detention of the *Leros Strength* by Port State Control in Rotterdam only a month after she had gone through the tough new survey recommended by the industry should have given rise to serious doubts as to how rigorously this survey was carried out. The refusal of some of her crew to sail any further than Murmansk and her subsequent loss in all too familiar circumstances must surely confirm that there were many things left undone that should have been done.

The sinking of the *Leros Strength* made the headlines in Gdynia, where twenty families mourned the loss of their breadwinners. Elsewhere, publicity of this tragic event was minimal. In Britain it rated a brief mention on early morning radio and half a column inch in one or two of the national dailies. Twenty-four hours later, the *Leros Strength* and her crew had receded into history.

Epilogue

In the House of Lords in 1981, Lord Trefgarne, then Parliamentary Under Secretary of State for Trade, said of the *Derbyshire*: "It has to be asked how can such a huge, modern and well-equipped ship virtually disappear without trace, or at least some last desperate signal. It appears from our inquiries that whatever happened to cause the loss of the *Derbyshire* was both immediate and catastrophic providing no chance for those on board to react. What this was can only be conjectured; a massive explosion, structural hull failure resulting in rapid sinking, or possibly the vessel was overwhelmed due to a sudden shift of the cargo. The fact is, regrettably, we do not know, and I have to tell the House that it has not been possible to adduce any evidence to support any one of these theories and, inevitably, the outcome of the inquiry has been inconclusive."

This was not good enough for the relatives of those who died in the *Derbyshire*, who from the outset had canvassed that the ship was lost through a structural break-up caused by faulty design. Their contention was that, as a result of economies made when the ship was building, her longitudinal strength had been compromised. It was said that, contrary to the original builder's plan, the wing tank side plating had not been continued through the watertight bulkhead immediately forward of the bridge (frame 65), but was cut and joined to the bulkhead on either side, thus saving time and money. This alteration–made with the approval of Lloyd's Register–in effect meant that the ship was two separate entities welded together, the long forepart containing the cargo holds, and the short after part the accommodation block and engine-room. The theory then advanced was that in the violent motion the *Derbyshire* must have experienced in the typhoon, she broke in two at her weakest part, i.e. at frame 65. The after part of the ship, with all those on board, then simply fell off and sank almost instantaneously. Cracks subsequently found in this same region in the *Kowloon Bridge* and *Tyne Bridge* added some weight to this scenario, for all the "Bridge" series, except the first-built, the *Furness Bridge*, were of the same construction. This was enough to launch the *Derbyshire* relatives, backed by the maritime unions and the International Transport Workers Federation, on a determined campaign to lay the blame for their grievous loss where it belonged. The ship's builder, Swan Hunter, her owners, Bibby Line, and the Department of Transport were all judged guilty of conspiring to send an unsafe ship to sea. That the relatives felt the need to hit out at someone is understandable but, unfortunately, there have been times in their campaign when they allowed the heart to rule the head.

The loss of the *Kowloon Bridge* in the full glare of the media floodlights in November 1986, served to concentrate minds in the Department of Transport, and in 1987 a formal investigation into the loss of the *Derbyshire* was convened. This lasted for forty-six days and heard evidence from scores of expert witnesses and people involved in the building and operation of the *Derbyshire* and her sister ships. The wheels of government grinding exceedingly slowly, a report on the investigation was not issued until January 1989. The summing up was as follows:

"The *Derbyshire* was a large, relatively modern (built 1976), fully equipped and well manned oil-bulk-ore (OBO) combination carrier which disappeared virtually without trace in the North West Pacific while on voyage from Canada to Japan in September 1980. At the time, it was the most serious UK marine casualty for many years because of the heavy loss of life (42 crew members and two wives).

"While at the time evidence as to the cause of the loss of the vessel was inconclusive, during the following five years the Department commissioned extensive research into the structural design of the *Derbyshire* and also investigated reports of defects in some of her sister ships. Despite this work, no firm evidence arose as to the cause of the loss. On December 12 1986, the Department announced that it was the government's intention to hold a formal investigation into the loss of the vessel. The investigation, under Wreck Commissioner Mr. Gerald Darling, QC, started on October 5 1987, and sat for 46 days, eventually closing on 10 March 1988. It reached the following conclusions: 'The *Derbyshire* was properly designed, properly built and constructed from material of approved standard. No inference can be safely drawn from the absence of any distress signal. The condition of the cargo when loaded and its loading were within the existing recommended parameters. The *Derbyshire* was caught in the worst part of Typhoon Orchid and may have encountered freak weather beyond what can be "hindcast."

The actions of her master were not unreasonable. The possibility that the *Derbyshire* was lost as a result of torsional weakness in her hull is extremely low. The combination of circumstances necessary to postulate separation of the hull at frame No. 65 is very unlikely, though some doubt must remain. It is improbable that immediate or even sudden structural failure of the forward hatch covers caused rapid sinking. Sequential flooding of holds is a possible cause of loss but not thought probable. If cargo liquefaction did occur, which is doubtful, it still cannot be concluded that that was a prime cause of loss. If the *Derbyshire* got beam-on to the weather, structural failure and/or cargo shift would have become much more likely. It is quite possible that that happened but it cannot be proved.'"

Quod erat demonstrandum. Every possible cause of the disaster had been examined in great detail but, not surprisingly, no hard evidence could be produced to substantiate any of them. The general inference of the report was that the *Derbyshire* had simply been overwhelmed by the weather, and this might well have been so, for the destructive power of a Pacific typhoon is enormous. It is well illustrated by a voice from the past in a letter written by an ex-crew member of the 7,924-ton British ship *Tacoma Star* and published in *Seaways*, the magazine of the Nautical Institute: "The findings of the *Derbyshire* inquiry reminded me of the occasion in 1941 when we were in a similar location to the *Derbyshire* in the Pacific Ocean.

"For five days we wallowed, broadside. The first of several miles of huge waves picked us up and threw us down again, into the uncanny deadly centre of the storm and then started the same process on the other side of the ship as the storm passed us by.

"The windlass had been shifted two feet to port, the No. 1 hatch boards had been broken–but luckily, as a refrigerated ship, we had insulated hatches immediately below and they stayed intact. We had a special funnel which could be taken in half for the Manchester Canal. We lost the top section. Our wireless aerial and one topmast had gone and eventually there was 20 feet of water in the engine-room. The waves towered some 50 feet above the bridge and as they slid under us, the ship leaned over more and more–reaching at least 45 degrees–and then slowly straightened up and swayed the other way as we slid down the other side of the wave. Two other things were quite sure. There was no way of contacting any safety station and if we had done, there was no way of getting an accurate position to give them and no rescue ship had yet been designed that could have got through those seas better than we did. Though old, the Tacoma was a tight ship, well manned and maintained.

"At one point before our engine-room flooded, Capt. Rhodes tried desperately to carry out the–up until then–recognised way of facing a typhoon: 'Put your bow into it and steam over.' He timed it well; the bow went up in the air at the top of the huge roller, then tipped over forward and we thought she was going right under the sea, with her propeller whirring away wildly in the open air. She dipped her foc'stle under the water (incidentally, the crew all lived there–luckily their doors were well battened down) then she suddenly sheered off, shook like a dog coming out of the water and went broadside on to the storm. We never got her back on course for five days.

"I've often wondered if, perhaps the *Derbyshire* had a similar experience and had failed to be turned away and had steamed right into the next vast rolling wave, never to come up. Anyone who has been through a storm like that would tell you that the strength of the vessel, the power of the engines or the use of radio could have saved us. I know that I and many others thought it was probably an answer to a prayer. It certainly was a miracle. After pumping out the engine-room with a small petrol engine, we staggered to Singapore for repairs."

It may have seemed like a miracle, but it is more likely it was the mould she came out of that saved the *Tacoma Star*. She was a ship of another age, and compared to the *Derbyshire* she was small–under 500 feet long and one fifteenth of her deadweight tonnage–she was also 22 years old, but she was a stout, riveted ship with an inbuilt strength rarely matched today. Like a true ship, she was able to "ride" the waves, unlike the barge-shaped *Derbyshire* and her kind who have no empathy with the sea. They are ships of up to 1,000 feet long, with perhaps 60 feet of their hulls below the water, archetypal "immovable objects," upon which the waves break with great force. Their great length could in many cases be their downfall. The average storm wave is about 600 feet from crest to crest, which means that there are times when the ship is balanced on top of two crests, one forward and one aft. This leaves the mid section only partly supported by the upthrust of the sea, thus subjecting the hull to immense stresses. If the ship is old, and her plates and frames badly wasted through corrosion and lack of maintenance, then it it feasible that a sudden and catastrophic break-up may occur.

It has become clear over the last 20 years or so that the average age of bulk carrier casualties is around 19 years. This is no great age for a ship, providing she is looked after–many of the old tramps of the first half of the 20th century went on for 40 years or more. But in the case of the large bulk carrier of today, commercial pressures do not allow for cossetting. These ships handle up to twelve ore cargoes in a year, leaving precious little time for the niceties of removing rust and painting that are an integral part of the operational routine of the well-run general cargo carrier. Below decks, at least, corrosion is allowed to go unchecked, eating away at the strength of the ship. And again, their loading is like no other, ores being poured into the holds from a great height at a rate of up to 12,000 tons an hour. Internal damage is inevitable. When unloading, huge grabs and bulldozers batter at the already weakened plates, frames and bulkheads. Many are the blind eyes turned on these ships in the interest of commercial expediency.

By the very nature of the loading practice of the trade these ships are under severe stress even in fair weather. In order to raise the centre of gravity of an ore carrier, and so reduce rolling, even numbered holds are usually left empty. This could feasibly result in up to 25,000 tons of cargo in one hold, with the holds on either side being completely empty. A bulk carrier young in years and well maintained may be perfectly able to stand these stresses, but age takes its toll.

After the belated publication of the results of the 1987 investigation into the loss of the *Derbyshire*, it seemed that her case had finally been laid to rest. The sea continued to reap its grisly harvest of the big bulk carriers—averaging one a month—but they were, almost without exception, flag of convenience ships manned by foreign crews, and they were no concern of the British Government. Then, on 15 March 1993, the *Gold Bond Conveyor* hit the headlines. Loaded with a full cargo of gypsum from Nova Scotia for Florida, she broke up and sank in a North Atlantic storm taking her crew of thirty-three with her. She was an old flag of convenience ship, and her sudden end would have resulted in no more than a few grim faces at Lloyd's, had not a number of her Hong Kong Chinese crew, including her master, carried British passports. This woke up the budding Plimsolls in the House of Commons, twenty of whom signed a motion urging the Government to reopen inquiries into the loss of the *Derbyshire*.

The Department of Transport's response to this renewed pressure was as non-commital as ever, but the *Derbyshire's* ghost had been resurrected and refused to go away. In the early summer of 1994, frustrated by the inactivity of government, the International Transport Workers Federation put up £380,000 to finance an expedition to find and examine the wreck of the *Derbyshire*. It was a bold project, involving the use of a towed sidescan vehicle and a deep ocean remotely operated vehicle (ROV) capable of diving to a depth of nearly 4 miles. After seven days searching an area of over 500 square miles, on 2 June a wreck was located 2 miles down near the position of the oil slick found after the *Derbyshire* went down. The ROV was launched, and its cameras confirmed that the remains of the ill-fated bulk carrier had been found, the letters SHIRE being clearly seen on the bow section of the ship. A plaque commemorating those lost in the ship was laid on the forecastle head by the ROV.

The ITF's money was limited, and the ROV was able to remain only just over six hours on the bottom. The conclusions reached in the report on the expedition threw an entirely new light on the *Derbyshire* enigma: "The distribution of the wreckage on the bottom rules out break-up on impact with the sea bed. It is more likely that break-up occurred at or near the surface with the release of the cargo of iron ore sand....

"The evidence, whilst not entirely consistent with the hypothesis set out earlier, does in our opinion confirm that whatever happened to the *Derbyshire* was sudden and catastrophic. The evidence would also indicate that the damage done to the ship occurred at or near the surface and not upon hitting the sea bed. The presence of hundreds of relatively small pieces of wreckage on the sea bed suggests an extremely violent break-up that must have occurred over a very short period of time, perhaps only seconds or minutes. Any other scenario would have permitted the crew to send out a distress message and would also have resulted in a much greater distribution of wreckage.

"The distribution of the cargo of iron sand on the bottom also holds clues as to what happened to the *Derbyshire*. It had initially been thought that the dense concentration of sonar targets within the wreckage field indicated that the cargo was giving a high sonar return and that some of the stronger targets could in fact represent mounds of cargo. Having viewed the video evidence it would seem that (at least in the area covered by the video) the cargo is evenly spread and has become incorporated into the indigenous bottom sediment. However, a provisional analysis undertaken by the University of Wales indicated that distinct patterns relating to the cargo may exist which could provide further clues to the sequence of events that caused the *Derbyshire* to sink.

"In addition, a shimmering effect was observed on the seabed as the light from the ROV's cameras was reflected by individual particles of iron ore sand. Not only is this shimmering phenomenon observed on the sea bed but also on the wreckage. These two facts have led to the conclusion that the cargo must have showered down from the surface taking longer to descend than the wreckage...."

So what calamitous event did cause the *Derbyshire* to sink? A close look at the fate of the other ships described in detail in this book may help find an answer to this vexing question.

Of them all, the *Antacus* scenario seems the most unlikely. Here was a clear case of negligence compounded by incompetence. She was an ageing flag of convenience bulker manned by a sub-standard crew of two different nationalities, a fatal combination of inadequacies. When her cargo of steel broke adrift, no one on board had the ability or the inclination to do anything about it. In the end, the cargo destroyed the ship.

The *Cumberlande's* end was also predictable. Fourteen years old, she was already living on borrowed time when she sailed from Australia in May 1987. By the admission of her own master and officers, she was in a deplorable state of repair. The stress she was subjected to by the long Pacific swells was enough to begin the breaking up process; the sea entering her holds did the rest. Nevertheless, she remained afloat for at least three days after the damage was done.

The *Yarrawonga* was 17 years old and had had five previous owners before ending up under the go-as-you-please flag of Cyprus with a far from enthusiastic crew of Filipinos. Evidence shows that she was pushed too hard in heavy weather, resulting in hatch covers lost and holds flooded. A free surface of thousands of tons of water smashed through plates wasted by corrosion, yet, for all that, the *Yarrawonga* did not sink, and reached port sixteen days later.

A similar fate befell the *Orient Pioneer*, 19 years old and caught in an Indian Ocean cyclone. Again, although holed below the waterline, this ship was still afloat three days later, and perhaps survived much longer.

The *Petingo*, a 23-year-old flag of convenience geriatric manned by a Third World crew, should not really have been allowed to sail in deep waters. Yet, when she lost hatch covers off the Cape, she sailed on for another 1,000 miles with her holds flooded. After running ashore, she then survived for another fifteen days before the sea, helped by the explosives of the salvage teams, broke her up.

With the *Kowloon Bridge*, it at first appeared that a definite comparison could be made. Here was a sister to the *Derbyshire*, out of the same yard and of identical construction. But there the similarity ended. The *Kowloon Bridge* was ten years old, had served under five flags, ending with the second register flag of Hong Kong, and was manned by a bi-national crew of Indians and Turks. No evidence was produced to say she was poorly maintained, but there is good reason to suspect that this was so. Alternate hold loading and violent rolling and pitching in an Atlantic storm must have put unacceptable strains on her hull, leading to severe cracking. She did in the end break at frame 65, but only after lying impaled on the Stags Rocks with her stern afloat in deep water for more than four days. Again, the end of this ship was not sudden or catastrophic.

All the ships so far mentioned had strong common links, in that they were of an advanced age and weakened by the rough usage of the trade and unchecked corrosion. Yet not one of them came to a sudden and catastrophic end. They all died hard but slowly, allowing ample time for their crews to be rescued. Why, then, did the *Derbyshire*, a comparatively new, first-rate ship not enjoy a similar unhurried exit from this world?

The *Cathay Seatrade*, caught in a freak Atlantic storm, apparently did not linger. But, then, she was a disaster waiting to happen. Fourteen years old, flag of convenience and manned by a Third World crew, she left port with her hull under stress through hogging, and her cargo of fine, dry ore untrimmed. By no stretch of the imagination could she be promoted into the same league as the *Derbyshire*.

The *Pasithea* and the *Derbyshire* were similar in size, both were oil/bulk/ore carriers, and both disappeared in a typhoon off Japan without sending out an SOS. And there the similarity ends. The *Pasithea* was a 19-year-old workhorse sailing under a flag with a poor record of complying with recognised maintenance standards. She had not carried an oil cargo for six years, which makes the possibility of destruction by explosion so remote that it may be safely disregarded. It seems more than likely that the *Pasithea* suffered a sudden capsize through shifting cargo and collapsing bulkheads. The *Derbyshire's* cargo might have shifted with the heavy rolling in Orchid, or, bearing in mind the high moisture content of her ore which necessitated frequent pumping of the bilges earlier in the voyage, through liquefaction of the lower part of the cargo. However, the *Derbyshire's* bulkheads will have been strong and unlikely to give way, making the likelihood of sudden and complete capsize remote.

That leaves only the *Berge Istra* and *Berge Vanga*. The similarities with the *Derbyshire* sinking and that of the two "Berge" sisters are very great. The three ships were much the same age, the *Derbyshire* 4 years, the *Berge Istra* 3 years and the *Berge Vanga* 5 years old. They were all oil/bulk/ore carriers owned by reputable and long-established shipping companies, and therefore presumably well maintained. In the case of the *Derbyshire*, however, she had not carried an oil cargo for eleven months, the last oil being discharged on 7 October 1979. In the intervening time, she had been through a major dry docking in Japan, in the course of which her slop tanks and pump-room were cleaned and gas freed. All oil ducts and pump strainers were cleaned out, 48 tons of residue wax being removed, and the cofferdams in the engine-room were examined and found to be clean. A considerable amount of welding and burning was then carried out in the after part of the hull, this apparently with no perceived danger of a gas explosion. Thereafter, until the day of her disappearance, the only oil the *Derbyshire* carried was in her bunker tanks. On the face of it, that appears to rule out the possibility of the ship being destroyed by a massive explosion. Or does it?

In March 1995, the British Government, under continued pressure, finally agreed that there was more to the loss of the *Derbyshire* than the much used and abused "perils of the sea" explanation. Lord Donaldson, a former leading judge well experienced in the investigation of shipping casualties, was called in to assess the case. After an exhaustive examination of the facts available, Donaldson concluded that the only means of establishing the cause of the sinking of the *Derbyshire* lay in a further examination of the wreck.

As is not unusual in matters concerning merchant shipping, money was hard to come by, and it was not until the end of July 1996 that an expedition financed by the British Government and the European Commission set out for the Pacific. A remote controlled mini-submarine equipped with three cameras was sent down to the *Derbyshire*, and in the course of a week-long operation, spent ten hours searching and photographing the wreckage. The bow and stern sections were found to be about 700 yards apart. The bridge and accommodation could not be located, and was thought to be lying to one side near the stern part. Assessors of the photographic evidence spoke of "a void" where the bulkhead between No. 9 hold and the pump-room had been.

Once again—and this time after the expenditure of £2 million, no firm conclusions could be drawn, and the fate of the *Derbyshire* remained a matter of speculation. The investigation of the wreck continued in 1997, but whether, on the basis of photographs taken 2 miles below the surface of the sea, structural failure in the region of frame 65 can be proven seems most unlikely.

What is already obvious from the video evidence collected is that the break-up of the ship was catastrophic, for the wreck was found to be in seven main parts, indicating that the ship had been torn apart by some tremendous force. The report on the ITF expedition in 1994 stated: "The presence of hundreds of relatively small pieces on the sea bed suggest an extremely violent break-up that must have occurred over a very short period of time, perhaps only seconds or minutes." And: "In addition, a shimmering effect was observed on the seabed as the light from the ROV's cameras was reflected by individual particles of iron ore sand. Not only is this shimmering phenomenon observed on the sea bed but also on the wreckage. These two facts have led to the conclusion that the cargo must have showered down from the surface taking longer to descend than the wreckage." Given that the expert assessment of the evidence revealed by the underwater cameras is correct, then the case for sinking by internal explosion is very strong. But an explosion caused by what?

It has already been established that, following the discharge of her last oil cargo in October 1979, the *Derbyshire's* tanks and holds were thoroughly cleaned of any oil or oily residues that might have led to a build-up of hydro-carbon gas. Any explosion of that nature seems therefore so unlikely as to be safely ruled out. There remains only one other possible explanation for the violent destruction of the ship, and that is an explosion of methane gas. It will be recalled that the *Derbyshire* discharged a cargo of coal in Fos-sur-Mer only three months before her disappearance. It is surely not beyond the bounds of possibility that a large pocket of coal gas may have still been lurking in the bowels of the ship—perhaps in one of the wing tanks. The working of steel on steel during the clash with Typhoon Orchid could have provided the spark necessary to set off a massive explosion. This hypothesis is not as absurd as it may seem at first sight. In the heyday of steam, ships loaded with coal frequently caught fire at sea; some just disappeared without trace, and may well have blown up. These were comparatively small ships, carrying only three or four thousand tons of coal. On her penultimate voyage, the *Derbyshire* had on board in excess of 100,000 tons–she could conceivably be likened to a small coal mine afloat. A great deal of explosive gas must have been generated on passage, perhaps enough of it left behind in the hidden reaches of the ship to blow her apart. When "Coal was King" in the Welsh valleys, devastating explosions in the mines caused by an accumulation of firedamp, or methane gas took a regular and heavy toll of lives. The blast that killed 265 men in the Gresford Colliery disaster of 1934 was said to have been set off by a spark from a hand-cranked telephone. In April 1942, what was then described as a "coal dust explosion" wiped out 1,572 men underground at the Hondeiko Colliery in China. At sea a demonstration of the destructive power of a coal gas explosion may have occurred when the 31,500–ton Cunard liner *Lusitania* was torpedoed off Ireland in May 1915. Only one torpedo was fired, but a few seconds after its impact another explosion tore the heart out of this great "unsinkable" ship and sent her to the bottom with the loss of 1,198 lives. At the time, the second explosion was attributed to the large amount of amunition the Germans claimed the liner was carrying–a claim later refuted. In a recent underwater examination of the wreck, Dr. Robert Ballard, of the Woods Hole Oceanographic Institute, established that the torpedo struck the *Lusitania* in one of her huge coal bunkers, which was nearly empty at the time. It is Dr. Ballard's opinion that the second, and fatal explosion was caused by the presence in the bunker of a large accumulation of coal gas. The possibility that the *Derbyshire* was destroyed in a similar manner cannot be ruled out.

The *Derbyshire* was one of a dying breed of national-flag bulk carriers manned by a first-rate crew. We may never see the likes of her again, for the flag of convenience ships with their half-trained crews now completely dominate the trade. As the years go by and these ships grow older and more neglected, so the harvest of the sea will increase. What a shameful way for the shipping industry to approach the third millenium!

Postscript

In the spring of 1997, a Woods Hole Oceanographic team carried out another extensive underwater examination of the *Derbyshire* wreck. The 57-day operation, costing some $4.5 million, was instigated by the Department of Transport, whose assessors then spent many months evaluating the 137,000 photographs and hundreds of hours of video film taken. Their conclusions, released in March 1998, shocked the maritime world.

The theory that the bulk carrier had been lost through an inbuilt structural weakness in the region of Frame 65–so assiduously promoted in some quarters–was thrown out of the window. In its place came the time-honoured hypothesis often used to explain away a disaster to which there are no living witnesses, human error.

As it probed the wreakage scattered across the sea bed 2.5 miles down, the eye of the underwater camera had found an open hatchway near the *Derbyshire's* bow, this being easily identifiable as the entrance to the forepeak store. The hatch cover of the 4-foot by 4-foot opening is missing, probably torn off in the sinking, but its securing dogs appear to be undamaged, indicating the hatch must have been open at the time. One of the ship's mooring ropes is still visable leading up through the hatchway onto the deck. The obvious inference to be drawn from this is that, sometime before Typhoon Orchard struck, the *Derbyshire's* crew had been bringing the mooring ropes up on deck ready for arrival at Kawasaki, and omitted to close the hatch when they finished the job.

The Department of Transport assessors needed little persuading to conclude that the open forepeak hatch was the primary cause of the loss of the *Derbyshire*. Their reasoning was as follows: mountainous waves breaking over the bows during the typhoon quickly flooded the forepeak store, which led to bulk carrier taking on a bow-down attitude. Subsequent seas coming aboard then landed further aft, eventually dislodging or smashing the hatch covers of the forward hold. Tens of thousands of gallons of water poured into this hold, and as the bows sank deeper as a result of this, the waves broke further aft again, beginning their assult on the covers of the next hold. And so each hold filled in turn until the ship sank under the weight of water she had taken on board.

If the assessors reasoning is correct, then the *Derbyshire's* crew must bear some responsibility for their own sad demise: the forepeak hatch should have been securely battened down before the ship entered Typhoon Orchid. But there is no explanation offered for the absence of any SOS or urgent communication from the ship.

As has been clearly shown in this book, the flooding of a bulk carrier's holds to the point of foundering is by no means instantaneous. In the case of a nearly-new, well maintained ship like the *Derbyshire*, many hours, perhaps days, would have passed before she became completely waterlogged in the manner envisaged by the assessors. Furthermore, Captain Underhill was a very experienced shipmaster, and had his ship been sinking by the bow, he would very quickly have been aware of this. At the very least, he would then have informed his owners of his predicament. Yet nothing was heard from him. This does not suggest that the sinking of the *Derbyshire* was a gradual process.

The wreckage of the bulk carrier was found strewn across the ocean bottom in some 2,000 pieces, and was described by the assessors as, "a picture of almost total destruction with parts of this huge ship ripped apart, lying torn and crumpled on the sea bed."

The theory advanced in this book that the *Derbyshire's* end was sudden and cataclysmic, possibly as a result of a violent explosion, still holds good.

Glossary

AFTER PEAK: Deep tank in the aftermost part of the ship. Usually used for water ballast.

BAREBOAT CHARTER: In effect, a transfer of the ownership of a vessel for the period of the charter. Charterer has the right to appoint his own master and crew.

BEAM-ON: Steering a course at right angles to sea or swell.

BEAUFORT SCALE: Admiralty scale of wind force.

BILGES: Drainage channels running the entire length of bottom of ship on both sides.

BILL OF LADING: A receipt for cargo carried signed by the master or owner.

BROACH-TO: To swing beam-on to wind and sea.

BULK CARRIER: Ship specifically designed for the carriage of cargoes in bulk, i.e. ore, grain, coal, etc.

BULKHEAD: Vertical partition between two compartments in a ship.

BULWARK: Steel parapet around open upper deck of ship to prevent seas breaking on board.

CHARTERER: Person who hires ship to carry his cargo.

CHARTER PARTY: Document specifying terms on which ship is hired.

CLASSIFICATION SOCIETY: Body which surveys ship to decide her seaworthiness.

COAMING: Steel parapet around a hatch opening.

COFFERDAM: Narrow watertight compartment between two tanks, or between tank and engine-room and tank and hold.

COLLISION BULKHEAD: Reinforced bulkhead in bows of ship.

DEAD RECKONING: Rule of thumb method of fixing position of ship using course steered, estimated speed and estimated drift of current or tide.

DEADWEIGHT: Measurement of ship's tonnage expressed in terms of maximum cargo, bunkers, fresh water and stores she is able to lift.

DECCA NAVIGATOR: Accurate system of fixing ship's position in coastal waters using radio waves from beacons ashore.

DISPLACEMENT: The weight of water displaced by a ship.

DOUBLE BOTTOM: Space between bottom of ship's hull and watertight floor of holds and engine-room. Used to carry water ballast and fuel oil.

DRAUGHT: The depth of water which a ship draws.

ECHO SOUNDER: Instrument using sonar pulses to determine depth of water under a ship's keel.

ETA: Estimated time of arrival.

EYE OF STORM: Centre or vortex of storm where wind is light but sea heavy and confused.

FATHOM: Six feet or 1.82 metres.

FLAG OF CONVENIENCE: Flag which allows the registry of foreign ships in order to avoid legal or financial restraints in the country of ownership.

FORECASTLE HEAD: Short raised deck in bows of ships.

FOREDECK: That part of the maindeck forward of the bridge.

FREEBOARD: Distance from the maindeck to the waterline.

GALE FORCE (8): Wind speed 34–40 knots (39–46 mph)

GREAT CIRCLE: The shortest distance between two points on the earth's surface.

GUNWALE: Uppermost part of the hull plating; where it joins the maindeck.

HATCHWAY: Opening in deck giving access to cargo hold.

HEAVE-TO: To stop the ship at sea.

HORSE LATITUDES: That part of the oceans which lies between the prevailing westerly winds of higher latitudes and the trade winds. Roughly 30° to 40° north and south.

HURRICANE FORCE (12): Wind speed 64 knots (74 mph) and over.

IN BALLAST: Carrying no cargo but trimmed to manageable draught with water ballast.

IN IRONS: As with sailing vessel–head to wind and temporarily unable to pay off on either tack.

KNOT: One nautical mile per hour, a nautical mile being 6080 feet or the length of one minute of latitude at the Equator.

LLOYD'S: Association of marine underwriters based in London and founded in 1601. The leading authority on the specification of ships.

LUTINE BELL: Bell of HMS *Lutine*, sunk in 1799, which hangs in the Underwriting Room at Lloyd's. The bell is rung whenever an important announcement–such as the loss of a ship–is to be made.

MAYDAY: Distress code word used on radio telephone meaning: "I require immediate assistance."

MAINDECK: Upper or weather deck of vessel.

METACENTRIC HEIGHT: The vertical distance between a ship's centre of gravity and her metacentre. This determines her ability to return to the upright when she rolls under the influence of wind or sea.

OPEC: Organisation of Petroleum Exporting Countries.

PIERHEAD JUMPER: Seaman who joins a ship at the last moment before she sails. Usually a substitute for a deserter.

PAN: Code word used on radiotelephone to prefix a message of considerable urgency, but less than distress.

PIPE TUNNEL: Central compartment which runs the length of the bottom of ship carrying piping from engine-room to tanks and hold bilges.

PRATIQUE: Clearance given to arriving ship whose crew is healthy and free of all notifiable diseases.

PUMP-ROOM: Compartment, usually immediately forward of engine-room, containing pumps and valves for loading and discharge of liquid cargoes.

ROARING FORTIES: Belt of strong westerly winds in the southern oceans between latitudes 40° and 50° South.

SATELLITE NAVIGATOR: Highly accurate system of position fixing using radio satellites circling the earth in fixed orbits at altitude of 600 nautical miles.

SECOND REGISTER: Flag having close links with the origins of a ship but offering the benefits of lower taxation and the freedom to employ a crew of any nationality.

SLOP TANK: Tank containing oil and water residues from tank washing.

STEERAGE WAY: The minimum speed at which a ship's rudder will have effect.

SWELL: Undulation of the surface of the sea caused by distant storm and persisting over long period. As when a stone is thrown into a pond.

TRADE WINDS: Winds between about 30°N and 30°S of Equator which blow consistently from one direction.

TRAMP: Ship not engaged in a regular trade, but picks up cargoes when and where available.

TROUGH: Hollow between the crests of two waves.

TURNBUCKLE: Rigging screw used for tightening wire stays and lashings.

VHF: Very high frequency radiotelephone used for short range communication.

VLCC: Very large crude carrier.

WING TANK: Tank for water or fuel at side of ship.

100A1: Highest classification at Lloyd's.

INDEX

INDEX

INDEX

INDEX

INDEX

INDEX

286

INDEX

Brick Tower Press
1230 Park Avenue
New York, NY 10128, US
Tel/Fax: 1-800-68-BRICK, bricktower@aol.com
For sales, editorial information, subsidiary rights information or a catalog, please write or phone or e-mail.

In the United Kingdom contact
Brick Tower Press
145 Springdale Road, Corfe Mullen
Wimborne Dorset BH21 3QQ
Tel/Fax: (01202) 692045